KIDS FEEDING KIDS
C O O K B O O K

A Collection of Recipes Designed For Kids By Kids
By the Kids Feeding Kids® Club

Photography by Ally Gruener

Look inside
for Recipes
submitted by Oprah,
Sean Hayes,
Maria Shriver &
Chris O'Donnell

Printed in the USA by Morris Press Cookbooks

98890-ls   1

Produced &
Published
by **Alyssa Pazdan**

Photography by **Ally Gruener**

Creative Direction & Styling
by **Alyssa Pazdan**

Art Direction & Graphic Design
by **Liz Benedetto**

Food Styling by **Sarah Roberts**

Kids Feeding Kids Club Logo
& Donor Design by
Karen Kardatzke

FIRST EDITION
ISBN 978-0-615-29434-6

For more information, contact
Kids Feeding Kids® Club
P.O. Box 313
Barrington, IL 60011-0313
www.kidsfeedingkids.info
kidsfeedingkids@hotmail.com
allygruenerphotography.com

Cookbook Promotion Team

Cindy Amerine, Liz Benedetto,
Shawna Binkowski, Jaime Brashler,
Purnima Bhogaraju, Natalie Clark, Cindy
Cramer, Nicole Daniels, Courtney Desmond,
Jan Faulkner, Barb Floyd, Ally Gruener, Jeff
Gruener, Kristin Hatch, Anne Horwath, Rich
Horwath, Sharon Henahan, Karen Kardatzke,
Chelsea LaRocco, Heather McCarty, Jen McVey,
Jaime Miller, Deborah Murray, Angela Nazha,
David Pazdan, Mary Rose Pazdan, Mia Peretta,
Laura Powroznyk, Kim Prell, Peg Prigge,
Sarah Roberts, Danielle Scheel, Anne
Schmitt, Jennifer Shimp, Shveta
Singh, Liz Szarek, Kara Wheaton,
Vanessa Wood

The Kids Feeding Kids® Club is a non-profit organization of children dedicated to feeding hungry youth through fundraising, volunteering and other charitable activities.

We encourage children to get involved so they are able to build awareness, compassion and a foundation of philanthropy to last a lifetime. It is our belief that the earlier we introduce community service, volunteerism, and charity work to kids, the more likely they will stay engaged in these activities into adulthood making this a better world.

The Kids Feeding Kids® Club was founded in 2008 by Carson Pazdan at the age of five. Inspired by his love to cook and experiment in the kitchen, Carson wanted to create his own cookbook featuring all of his recipes as well as those from other kids. He dreamed of a cookbook designed FOR kids BY kids. This idea evolved into a vision of creating a club for kids where they can directly impact the lives of other children and help stop hunger.

100% of the profits from the sale of this cookbook will be donated to the Northern Illinois Food Bank – Youth Nutrition Program.

Northern Illinois Food Bank
delivering food assistance to your community

Special Thanks

A special thanks needs to be made to all of the kids, families, schools, churches and communities who have rallied together with their enthusiastic support and involvement to make this cookbook a reality. It is with their charitable hearts that we will help feed our hungry neighbors, especially children. Kudos to all of the parents who have embraced this opportunity to get their kids involved to show them that they truly can make a difference in the world!

Expression of Appreciation

To Dave & Cindy Amerine, Ally Gruener, Liz Benedetto, Karen Kardatzke, Sarah Roberts and everyone on the Cookbook Promotion Team, enough gratitude cannot be expressed for your involvement and participation. Your time, talent and compassion fill the pages of this book with friendship and love.

To Oprah Winfrey, we thank you for your acknowledgement of the amazing efforts by these children. Your philanthropy and generosity to children around the world is admirable and inspiring.

To Maria Shriver, Sean Hayes and Chris O'Donnell, your participation will help countless children in your home state and we thank you.

Acknowledgement

Countryside Elementary School, St. Mark's Day School, Barrington Middle School – Prairie Campus, Lake Zurich Community Unit School District 95, Lisle Community School District 202, Fox River Grove School District 3, St. Michael's Little Angels Christian Preschool, Noah's Ark Christian Preschool, Salem Methodist Preschool, Science and Arts Academy, Crossway's Preschool, Knox Presbyterian Church, Westchester Intermediate School, Park City Teen Center Cooking Club, Gurnee Teen Center Cook Club

Delivery Truck Donor

Dave & Cindy Amerine
Margaret Amerine
John & Melissa Anton
Ananth & Purnima Bhogaraju
Brett & Shawna Binkowski
Jeff & Ally Gruener

Cole, Graham & Hayden Hamilton
Mrs. Floyd's Second Grade Class
Mrs. McVey's 7th Grade Media Class
Dave & Alyssa Pazdan
Jerry & Mary Rose Pazdan
Kim Prell's Girl's Night Out

Grocery Cart Donor

Barrington Bank & Trust Co.
The Kathleen Kolb Bonham
Private Charitable Foundation
John & Gretchen Brashler
Bill & Karma Crowell
Jeff & Gina Deignan
John & Laura Denk
Mark & Kristin Hatch
Janet Herr
Brian & Courtney Desmond Keuer

Steve & Chelsea LaRocco
Larry & Michelle Lio
Judy Pazdan
Michael & Vicki Pesch
Steve & Laura Powroznyk
Daniel & Lee Ann Senese
Amarik & Shveta Singh
Damon & Mary Skyta
South Barrington Ladies Bunco
Paula Viola

Shopping Bag Donor

Doug & Robyn Angelbrandt
Josh & Heather Bastin
Monsignor Paul Brigandi
Steve & Jennifer Carroll
Charles & Joan Cope
Oliver & Erin Cotter
Tom & Keri Culhane
Craig & Laura Elpers
Cade Fetzer
Camryn Fetzer
Growning Cents of Style
Clifton & Erica Horn
Dan & Karen Kardatzke
Gene & Rose Koch
Rich & Linda LaRocco
Lovey & Peanut

Joe & Mary Ann Macino
Matt & Melissa Marquis
Whit & Taylor Moloney
Brad & Debbie Murray
Rachel Nazha
Craig, Julie, Annabel,
Abby & Atley Pittman
Kyle & Brandon Powroznyk
Tom & Mary Roberts
John & Kim Ruskusky
Paisley Schmitt
Justin Spiegel
Korry & Sharon Stagnito
Dean & Patty Thorsen
Welcome Baby Darling

elizabeth ashby
incorporated

VISUAL DESIGN
Specializing in eye-candy

773.428.6474

lizbenedetto@elizabeth-ashby.com

coming soon...

FIREFLY • INK

Images for All Reasons | Cards for All Seasons

Ally Gruener
P H O T O G R A P H Y

Specializing in
CUSTOM PORTRAITS, FOOD & COMMERCIAL
PHOTOGRAPHY

847.421.0446
WWW.ALLYGRUENER.COM

OPRAH'S CORN FRITTERS
Oprah Winfrey

2/3 cup yellow cornmeal
1/3 cup self-rising flour
1 cup buttermilk
1 egg, beaten
2 ears of corn, shucked or 1/2 cup frozen or canned corn
2 tblsp. unsalted butter, melted
milk or water, if needed (optional)

Microwave the corn on high for 2 or 3 minutes. Slice off the kernels, and set them aside. In a bowl, mix the cornmeal and the flour well, using a wire whisk. This will make your fritters very light. In a separate bowl, whisk together the buttermilk and the egg. Gradually add the wet ingredients to the dry. Don't worry if the batter isn't completely combined; you want to be careful not to over mix it. Fold in the corn and add the butter if desired. If the result is thicker than pancake batter, thin it with a little milk or water. Heat a skillet or a griddle to medium, spray with Pam, and add spoonfuls of batter. Cook the fritters for 2 minutes per side. A great way to tell if they're ready to turn is to look for little bubbles all over the surface. You might have to make a few fritters before they start coming out perfectly. Serve with honey or your favorite syrup.
Makes 4 servings.

CHRIS O'DONNELL'S TERRIFIC TURKEY TACOS
Chris O'Donnell & Family (Caroline, Lily, Chip, Charlie, Finn, and Maeve)

1 pkg. Lawry's Taco Seasoning
1 tblsp. olive oil
2 garlic cloves, finely chopped
1/4 cup onion, finely chopped
1 lb. ground turkey taco shells
shredded cheddar cheese
shredded lettuce
diced tomatoes

Saute onions, olive oil, and garlic. Remove from pan and set aside. Brown ground turkey in the same pan. Add taco seasoning (and water as directed on package). Stir in onion mixture until blended. Serve with taco shells and your favorite taco fixin's! Enjoy!

MARIA SHRIVER'S ORIENTAL CHICKEN SALAD

(Schatzi Recipe, in Famous Friends of Wolf Cookbook)
Maria Shriver, First Lady of California

Chicken Breasts

2 lbs. boneless chicken breasts
1/4 - 1/2 lb. mixed lettuce greens
1 bunch watercress, tops only
1 bunch cilantro

1 bunch mint, leaves only
1 large carrot
1 small cucumber
2 large oranges

Marinade for Chicken

1 cup low sodium soy sauce
3 oz. green onions, chopped
1 1/2 oz. ginger, peeled and julienned

2-3 oz. dark sesame oil
salt and pepper to taste

Sesame Rice Wine Vinaigrette

1 cup rice wine vinegar
1/2 cup peanut oil
1/2 cup sugar or to taste
2 tblsp. dark sesame oil
1 tblsp. low-sodium soy sauce

salt and pepper to taste
1/2 tsp. crushed red chile pepper
1/2 cup toasted slivered almonds
1 pinch pickled ginger
fried wonton skins for garnish

To prepare chicken:

Combine all marinade ingredients in a baking dish. Add salt and black pepper to taste. Place chicken breasts in the dish, and refrigerate, preferably overnight. Preheat oven to 350°. Pour off and discard marinade. Bake chicken, skin side up, for 30 minutes, or until cooked through. Cool, and remove skin. Shred Chicken. To prepare salad: Clean lettuces, spin dry, and chill for crispness. Mix watercress, mint and cilantro with lettuce. Peel and julienned the carrot and cucumber. Peel and segment the oranges. To prepare vinaigrette: Whisk all ingredients together in a bowl. To assemble salad: Place all ingredients except wonton skins in a large mixing bowl. Dress lightly with vinaigrette and toss gently. Add more dressing as required. Garnish with crumbled wonton skins.

CARYN BURKHARDT'S GRANDMOTHER'S SLOPPY JOES

Sean Hayes, Actor

1 1/2 - 2 lbs. ground beef
1/2 onion, chopped
1/2 green pepper, chopped
1 can tomato soup
1 sm. can tomato paste
1/4 cup chili sauce
1/4 cup brown sugar
1/2 tsp. salt
1/4 tsp. pepper
2-3 tblsp. dark molasses
1 tblsp. vinegar

Brown 1 1/2 - 2 lbs. ground beef, drain and set aside. Saute chopped onion with chopped green pepper for a few minutes and add ground beef back to pan with onion and pepper. Add the can of tomato soup, can tomato paste, chili sauce, brown sugar, salt, pepper, dark molasses, and vinegar. Heat together and simmer until flavors combine. Add Sloppy Joe mixture to your favorite hamburger buns.

I call this Caryn Burkhardt's grandmother's Sloppy Joes. Cause they're not mine. They're Caryn Burkhardt's grandmother's Sloppy Joes.

Tastes best with a glass of Caryn Burkhardt's grandmother's milk. Go nuts!

Sean Hayes

Table of Contents

APPETIZERS
&
BEVERAGES

Helpful Hints

- To add flavor to tea, dissolve old-fashioned lemon drops or hard mint candies in tea. They melt quickly and keep the tea brisk.

- Make your own spiced tea or cider. Place orange peels, whole cloves, and cinnamon sticks in a 6-inch square piece of cheesecloth. Gather the corners and tie with a string. Steep in hot cider or tea for 10 minutes or longer if you want a stronger flavor.

- Always chill juices or sodas before adding them to beverage recipes.

- Calorie-free club soda adds sparkle to iced fruit juices and reduces calories per portion.

- To cool your punch, float an ice ring made from the punch rather than using ice cubes. It appears more decorative and also inhibits melting and diluting.

- Place fresh or dried mint in the bottom of a cup of hot chocolate for a cool and refreshing taste.

- When making fresh orange juice or lemonade, one lemon yields about ¼ cup juice, and one orange yields about ⅓ cup juice.

- Never boil coffee; it brings out acids and causes a bitter taste. Store ground coffee in the refrigerator or freezer to keep it fresh.

- Always use cold water for electric drip coffee makers. Use 1–2 tablespoons ground coffee for each cup of water.

- How many appetizers should you prepare? Allow 4–6 appetizers per guest if a meal quickly follows. If a late meal is planned, allow 6–8 appetizers per guest. If no meal follows, allow 8–10 pieces per guest.

- If serving appetizers buffet-style or seating is limited, consider no-mess finger foods that don't require utensils to eat.

- Think "outside the bowl." Choose brightly-colored bowls to set off dips. Or get creative with hollowed-out loaves of bread, bell peppers, heads of cabbage, or winter squash.

- Cheeses should be served at room temperature, approximately 70°.

- To keep appetizers hot, make sure you have enough oven space and warming plates to maintain their temperature.

- To keep appetizers cold, set bowls on top of ice or rotate bowls of dips from the fridge every hour or as needed.

APPETIZERS & BEVERAGES

"BERRYLICIOUS" SMOOTHIES

Angelina Pascente - Age 12

1 container (6 oz.) strawberry
low-fat yogurt
1 stick (o.27 oz.) Kool-Aid
Singles Cherry Flavor Soft
Drink Mix

6 strawberries
1 cup ice cubes

Place all ingredients in a blender; cover. Blend 30 seconds or until thickened and smooth. Serve immediately. Substitute: This also tastes great prepared with Kool-Aid Singles Tropical Punch Flavor Drink Mix.

1-2-3 SNACK MEATBALLS

Nicholas Lawrence - Age 8
Jack Patrick - Age 8
Noah Matthew - Age 5

1½ lbs. hamburger
⅔ c. evaporated milk
2 tsp. Worcestershire sauce
1 env. onion soup mix

2 c. ketchup
1 c. brown sugar
1 T. Worcestershire sauce

Mix first four ingredients together. Shape into balls 1 Tbls. each. Bake on broiler pan in 350 degree oven 10-15 minutes or until done in the middle. For the sauce, mix the last three ingredients together and pour over cooked meatballs. Keep warm in the crockpot. Great for parties!

A BERRY HEALTHY SNACK!

Luke Richard - Age 6
Jessica Janice - Age 4

1 Graham Cracker Square
1 (2-oz.) tblsp Peanut Butter

8 Frozen Blueberries

Spread peanut butter onto 1 square graham cracker. Add approximately 8 Frozen Blueberries. Enjoy!

ANTS ON A LOG

Rachel Sue - Age 5

Celery Sticks
Peanut Butter

Raisins

Doesn't get much simpler than this! Spread the peanut butter on the celery sticks and add as many "ants" (raisins) as you want. This is

(continued)

one of Rachel's favorites and she loves that she can make them all by herself!

ANTS ON A LOG

Gianna Maria Keuer

2 sticks Washed Celery
4 tblsp Peanut butter

1 box Raisins

Cut each celery stick to how long you like your snack (Gianna likes it in thirds). Put the peanut butter on the celery (spread the peanut butter inside the concave part of the celery). Put raisins on top of the peanut butter so it looks like ants sitting on a log. EAT! YUM!!

ANTS ON A LOG

Kelsy Elizabeth - Age 11

1 bunch celery, cleaned and
**   stalks separated**

creamy peanut butter
raisins

Cut each stalk of celery in half. Fill with peanut butter. Sprinkle the raisins on the peanut butter. Now you have a delicious and healthy snack.

ANTS ON A LOG

Rocco Napoli - Age 9
Isabella Napoli - Age 5

1 celery stalk
1 cup raisins

2 cup peanut butter

Take celery and use spoonful of peanut butter to spread across. Then place raisins along the top of the peanut butter.

ANTS ON A SNOWY LOG

Harrison Mosier - Age 2
Mary Frances - Age 8 months

5 sticks celery
lots of cream cheese

lots of raisins

Spread cream cheese (snow) onto celery sticks (logs) and cover with raisins (ants) and enjoy!

APPLE CRUNCHIES

Jessica Lynn - Age 6
Ryan Robert - Age 4

1 apple

1 bag bagel chips

(continued)

98890-09

Have an adult slice an apple into thin, wide slices. Take out approximately 3 bagel chips from the bag. Place a bagel chip on a plate, then stack an apple slice on top of the chip. Repeat 1 or 2 more times. Voila! Apple Crunchies! Make a bunch and share with your friends or family!

APPLE PIE PARTY DIP

Timothy Sebastien - Age 5
Sophia Claire - Age 3

1⅓ c. peeled, cored and diced apples
1 tsp. lemon juice
2 tsp. brown sugar
2 tsp. apricot preserves

⅛ tsp. cinnamon
5 6" tortillas
2 T. butter, melted
½ tsp. cinnamon
1½ T. sugar

Combine apples, lemon juice, brown sugar, preserves, and cinnamon in a bowl. Cover and refrigerate until chilled. Brush the tortillas with butter; cut into wedges. Arrange on greased cookie sheet. Sprinkle with cinnamon and sugar, and bake at 350° until golden, about 10 minutes. Cool before serving. Arrange tortilla wedges around the bowl to dip and enjoy.

AUNT ERICA'S CHEX MIX

Bodhi F. Bykowski - Age 1

1 stick butter
3 tblsp Worcestershire sauce
2 tsp. seasoned salt
1 tsp. garlic powder
¾ tsp. onion powder
2 cups Corn Chex cereal

2 cups Rice Chex cereal
2 cups Wheat Chex cereal
2 cups mixed nuts
3 cups pretzels
1 cup garlic-flavor bite-size bagel chips

Heat oven to 250 degrees. Melt butter in large roasting pan in oven. Stir in seasonings. Gradually stir in remaining ingredients until evenly coated. Bake 1 hour, stirring every 15 minutes. Spread on paper towels to cool. Store in airtight container.

BACON SWISS DIP

John Thomas Blanke - Age 12

1 brick cream cheese
3 green onions, chopped
1 tsp. mayonnaise

8 strips of bacon
5 oz. shredded Swiss cheese
deli rye Triscuits

First, cook the bacon. Mix all other ingredients together and then add the bacon. Cook in the microwave for 3 minutes or until it is melted. Serve with deli rye Triscuits.

BACON WATER CHESTNUTS

Crystal Marie - Age 13

1 lb. bacon
1 (8-oz.) bottle Bennett chili
  sauce

2 (6-oz.) can whole water
  chestnuts
1 cup brown sugar

Cut bacon in half. Drain chestnuts. Roll chestnut up in a half slice of bacon. Hold together with a wood toothpick. In a shallow pan, bake in 350 degree oven for 40 minutes. Microwave brown sugar for 1 minute, then add chili sauce. Mix well. Drain grease from bacon. Dip bacon chestnuts in sauce, then return to oven for 10 minutes.

BACON WRAPPED SMOKEY LINKS

Issac Noah - Age 7

1 pkg. Cocktail Smokey Links   **1 lb. Bacon**

Cut bacon into thirds. Wrap a piece around each cocktail smokey link, secure with a toothpick. Place on baking sheet. Bake at 350 degrees for about an hour. Turn several times while cooking. When the bacon is crisp they are done. Enjoy!

BANANA CATERPILLAR

Amanda Leigh Dern - Age 8

1 banana
10 thin pretzel sticks

¼ cup peanut butter (optional)
3 raisins

Peel banana and slice into ½ inch slices. Break pretzels in half and insert into banana on both sides of each piece for legs. (optional) Dab peanut butter between each banana piece. Put raisins on head to make 2 eyes and a mouth.

BANANA SHAKE

Lizbeth P. - Age 13

2 bananas
milk

1 spoonful of Nesquik

Chop the bananas into little pieces and put them in a blender. Add as much milk as you need and one spoonful of Nesquik. Blend. There you have a great SHAKE!!!!!!!!!!!!

98890-09

BERRY BANANA SMOOTHIE

Xavier Mendoza - Age 13

1 ripe banana, cut into pieces
2 cups blueberries (fresh or
  frozen), strawberries, or any
  other kind

2 cups plain yogurt
¼ cup honey

Put all ingredients into a blender and blend until smooth.

Note: If using fresh fruit, add ½ cup crushed ice.

BERRY SMOOTHIE

Daniella Dolores - Age 12

1 or 2 bananas
2 cups blueberries
2 cups strawberries
1 cup milk

1 cup vanilla ice cream or
  vanilla yogurt
½ cup fruit juice (apple or
  orange), optional

Cut fruit into pieces and place in a blender. Add yogurt or vanilla ice cream and juice (if used). Blend and serve. Serves 4. Enjoy!

BEST BLUEBERRY SMOOTHIE

Madeline - Age 12
Emily - Age 10
Miah - Age 8

extra large Container of
  Blueberries (can be frozen)
extra large Container of Dannon
  Vanilla Yogurt

splash orange juice
handful of ice cubes
½ banana

Get out the blender and add all ingredients! Blend thoroughly and serve. Sample and add more of something if needed! Strawberries work well too. Very healthy and delicious!

BLUEBERRY & RASPBERRY SODA

Daniel Mies

1 cup blueberries
1 cup raspberries

2 cups sparkling water

Place blueberries and raspberries in a large bowl and mash well with a potato masher. Pour contents of the bowl through a fine mesh sieve to remove the solids, pressing down on the mashed blueberries and raspberries to extract all the juices. Transfer juice to a pitcher and add sparking water. Serve over ice and enjoy!

BUFFALO CHICKEN DIP

Issac Noah - Age 7

2 cans Chunk Chicken, drained
2 (8-oz.) pkgs. Creamed Cheese, softened
1 cup Ranch Dressing

¾ cup Red Hot Sauce
1½ cups Shredded Cheddar Cheese

Heat chicken and hot sauce in a skillet over medium heat, until heated through. Stir in cream cheese and ranch dressing. Cook, stirring until well blended and warm. Mix in half of the shredded cheese and transfer mixture to a slow cooker. Sprinkle the remaining cheese over the top, cover on LOW setting until hot and bubbly. Serve with celery sticks or pita chips. Enjoy!

BUFFALO CHICKEN WING DIP

Reece William - Age 7

1 cup Ranch Dressing
1 cup Frank's Red hot Buffalo Wing Sauce
2 cans chicken chunks
2-4 cups shredded cheddar cheese (preference to cheesiness)

8 oz. cream cheese
tortilla chips

Drain chicken and cut up cream cheese. Mix all ingredients together. Bake at 350 for 30 - 35 minutes. Enjoy with chips!

CHAMPIONS OF ITALY

Tristan Stephan - Age 13
Stephanie Hammond

4 Roma Tomatoes Chopped
3 Green Onions Chopped
3 tblsp Chopped Cilantro
1 small can Chopped Jalapeños (drained)

1 (16-oz.) pkg. Thick Shredded Colby-Jack Cheese
1 pkg. Good Seasons Italian dressing (prepared)

Mix all ingredients except dressing together in a large bowl. Add about ¾ of the prepared dressing. Refrigerate at least 3 hours. You can make it the night before. Serve with tortilla chips.

CHEERIO BITES

Jeremy Glavanovits

1 box Cheerios
peanut butter

sugar

(continued)

Take a Cheerio out of the box. Put a little bit of peanut butter on the Cheerio. Take a pinch of sugar and sprinkle it over the peanut butter.

CHEESY MOVIE POPCORN

Rachel Sue - Age 5

2 tblsp vegetable oil
1 cup popping corn kernels

3 tblsp melted butter
½ cup Parmesan cheese

Heat oil in deep pot over medium heat. Add corn. Cover pot and pop the corn, shaking pan often. Remove from heat. Drizzle with melted butter and sprinkle evenly with cheese. Serve hot. Makes 4 BIG servings. Put in your favorite movie and enjoy!!

CHEESY SALSA FLIP

Camryn Danielle - Age 9

1 Tortilla
2 tblsp Salsa

2 handful of Shredded Cheese

Put shredded cheese and salsa on half of tortilla. Fold the other half of the tortilla on top. Microwave for 30 seconds. It's like a quesadilla you don't have to dip!

CHERRY POP

Crystal Marie - Age 13

Sprite
Cherries

Ice

Pour sprite into a large cup. Then put as many cherries in the cup with the sprite as you would like. Put at least 3 ice cubes into the cup. Then put the cup into the freezer for at least 30 minutes. Take it out when the 30 minutes is up. Take a spoon and crush the ice. Now you have a delicious cheery pop slushy.

CHILE - CHEESE DIP (AUNTI KAREN'S DIP)

Jacob - Age 10

1 can chile with beans
1 (8-oz.) pkg. cream cheese

1 (8-oz.) pkg. shredded Mexican blend cheese

You need one 9-inch glass pie dish. Spread cream cheese equally to cover pie dish. Pour chile on top of cream cheese. Spread shredded cheese on top. Put in microwave for 5 minutes. Take out of microwave, it will be hot. Then serve with tortilla chips and enjoy! Makes 4-6 servings.

CHILI CHEESE DIP

John Thomas Blanke - Age 12

1 pkg. cream cheese
2 cups shredded cheese

1 can turkey chili with no beans
1 bag tortilla chips

In a dish, spread cream cheese then put the turkey chili on top of that and finally sprinkle cheese over the top. Cook in the microwave for 3 minutes or until the cheese is melted. Eat with tortilla chips.

CHIP BEEF DIP

Elizabeth Lauren - Age 6

1 pkg. chip beef lunch meat (cut up)
1 (8-oz.) pkg. cream cheese (softened)
1 c. sour cream

1/2 c. green pepper (chopped up)
1 tsp. grated onion
1 tsp. garlic salt
1 pinch salt

Combine all of the ingredients in a sprayed casserole dish. Back at 350 in the over for 30 minutes until hot. Serve hot with all types of crackers.

CHUTNEY CHEESE BALL

Melissa Adair, Memphis, TN

1 lb. shredded sharp cheese
1 tsp. salt
12 green onions, chopped
1 c. slivered almonds

1 1/2 c. mayo
1 jar chutney
12 oz. bacon, fried and crumbled

Mix cheese, salt, onions, almonds, and mayonnaise together. Shape into a ball. Top with chutney, then place bacon on top of chutney. Serve with crackers.

CRAZY DRINK

Emily M - Age 13

1/2 cup milk
1 slice banana

1/4 cup juice (your choice)

A drink fit for a king. The crazy drink is a good way to get your fruit servings for the day. All you have to do is blend the milk, banana and juice in a blender and wait until smooth.

(Tip: the riper the banana the sweeter).

8

98890-09

CREAMY CRAB DIP!

Erica McCathy

1 can Canned Crab Meat
1 pkg. Cream Cheese

¾ cups Cocktail sauce

Open and drain crab meat. Soften cream cheese in microwave for between 20 and 40 seconds. Mix together [in a medium bowl] the cream cheese and crab meat. Flatten the top and pour over cream cheese/crab mix. Spread evenly. Eat chilled with crackers!

CRUNCH AND MUNCH YOGURT PARFAIT

Candace J. Liu - Age 13

granola bar
fresh strawberries

1 cup plain yogurt

It's quick and simple! Grind the granola in a bowl and top with fresh strawberries. After that, add the cup of plain yogurt and get mixing! You now have a delicious and nutritious yogurt parfait!

CUCUMBER SANDWICHES

Rachel Sue - Age 5

1 cucumber
1 pkg. garlic &herb cheese
spread (Rondele)

1 small loaf pumpernickel bread
1 pinch dill weed

Rachel LOVES these little sandwiches. Peel and slice cucumber. Spread approx. ½ tablespoon cheese on the small pumpernickel bread slices; add cucumber slice on top and sprinkle with dill.

CUCUMBER SANDWICHES

Elleana Elisabeth - Age 6

Slices of Whole Wheat bread
1 container Sour cream
1 pkg. Hidden Valley Ranch
dressing

1 Seedless cucumber, thinly
sliced

Mix together sour cream and ranch dressing in a medium bowl. Spread sour cream mixture on each slice of bread. Arrange cucumber slices on one slice of bread. Place two slices together and enjoy.

DELANEY'S FIVE-LAYER MEXICAN DIP

Delaney Elizabeth - Age 8

1 can refried beans
3 avocados, peeled
1 tblsp. lemon juice
1 env. taco seasoning mix
2 cups sour cream

1 cup shredded cheddar cheese
2 tomatoes, chopped
1 (2-oz.) can sliced black olives,
  drained
chips

Spread bean dip in 9 x 13 inch pan (layer 1). Mash avocados with lemon juice in a bowl then spread over refried beans (layer 2). Stir taco seasoning mix with sour cream then spread over the avocado layer (layer 3). Top with cheese and tomatoes (layer 4). Sprinkle with olives (layer 5). Serve with chips.

DELUXE FAJITA NACHOS

Jose Hernandez - Age 12

2½ cups shredded cooked
  chicken
1 (1.27 oz.) pkg. Lawry's
  Spices & Seasonings for
  Fajitas
⅓ cup water
8 oz. tortilla chips
1¼ (5-oz.) cups grated Cheddar
  cheese

1 (4-oz.) cup grated Monterey
  Jack cheese
1 large tomato, chopped
1 (2.25 oz.) can sliced ripe
  olives, drained
¼ cup sliced green onions
salsa
guacamole
sour cream

Makes 4 appetizer or 2 main-dish servings. In medium skillet, combine chicken, spices & seasoning for Fajitas and water; blend well. Bring to a boil; reduce heat and simmer 3 minutes. In large shallow ovenproof platter, arrange chips. Top with chicken and cheese. Place under broiler to melt cheese. Top with tomato, olives, green onions and desired amount of salsa. Serve with guacamole and sour cream.

Substitution: 1 ¼ pounds cooked ground beef can be used in place of shredded chicken. HINT: For spicier version, add sliced jalapeños.

DEVILED EGGS

Kaley Murphy - Age 7
Lia Murphy - Age 5

6 hard-cooked eggs
¼ cup mayonnaise
¼ tsp. salt

pinch pepper
¼ tsp. prepared mustard
pinch paprika (optional)

Peel Hard-Cooked Eggs (eggs boiled in water for 15 minutes), cut in half lengthwise and remove yolks. Place yolks in a bowl and mash with a fork. Add mayonnaise, mustard, salt and pepper; mix well. Stuff egg-white halves with yolk mixture. If desired, garnish with paprika.

98890-09

DEVILED EGGS

Caius - Age 10

eggs **mayo**
relish

Boil eggs until cooked. Remove the shells. Cut the eggs in half and scoop out the yolk. Place yolks in a bowl. Add mayo and relish to the yolks. Mix thoroughly and fill the eggs with the mixture.

E & E'S POMABERRY SMOOTHIE

Emily Arwen - Age 4
Elise Annabelle - Age 2

1 ripe banana
1 cup strawberries or
blackberries, fresh or frozen
1 cup low fat vanilla yogurt

1 cup pomegranate blueberry
juice*
³/₄ - 1 cup low fat milk
honey - to taste

Place sliced banana and sliced strawberries (or whole blackberries) into blender. Add remaining ingredients using ³/₄ cup of milk to start. Blend until well mixed. If desired, add additional ¹/₄ cup of milk for thinner consistency; blend again. Enjoy! Makes about 4 servings. *We use Minute Maid Pomegranate Blueberry Flavored 100% Fruit Juice Blend.

EASY LAYERED TACO PIE

Ashley Richards - Age 13

1 pound lean ground beef
1 pkg. taco seasoning mix
¹/₂ cup water
4 flour tortillas, cut into quarters
1 cup cheddar jack Mexican
style shredded cheese

2 cups shredded lettuce
¹/₄ cup sliced green onions
¹/₄ cup sour cream

Place meat in microwaveable (plastic) colander set over microwaveable bowl. Microwave on HIGH 8 min., stirring and breaking up every 2 min. Discard any fat that collects in bowl. Transfer crumbled meat to 9-inch microwaveable dish. Stir in seasoning mix and water. Microwave for 5 min., stirring after 3 min. Remove half of the meat mixture; set aside. Place 8 tortilla quarters on top of remaining meat mixture in pie plate. Top with reserved meat mixture and remaining 8 tortilla quarters. Top with salsa and cheese. Microwave for 4 min. Top with lettuce, green onions, and sour cream just before serving. Makes 4 servings.

ELLA'S SMOOTHIE

Ella Albright - Age 11

3 Bananas
1 cup Strawberries

1 cup Yogurt
1 - 2 cups Pomegranate

Combine bananas, strawberries, yogurt and pomegranate in a blender until smooth.

FILLAT CRACKERS

Carson Bruce - Age 5

1 dozen saltine crackers
peanut butter
cinnamon

2 dozen chocolate chips
1 dozen marshmallows

Arrange crackers on cookie sheet. Spread peanut butter on each cracker and give each a dash of cinnamon. Arrange 3 chocolate chips per cracker. Top with a marshmallow. Bake at 350 degrees for 7 minutes or until marshmallow and chocolate chips have melted.

FOUR FRUIT SMOOTHIE

Emily Michelle - Age 13

1 Banana
8 Strawberries
½ c. Blackberries
½ c. Blueberries
1 (8-oz.) container Strawberry
  yogurt

½ c. Skim Milk
6 Ice cubes
1 tblsp. Honey

Put all ingredients in the blender. Blend on high power for 25 seconds or until the ice is crushed. Pour into glasses and enjoy!!!

FROZEN BERRY SLUSHY

Anthony Raven - Age 6
Jaydon Mateo - Age 5
Brandon Michael - Age 2

2 cups frozen berries: any kind
  or a combination
1 tblsp honey
1 cup crushed ice
½ cup sugar

1 tsp. vanilla (optional)
¼ cup orange juice (optional)
1 tsp. lemon juice
2 cups water

In a blender, combine all the ingredients listed. Blend completely. You can add more water for a thinner slushy or less water for an even thicker slushy. My kids like the strawberry or mixed berry slushy the best.

98890-09

FROZEN FRUIT SMOOTHIE

Annabel Marie - Age 7
Abigail Leigh - Age 4
Atley Catherine - Age 2

1½ c. Vanilla Yogurt
1 Banana
¾ c. Orange Juice
½ c. Milk

2½ c. Frozen Mixed Fruit
(raspberries, blueberries,
strawberries)

Place all ingredients in a blender and mix until smooth! Makes approximately four cups.

FRUIT MINGLED SMOOTHIE

Candace J. Liu - Age 13

2 cups fruit (your choice)
2 cups milk

2 tblsp. sugar
1 cup plain yogurt

Processing is easy! First, chop all of the fruit and put it into the blender. Then, pour in milk and yogurt. Finally, add a little bit of sugar to make it a little bit sweeter. Blend it all together and presto! Serves about 5 cups.

FRUIT PUNCH

Bennett John - Age 4
Annabelle Kady - Age 2

3 qts. orange juice
2 qts. pineapple juice
1 (2-liter) lemon-lime soda
½ cup grenadine syrup

4 cups ice cubes
1 orange - sliced
1 lemon - sliced
1 lime - sliced

Combine juices, soda and grenadine in a punch bowl. Add ice. Lay slices of fruit on ice to garnish. Enjoy! (serves 40)

FRUITFUL SMOOTHIE

Shivani S - Age 9
Sanjiv N - Age 6

1 cup vanilla yogurt
1 cup chocolate soy milk or
  plain milk
2 tblsp honey

1 banana
¼ cup blueberries
¼ cup strawberries

Put all the ingredients in your blender and process until smooth! You can add other berries or fruits to your liking. Enjoy!

FRUITY SMOOTHIE

Luke Richard - Age 6
Jessica Janice - Age 4

1 cup Frozen Strawberries
¼ cup Frozen Blueberries

¾ cup Berry Blend Fruit Juice
½ cup Yogurt

Place all ingredients into blender. Blend until smooth. YUM!

GOLDFISH SWIMMING

Harrison Mosier - Age 2
Mary Frances - Age 8 months

5 sticks celery
lots of cream cheese

lots of goldfish crackers

Spread cream cheese onto celery sticks and top with as many goldfish as you would like. Enjoy!

GRAHAM CRACKER AND PEANUT BUTTER TEA SANDWICHES

Emily Miller - Age 5

4 large Graham Crackers
lots of Peanut Butter

⅓ cup chocolate chips

Snap Graham Crackers in half, enough for 4 sandwiches. Spread peanut butter on bottom crackers. Add a few chocolate chips. Place top cracker on sandwich. Make four tea sandwiches. Serve with ice cold milk for a great afternoon snack.

GRAMMIE'S SHRIMP BALL

Grier - Age 1

1 (12-oz.) pkg. Cream cheese
3 stalks Green Onions
1½ tblsp Horseradish sauce

1 can Tiny Shrimp
1 bottle Cocktail Sauce
1 box crackers

Drain Shrimp. Chop green onions. Mix softened cream cheese, shrimp, green onions and horseradish sauce in a bowl. Form ball with mixture and place in refrigerator. When ready to serve, drizzle cocktail sauce on top of the bowl. Serve with crackers.

14

GRANDMA'S SWEDISH MEATBALLS

Jenna C. - Age 13

1 lb. ground beef
3/4 cup bread crumbs
1 egg, beaten lightly

1/2 onion, finely chopped
salt and pepper to taste
2 tblsp. parsley

Fold raw ground beef with all other ingredients until evenly mixed. Shape into small meatballs. Place on shallow pan. Bake 15-20 minutes at 350° or until brown.

GRANDMA'S TUNA DELIGHT

Madeline - Age 12
Emily - Age 10
Miah - Age 8

1 can Tuna
4 tblsp. Miracle Whip Light
1 tsp. ketchup
2 tsp. pickle relish

pinch garlic salt
tsp. minced onion
pinch black pepper

Gently mix all ingredients together. You can add sliced grapes and celery for extra yummy flavor. Serve on Ritz crackers or your favorite bread! A tuna lover's delight!

GRANDMA'S CHEESE BALL

Crystal Marie - Age 13

1 (3-oz.) wedge of Roquefort
1 (5-oz.) glass jar of Old English Cheese (Kraft)
2 (3-oz.) pkg. cream cheese

1 tblsp. Worcestershire sauce
1 sm. onion, grated
1 1/2 cup pecan pieces

Blend all ingredients together except for pecans and roll into a ball. Then wrap cheese ball in wax paper and refrigerate over night. When firm, role in pecan pieces and serve on platter with your favorite crackers.

GREEN APPLES & TUNA

Piper Patellis - Age 1

2 (6-oz.) can Tuna in Spring Water

2 medium Crisp Green Apples
1 cup Light Miracle Whip

Cut the green apples into small chunks and put them into a mixing bowl. Drain the tuna and add the tuna to the apples. Add the miracle whip and mix well. Serve as a sandwich or with crackers. This is a healthy snack or meal.

GUACAMOLE

Timothy Sebastien - Age 5
Sophia Claire - Age 3

4 avocados
3 limes
4 T. red onion, chopped
½ large orange

1 tsp. salt
4 tomatoes, roasted
½ poblano pepper
⅓ c. cilantro, chopped

Roast the tomatoes by cutting them in half, drizzling some olive oil over them, adding some dried Italian seasonings (ironic, I know) and put them in the oven at 300 degrees for twenty minutes. Put the seeded and halved poblano so it gets roasted at the same time. Cut the avocados in half and remove the seed. Pull them out of the skin and dump them in a bowl. Juice the lime and orange over the avocado. Use a knife to cut the avocado into ½" pieces (or so). Chop the tomatoes and poblano, and add them to the avocado mix. Add the salt and chopped cilantro. Stir the mixture gently, and you're done.

HALLOWEEN PUNCH

Ella Albright - Age 11

¼ cup Ginger Ale
¼ cup Apple Juice

Orange Slices

In a tall glass with ice add ginger ale and apple juice. Float orange slices on top and serve.

HOMEMADE LEMONADE FOR ONE

Max Tarasewicz

1½ cups of water
4 tblsp. sugar

3 tblsp. natural lemon juice

Pour water and lemon juice into a cup with a generous helping of ice. Add sugar and stir until dissolved. Put lemonade in the fridge for approximately 15 minutes. Enjoy!

HOT ARTICHOKE DIP

Stephanie - Age 10

1 (8-oz.) pkg. Cream Cheese, Softened
1 (14-oz.) can Artichoke Hearts, Drained and Chopped
½ c. Mayonnaise
½ (2-oz.) c. Grated Parmesan Cheese

2 T. Finely Chopped Fresh Basil or 1 tsp. Dried Basil Leaves
2 T. Finely Chopped Red Onion
1 clove Garlic, Minced
1 Tomato, Chopped

(continued)

98890-09

Mix cream cheese and all remaining ingredients, except tomato, with electric mixer on medium speed until well blended. Spoon into a 9-inch quiche dish or pie plate. Bake at 350° for 25 minutes. Sprinkle with tomato. Serve with assorted cut-up vegetables or toasted pita bread wedges. Garnish if desired.

INCREDIBLE PUNCH

Ashley Ann - Age 5½
Matt - Age 8½
Mom - Age Unimportant :)

1 (46-oz.) bottle Cranberry-Raspberry Juice
½ (32-oz.) bottle Pina Colada Mix (non-alcoholic of course)

1 (2-liter) bottle Raspberry Ginger Ale Soda
1 (10-oz.) approx. frozen mixed berries

1. In a large bowl, stir cranberry-raspberry juice with the pina colada mix. Transfer to large gallon-size zip bags and freeze overnight. (Keep flat in freezer.) 2. Fill mini ice cube trays with either cranberry juice or ginger ale ¾ full. Then top with a frozen berry (no thawing needed). (You are making frozen berry cubes to float and serve with your punch.) 3. The next day... Remove the punch from the freezer 30 minutes prior to serving. Place frozen slush in a nice punch bowl and slowly add raspberry ginger ale to mixture. (I usually add more, as it tends to be on the sweet side.) Go ahead and use a potato masher to help it slush down quicker. After the punch is a nice consistency and no longer in a clump, add those pretty berry cubes and enjoy! The kids LOVE this punch and it goes quickly, so I usually double this recipe! The adults like it too with a little something added to it! :)

IZZITAS

Izzy - Age 11

Flour Tortillas
Cheese Sticks

salsa (optional)

Place tortilla in microwave and put a cheese stick on tortilla at one end. Microwave for five seconds. Roll up tortilla with cheese stick in the middle. Microwave for ten more seconds or until cheese is melted. You can also serve with salsa on the side.

JALAPEÑO POPPERS

Nikki Morgan Brown - Age 16

2 lbs. Jalapeños
5 - 6 (8-oz.) boxes cream cheese

2 pkgs. bacon
several toothpicks

Preheat oven to 325°. Cut the Jalapeños down the sides. Then take a spoon and take all the seeds out and fill with the cream cheese. Put

(continued)

the peppers on a tray with aluminum foil. Cut the bacon in medium size slices. Wrap each Jalapeño with a slice of bacon. Place tray in oven, and cook for 60 minutes. Let cool. Enjoy!

KLAYICE NADAY CRACKERS

Carson Bruce - Age 5

1 sleeve Saltine Crackers
1 can squeezable cheese

1 jar sunflower seeds

Spread cheese on each saltine cracker. Top with sunflower seeds. Easy, simple, and something every kid can make themselves!

LEMONADE

Ella Albright - Age 11

1 Lemon
2 cups Water

1 cup Sugar

Cut a lemon in half. Squeeze the lemons into a pitcher. Add a cup of sugar. Then stir.

MAMA MIA

Tristan Stephan - Age 13
Stephanie Hammond

1 (8-oz.) pkg. Cream Cheese
1 (8-oz.) tub Sour Cream
Garlic Powder
Onion Salt
Chives

Salt and Pepper
1/4 cup Chopped Pepperoni
1/4 cup Marinara Sauce
Mozzarella Cheese
French bread slices or crackers

Spread cream cheese on a microwaveable plate. Spread sour cream on top. Sprinkle on garlic powder, onion salt, salt and pepper, and chives to taste. A lot or a little depending on how you like it. Pour on the marinara sauce and top with chopped pepperoni and shredded mozzarella cheese. Microwave until cheese has melted. Serve with French bread slices or crackers.

MANGO LASSI

Ankur K. - Age 9

2 mangos
1 (16-oz.) container plain yogurt

sugar, to taste
2 cups water

Take fully ripe mangos and remove pulp. Put pulp in blender. Add plain yogurt and water and sugar. Blend for 2 minutes or until smoothie is done. Add cubes of ice and serve chilled. Serves 6.

98890-09

MANGO SMOOTHIE

Jasmine Patel - Age 9

2 Mangos, peeled
200 grams Plain Yogurt

12 Ice cubes
4 tsp. Sugar

Peel mangos and slice into blender. Add 200 grams plain yogurt, 12 ice cubes and 4 teaspoons of sugar. Blend until smooth. Makes two servings. Enjoy your mango smoothie!

MINI CORNDOGS

Lane - Age 8
Mackenzie - Age 5

1 can Pillsbury refrigerated
   breadsticks

1 pkg. mini cocktail wieners

Heat oven to 375 degrees. Open a can of breadsticks, separate them and using a kitchen scissors, cut each strip into two. Take a piece of the breadstick dough and place a mini wiener at one end. Roll up the wiener the full length of the dough. Give it a quick squeeze to keep the dough secure. Repeat with the remaining pieces of dough and wieners. Spread out the wrapped wieners on a non-stick baking sheet and back for 10-12 minutes until golden. Serve with dipping sauces.

MINI CUCUMBER SANDWICHES

Brandan Michael - Age 17
Allie Marie - Age 10
Avery Madison - Age 7

1 large Cucumber
1 pkg. Cream Cheese (one brick
   softened)
1 tblsp Mayonnaise

1 packet Good Seasons Italian
   Salad Dressing Mix (dry)
few shakes Dill Weed
1 loaf Cocktail Rye

Peel cucumber and cut into slices about 1/4" to 1/2" thick. Combine softened cream cheese, mayonnaise and salad dressing in a small bowl. Spread onto slices of cocktail rye. Top with a slice of cucumber and sprinkle of dill weed.

MINI FRUIT KEBOBS

Candace J. Liu - Age 13

any 3 fruits

toothpicks

Just pick your favorite fruits and chop them up into slices. Then, cut those slices into fun shapes like squares or triangles. Come up with as many different shapes and sizes of fruit you can think of! Put each little piece of fruit on each tooth pick and you have the mini fruit kebobs!

MINI QUICHE

Allison Lynn - Age 11
Mallory Jean - Age 8
Ryan - Age 4

8 ounce small curd cottage
  cheese
¼ cup sour cream
¼ cup melted butter
4 ounce shredded sharp
  cheddar cheese

½ cup Bisquick
3 eggs
¼ cup chopped onions
¼ cup bacon bits
¼ cup chopped mushrooms

Last three ingredients are optional, depending on your taste preferences. Other items may be substituted. Preheat oven to 350°. Combine all ingredients with mixer. Grease mini muffin tins with Crisco and fill ¾ full. Bake 18-20 minutes. Quiche freezes very well.

MINI TACOS

Elise Marie - Age 13

1 lb. ground beef
1 pkt. taco seasoning mix
2 cups French Fried Onions
¼ cup chopped fresh cilantro
32 bite-size round tortilla chips

¾ cup sour cream
1 cup shredded cheese
¾ cup water
red bell pepper (optional)

Cook the ground beef in a skillet over medium-high for 5 minutes (until browned); then drain it. Stir in the taco seasoning mix, ¾ cup water, 1 cup French fried onions, and cilantro. Cook this on low for 5 minutes until all flavors are blended. Preheat the oven to 350 degrees. Arrange tortilla chips on a foil-lined baking sheet. Top with beef mixture, sour cream, and cheese. Bake this for 5 minutes or until the cheese is melted. Sprinkle it with chopped red bell pepper (optional). Tada! You now have bite size appetizers for your party!

MIXED FRUIT SALSA

Christopher Rosenberg - Age 14

1 (16-oz.) pkg. mixed frozen
  berries, thawed and chopped
2 medium peaches, diced
2 medium kiwifruit, peeled and
  diced
3 tblsp. sugar

2 tblsp. lemon juice
1½ tsp. grated lime peel
8 flour tortillas (7 inches)
3 tblsp. butter, melted
3 tblsp. sugar
1½ tsp. ground cinnamon

In a large bowl, combine the first six ingredients and set aside. Brush both sides of tortillas with butter. Combine the sugar and cinnamon; sprinkle over both sides of tortilla. Cut each into six wedges. Place on ungreased baking sheets. Bake at 400° for 6-8 minutes on each side until crisp. Drain salsa; serve with tortilla chips. Makes 6-8 servings.

98890-09

MOM SURPRISE

Aidan Francis - Age 6

½ cup 100% fruit juice, any flavor

½ cup lemon-lime soda
4-6 cubes ice

Add all ingredients to a "fun" cup. Garnish the cup and add a straw. Enjoy! The surprise comes in because the flavors are always changing based on the type of fruit juice you have on hand at the time.

MOM'S EASY CORN AND BEAN DIP

Bodhi F. Bykowski - Age 1

2 cans black-eyed peas
2 cans white corn
1 can Rotel Tomatoes
2 tblsp Mrs. Dash
¼ red onion

1 can black olives
½ cup Paul Newman's Family Recipe Italian Salad Dressing
½ cup finely shredded Jack cheese

Drain and rinse the peas and corn well. Drain the tomatoes. Finely chop the red onion. Dump all in bowl. Add black olives, salad dressing and Mrs. Dash. Mix well. It is better if you let it sit overnight -- refrigerate. Add cheese when ready to serve. (I don't usually add cheese at all. We prefer it without, and leftovers keep well.) Serve with nacho chips. The original recipe didn't come with amounts for most of the ingredients. I have included the amounts that we have honed in on, but you may adjust them for your personal taste! Enjoy!

MUSHROOM CUPS

Carson Bruce - Age 5

1 dozen mushrooms
1 dozen saltine crackers
1 cup shredded cheddar cheese
½ cup grated Parmesan cheese

⅓ cup soft butter
⅓ cup mayonnaise
⅓ cup mustard
salt and pepper

Wash and dry mushrooms. Pull out stalk and arrange on a cookie sheet. In a bowl, mix the cheddar cheese, Parmesan cheese, butter, mayonnaise and mustard. Fill each mushroom with the mixture. Salt and pepper to taste. Bake at 350 degrees for 15 to 20 minutes.

OVER THE TOP POPCORN

Timothy Sebastien - Age 5
Sophia Claire - Age 3

4 slices bacon
¹/₄ c. popcorn kernels
1 T. oil
4 T. butter, melted
¹/₄ c. Parmesan cheese, grated
  (not from the can)

2 tsp. buttermilk Ranch dressing
  mix
¹/₄ tsp. pepper

Cook bacon in a large skillet over medium-high heat 10 minutes or until crisp. Remove bacon, and drain on paper towels. Coarsely chop bacon. Pour oil into a large metal bowl, add popcorn kernels. Cover with tin foil, and poke holes in the tin foil. Heat on medium high, shaking constantly until all kernels are popped. Remove foil. Toss with bacon, Parmesan cheese, melted butter, dressing mix, and pepper. Serve immediately.

PEANUT BUTTER AND BANANA WAKEY-SHAKEY

MaryFaye Margaret - Age 8

1 banana
1 heaping T. smooth peanut
  butter

¹/₂ cup milk
whipped cream (optional)
candied cherries (optional)

Before you go to bed, peel and chop banana into bite-sized pieces. Put in a plastic bag and leave in the freezer overnight. When you wake up, put all ingredients in the blender. Get a grown-up to help you whiz it up for about a minute, or until it's really thick and smooth. Makes sure you hold the lid down or your shake might end up all over the kitchen! Top shake with whipped cream or cherries if you want to. EXTRAS: try swapping the peanut butter for any of these: ¹/₄ cup strawberries, blueberries or raspberries and 1 teaspoon of honey. Add 1 heaping tablespoon sweetened cocoa powder.

PEANUT BUTTER BANANA SMOOTHIE

Carson Bruce - Age 5

4 cups ice
1 cup peanut butter
1 tblsp cinnamon

1 banana
1 cup vanilla ice cream
1 cup milk

Add all ingredients into a blender. Blend until smooth. Serve in a large glass with a straw and probably a spoon. Delicious, delicious, delicious!

98890-09

PEANUT BUTTER BANANA SURPRISE

Allison Hope - Age 5
Natalie Barbara - Age 3

1 banana
Peanut butter

1 handful of crunchy snacks

Peel the banana and slice it into round pieces. Spread some peanut butter onto each piece. Then top it with your favorite crunchy snack such as goldfish, animal crackers, teddy grahams or pretzels. Enjoy!

PINEAPPLE NUT BALL

Jack S - Age 13

2 (8-oz.) pkgs. cream cheese
2 cups finely chopped pecans
1 (8-oz.) can crushed pineapple

¼ cup green pepper, diced
1 tblsp onion, diced
1 tsp. seasoned salt

In a bowl, combine cream cheese, 1 cup of pecans, pineapple, green pepper, onion, and salt and mix well. Refrigerate for 1 hour. Divide in to bite-sized balls. Roll balls in remaining cup of pecans. Place back in refrigerator. Remove from refrigerator 30 minutes before serving.

PINK FLOAT SHAKE

Meagan Reigh - Age 12

1 frozen banana
½ cup milk

1 T. strawberry syrup (like
Nesquik)

Place ingredients in blender. Blend until smooth.

PIZZA BARS

George Wight XI

2 cups Milk
2 Eggs
Pepperoni slices (thin)
1¼ cup Flour

8 oz. Munster cheese (grated)
8 oz. Mozzarella cheese (grated)
4 oz. Cheddar cheese (grated)

Yields 24 bars (slices). Preheat oven to 350 degrees and grease cookie sheet. Mix eggs and flour. Add grated/shredded cheese to mixture. Fold in ½ of pepperoni slices and pour into cookie sheet, spread evenly. Add additional pepperoni to the top of mixture. Bake for 30 minutes - slice and serve hot or at room temperature.

PURPLE COW

Emma Janina - Age 7

4 cups Vanilla Ice Cream
¼ cup Purple Grape Juice

½ cup Blueberries
10 Mini Marshmallows (optional)

In a blender, mix ice cream, grape juice and blueberries. Blend until smooth. Pour into a glass and garnish with mini marshmallows.

ROOT BEER FLOAT

Connor Corrigan

2 scoops vanilla ice cream

1 can of root beer soda

Put 2 scoops of vanilla ice cream in a tall glass. Pour root beer in the cup. Add a straw and spoon.

SEAFOOD NACHOS

Hunter - Age 4

1 bag Tortilla Chips
1 can Crab meat
2 cups Shredded Cheddar Cheese

1 container Sour Cream
Taco Sauce

Line baking tray with tin foil. Spread chips on tray. Drain crabmeat, mix crabmeat with shredded cheese in a bowl. Sprinkle mixture over chips. Put tray in oven (low broil) until cheese is melted. Remove tray and top nachos with sour cream, taco sauce, olives, peppers, anything you like!

SENSATIONAL FRUIT SMOOTHIE

Michael Vitale - Age 5
Matthew Vitale - Age 3

2 cups Frozen strawberries
2 cups Frozen raspberries
1 cup Vanilla yogurt
4 tblsp Strawberry yogurt

5 cubes Pineapple
8 oz. Apple juice
1 Banana

Blend fruit, yogurt, and juice together on high speed in a blender. Add ice and mix again. Serve in fancy glasses with straws. Cheers!

SMOOTHIE HEAVEN

Ashley - Age 12

½ cup any flavored sherbet
10 strawberries

½ cup pineapple chunks
1½ cup orange juice

(continued)

98890-09

Cut strawberries in half. Mix sherbet, strawberries, pineapple chunks, and orange juice together in blender until smooth. Add a couple ice cubes at end to turn smoothie heaven into a chilling drink.

SOMBREROS

David Stuart - Age 7

2 slices Bologna
1½ tblsp Soy Sauce

1 tsp. Water

In a skillet, sauté bologna in the soy sauce and water. When very hot, the bologna forms a shape like a hence the name Sombrero! Remove bologna from pan and place on plate. Let it cool a little bit and it is ready to eat!

SOY MILK SMOOTHIE

Daniel Mies

2 (8-oz.) cups unsweetened soy milk
1 banana

½ cup chopped mango
½ cup chopped strawberries
2 T. honey

Put the soy milk, banana, mango, strawberries and honey in a blender. Have your grown-up helper help you blend it until it is smooth. Divide among four cups and enjoy!

SPINACH-ARTICHOKE DIP

Wyatt - Age 13
Morgan - Age 7

1 cup miracle whip
1 cup sour cream
1 (14-oz.) can artichoke hearts drained and chopped
1 (10-oz.) box frozen, chopped spinach well drained

1 cup shredded cheddar cheese
1 cup grated Parmesan cheese
1 clove minced garlic
chopped tomato
sliced green onions

Mix all ingredients except tomato and onions. Spoon into two separate 9-inch pie plates. Bake at 350 degrees for 20-25 minutes. Sprinkle with tomato and onions. Serve with crackers or toasted pita bread. Serve one pie and freeze the other if desired.

STRAWBERRY BANANA SMOOTHIE

Mckenna Grace - Age 2

1 banana
1 cup frozen (or fresh)
 strawberries
1 cup milk

1 cup vanilla ice cream (or
 frozen yogurt)
splash of apple or orange juice

Add all ingredients into blender and blend until smooth.

STRAWBERRY KOOL-AID

Gabi Chatman

1 packet Strawberry Kool-Aid
1 cup sugar

2 cups water
4 strawberries

Pour contents of Kool-Aid packet into a pitcher. Add sugar and water.
Serve in a glass with ice and strawberries on the side.

STRAWBERRY SMOOTHIES

Elleana Elisabeth - Age 6

2 cups soymilk or 2% milk
1½ cups frozen or fresh
 strawberries (optional - use
 blueberries, raspberries)

2 (6-oz.) containers berry yogurt
4 tblsp sugar

Combine all ingredients in blender. Stir and blend again. Pour in 8 oz.
glass, top with whip cream and enjoy. Makes about 4 - 8 oz. cups

STRAWBERRY-MANGO SMOOTHIE

Rachel Haraldsen

1 cup Milk
1 can Yogurt
10 Strawberries

2 Mangos (remove pit and skin)
2 cups Ice
Sugar (to taste)

Put all ingredients in a blender and mix until no chunks are left. Pour
into cup and enjoy!

STUFFED CRESCENT ROLLS

Izabela Urszula Presta - Age 9

1 can refrigerated crescent rolls
2 tsp. flour for work area
2 tblsp. butter, softened
8 thin slices deli ham or turkey

4 stick string cheese, cut into 4
 pieces
poppy seeds (optional)

(continued)

98890-09

Preheat oven to 375°. Unroll each crescent roll on a lightly floured work area. Turn to coat each side of roll. Put ½ tsp. softened butter on each piece of dough. Top with 1 slice of ham or turkey and finish with 2 small chunks of string cheese. Roll up dough from the widest side and form into a straight horn shape. Add poppy seeds on top if desired. Bake rolls as directed on package.

THE CHAMPION SMOOTHIE

Kamren Christopher - Age 5½
Keaten Lawrence - Age 7

2 scoops rainbow sherbet
1 cup Tropicana Healthy Kids
orange juice

½ cup apple juice
½ cup frozen mixed berries

Combine all ingredients in a blender. Blend until smooth. Makes 2 yummy servings.

TROPICAL TWISTER SHAKE

Michael - Age 10

1 c. Dole tropical fruit salad
1 c. lowfat vanilla frozen yogurt
or ice milk

½ medium banana
½ c. skim milk
⅓ c. syrup from fruit salad

Drain fruit salad, reserve ⅓ cup syrup. Add syrup and remaining ingredients to blender. Blend until smooth. Makes 2 servings.

TZATZIKI
(Greek Cucumber Dip)

Baylor George - Age 5

1 (16-oz.) container plain yogurt
1 large cucumber
2 tblsp. fresh lemon juice
2 tsp. olive oil

1 tsp. dill
2 tsp. fresh minced garlic
Pita chips, pita bread or veggies
for dipping

In a large bowl, combine yogurt, lemon juice, olive oil, dill and garlic. Peel and slice cucumber in half the long way and scrape out all the seeds with a teaspoon. Dice cucumber into small pieces. Combine cucumbers with yogurt mixture. Serve well chilled. Serve with pita chips, fresh pita bread, veggies, etc. Also great with gyros or chicken. (This is my favorite after school snack!)

VEGETABLE SAMOSA

Arjun Varma - Age 12

Dough ingredients as follows:
1 cup flour
½ tsp. carom seeds (optional)
3 tblsp oil
salt to taste
Stuffing ingredients as follows:
½ cup shelled green peas
2 tblsp oil (for frying)
1 tsp. cumin seeds

1 tsp. chopped ginger
1 tsp. chopped green chilies
2 cups potato cubes (½ centimeters)
1 tsp. red chili powder
salt to taste
1 tsp. dry mango powder
1 tsp. garam masala powder
1 tblsp chopped cilantro leaves

Mix the dough ingredients. Add water little by little and make a hard dough. Keep it under a wet cloth for ten to fifteen minutes. Next, cook green peas in salted boiling water till it is soft. Refresh the peas in cold water. Drain out excess water. Heat oil in a pan, add cumin seeds and when they start to change color, add chopped ginger, chopped green chilies and diced potatoes. Add red chili powder, salt, dry mango powder and garam masala powder. Stir well. Sprinkle with water and cook covered until the potatoes are done. Add the shelled green peas and mix them well. Divide the dough into sixteen equal portions and roll them into balls. Apply a little flour and roll them into four-inch diameter elongated diskettes. Cut them into half and apply water on the edges. Shape it into a cone and stuff it with the potato and peas filling. Seal the edges and deep fry in medium hot oil until they are crisp and golden brown. Serve hot with tamarind chutney as an appetizer.

WALKING SALAD

Ava Mary - Age 2

Iceberg Lettuce
Peanut Butter

Raisins
Apple Slices (green or red)

Spread a dollop of peanut butter on one leaf of iceberg lettuce, lay apple slices & raisins on top of lettuce & peanut butter then roll up. Walk, Eat & Enjoy!

98890-09

Soups & Salads

Helpful Hints

- If the soup is not intended as the main course, count on 1 quart to serve 6. As the main dish, plan on 1 quart to serve 2.

- After cooking vegetables, pour any water and leftover vegetable pieces into a freezer container. When full, add tomato juice and seasoning to create a money-saving "free soup."

- Instant potatoes help to thicken soups and stews.

- A leaf of lettuce dropped in a pot of soup absorbs grease from the top. Remove the lettuce and serve. Or make the soup the day before, chill, and scrape off the hardened fat that rises to the top.

- To cut down on odors when cooking cabbage or cauliflower, add a little vinegar to the water and don't overcook.

- Three large stalks of celery, chopped and added to about two cups of beans (navy, brown, pinto, etc.) makes the dish easier to digest.

- Fresh is best, but to reduce time in the kitchen, use canned or frozen broths or bouillon bases. Canned or frozen vegetables will work well, such as peas, green beans, and corn.

- Ideally, serve cold soups in chilled dishes.

- Perk up soggy lettuce by spritzing it with a mixture of lemon juice and cold water.

- You can easily remove egg shells from hard-boiled eggs if you quickly rinse the eggs in cold water after they are boiled. Also, add a drop of food coloring to help indicate cooked eggs and raw ones.

- Your fruit salads will look better when you use an egg slicer to make perfect slices of strawberries, kiwis, or bananas.

- The ratio for a vinaigrette is typically 3 parts oil to 1 part vinegar.

- Cook pasta for salads al dente (slightly chewy to the bite). This allows the pasta to absorb some of the dressing and not become mushy.

- Fresh vegetables require little seasoning or cooking. If the vegetable is old, dress it up with sauces or seasoning.

- Chill the serving plates to keep the salad crisp.

- Fruit juices, such as pineapple and orange, can be used as salad dressing by adding a little olive oil, nutmeg, and honey.

SOUPS & SALADS

APPLE CRAISIN SALAD

Sophie Clark - Age 6
Ian Clark - Age 4

Salad:
1 bag spinach
3 red apples
1 bunch romaine
(4-oz.) fresh grated mozzarella
1 package dried cranberries or
  Craisins
cashews

Dressing:
³/₄ cup sugar (I use less)
¹/₃ cup cider vinegar
1 tsp. dried mustard
1 cup vegetable oil
1 tsp. salt
1 tblsp. poppy seeds
1¹/₂ tblsp. fresh grated onion

Dice apples leaving skins. Mix together all salad ingredients. Use own judgement on amount of cashews and Craisins. Combine dressing ingredients in a jar; add to salad just before serving. May not want to use all dressing or serve dressing on the side.

BACON POTATO CHOWDER

Issac Noah - Age 7

8 slices Bacon cut into
  ¹/₂"pieces
1 cup Onion chopped
2 cups Potatoes diced with skin
  on
1 cup Water

1 tsp. Salt
¹/₈ tsp. Pepper
1 (10-oz.) can Condensed Cream
  of Chicken Soup
1 cup Half and Half
1¹/₂ cups Milk

In a 3 qt sauce pan fry bacon until brown. Add onions and cook until tender. Add potatoes, water, salt and pepper. Cook until potatoes are fork tender. Reduce heat to low and stir in soup, half and half and milk. Continue to cook on low and stir occasionally. Garnish with chopped green onions and shredded cheddar cheese. Enjoy!

BEST CHICKEN SALAD EVER

John W. - Age 13

1 Roasted Chicken
¹/₂ cup extra virgin olive oil
1 tsp. dried oregano
juice of 1 lemon
¹/₂ cup imported black olives
2 tblsp drained tiny capers

8 grape tomatoes (yellow or
  red), halved lengthwise
¹/₄ lb. thin green beans
Romaine Lettuce leaves, cooked
2 tblsp chopped parsley, for
  serving

First, remove the skin from the chicken and tear the meat into large pieces. Place chicken in a bowl. Combine with the oil, oregano, and

(continued)

lemon juice. Let stand for 1 hour. Toss the chicken with the olives, capers, tomatoes, and beans. Season with salt and pepper. Arrange the salad on romaine lettuce.

BLAKEY SNAKEY'S WORLD FAMOUS CHICKEN NOODLE SOUP

Braelyn Grace - Age 6
Blake Emmitt - Age 4

5 qt. Water
1 Whole Chicken quartered
1/2 cup Kosher Salt
1 Bay leaf
1 cup Carrots-diced
1 cup Celery-diced

1 cup Onion-chopped
2 tblsp Olive Oil
Salt and pepper to taste
3 cups Egg Noodles
Cracked Black Pepper

BROTH- Fill large stock pot with 5 qt's of fresh water, add 1/2 cup of salt, 1 bay leaf and chicken parts (you may want to remove some or all of the skin before boiling to minimize grease) bring to boil and simmer for 1-2 hours; this will be your broth (you may want to add salt based on your taste). Remove chicken parts and let cool to touch. Take meat off of bones, chop and put aside. You may want to add the remaining chicken bones back to the broth to add additional flavor. VEGGIES- In another large stock pot (large enough to incorporate broth later to finish the soup) heat olive oil and sauté Onions, Carrots and Celery, salt and pepper to taste. Add chopped Chicken and sauté for 2-3 minutes. SOUP- Strain the broth into the pot with the veggies and chicken add salt and pepper to taste. Cook Egg Noodles as directed on package. Add noodles to the soup when served to prevent the noodles from absorbing the broth and thickening the soup. Enjoy with your family and friends!

BROCCOLI SALAD

Stephanie Ann - Age 16

1 bunch broccoli (in a bag, buds only)
1 sm. white onion, chopped finely
1/2 cup grated cheddar cheese
1/2 lb. bacon, cooked well, drained, cooled & diced

1 1/2 cup mayonnaise
2 tblsp. sugar
1/2 tsp. salt
1/2 tsp. pepper
2 tsp. white vinegar

Toss together broccoli, onion, cheese and bacon in large bowl. Mix together; mayonnaise, sugar, vinegar, salt and pepper. Add to broccoli mixture and toss until blended. Make 24 hours ahead and refrigerate. Serves 6-8.

98890-09

CAESAR SALAD WITH SLICED CHICKEN BREASTS

Kaitlyn N - Age 7

½ cup nonfat mayonnaise
¼ cup skim milk
1 tsp. lemon juice
1 tsp. balsamic vinegar
1 tsp. Dijon mustard
½ tsp. Worcestershire
1 clove garlic

2 T. Parmesan cheese
black pepper to taste
4 boneless, skinless chicken
  breasts
1 head Romaine lettuce
croutons (optional)

Blend mayonnaise, milk, lemon juice, vinegar, mustard, Worcestershire, garlic, Parmesan cheese and pepper in blender until smooth. Chill for one hour. Broil chicken breasts - six minutes on each side or until golden brown and juices run clear. Let cool and slice. Tear lettuce into bite size chunks. Toss with chicken and dressing and sprinkle with grated Parmesan cheese. Serve with croutons if desired.

CARAMEL APPLE SALAD
(TAFFY APPLY SALAD)

Issac Noah - Age 7

1 (8-oz.) Cool Whip
1 pkg. Instant Butterscotch
  Pudding
1 (8-oz.) can Crushed Pineapple
  with juice

3 cups Diced Apples
1 cup Dry Roasted Nuts
1 cup Marshmallows

Mix Cool Whip, Instant Pudding and Pineapple with juice together. Add Apples, Nuts, and Marshmallows. Refrigerate until ready to serve. Enjoy!

CHICKEN NOODLE SOUP

Mike Groth - Age 12

2½ lb. Frying chicken, cut up
10 cups Water
2 Chicken-flavor bouillon cubes
½ cup Onion, chopped
1½ tsp. Salt
½ tsp. Pepper

1 Bay Leaf
1 cup Celery, sliced
1 cup Carrots, thinly sliced
3½ oz. Wide Egg Noodles,
  uncooked

In 5-quart Dutch oven, combine chicken and water. Bring to a boil; reduce heat. Cover; simmer 15 minutes. Skim surface of broth, if necessary. Add bouillon cubes, ½ cup onion, salt, pepper, and bay leaf. Cover; simmer an additional 35 to 40 minutes or until chicken is tender. Remove chicken from bones; cut into bite-sized pieces. Skim fat from broth. Return chicken to broth. Stir in celery, carrots, and ¼ cup onion. Bring to a boil; reduce heat. Cover; simmer for 15 minutes or until

(continued)

carrots are crisp-tender. Remove bay leaf. Bring to a boil. Drop noodles into boiling soup. After soup returns to a boil, cook uncovered for 5 to 10 minutes or until noodles are tender, stirring occasionally. Makes 7 servings.

CHRISTOPHER'S FRUIT SALAD

Christopher John - Age 5
Ryan Raymond - Age 3

2 cups romaine lettuce,
  chopped
2 cups fresh spinach
¼ cup mandarin oranges
½ cup strawberries, sliced

½ of a pear, diced
¼ cup dried (or fresh)
  blueberries
4 tblsp raspberry flavored salad
  dressing

Place romaine and spinach in a big bowl. Add oranges, strawberries, pear, and blueberries. Drizzle dressing on top, mix and serve.

COLD PASTA SALAD

Jay Torres - Age 15

1 box Tri-Color Rotini
Broccoli, Carrots, Cucumber,
  Zucchini, and Cherry Tomato's
4 sticks Mozzarella Cheese
1 pkg. Good Seasons Italian
  Salad Dressing mix prepared
  according to the package.

Add any other vegetable that
  your family enjoys

Cook pasta according to directions on package. Drain the pasta and rinse in cold water. While pasta is cooking, cut up vegetables and cheese into bite size pieces and put into large bowl. Make Italian Salad Dressing and chill until pasta is ready. Mix cold pasta, vegetables, cheese and Italian Salad Dressing and mix well. Cover bowl with foil. Chill for 2 hours. Mix well before eating. Options: You can add Chicken Strips for a yummy Chicken Cold Pasta Salad. You can use your favorite pre-made Italian Salad Dressing. You can make 2 boxes of pasta and add more vegetables for a large family or party. This can be a side dish or as a meal.

CREAM OF POTATO SOUP

Katie - Age 12

1 can Campbell's cream of
  potato soup

1 can of milk

First put the can of cream of potato soup in a bowl. Then slowly pour the can of milk in the same bowl while stirring the soup. Put it in the

(continued)

microwave for 3 minutes to 3 minutes and 30 seconds. Then let it cool for 30 seconds.

CREATIVE BEGINNINGS STONE SOUP

Sean - Age 5
Meghan - Age 3

1 large CLEAN stone
4 cups water
1 can sliced carrots-cut small
1 can potatoes-cut small
dash of onion flakes
1 large can stewed tomatoes
3 chicken bouillon cubes

1 can corn
1 can peas
some pasta
some celery
1 tsp. salt
½ tsp. pepper

Put water and stone in large pot. Add vegetables which kids have helped prepare. Add rest of ingredients. Cook 20 minutes. Remove stone and serve.

CUCUMBER AND TOMATO SALAD

Katie Pantaleo

2 cups cucumber
2 cups tomato
1 cup white onion
½ cup balsamic vinegar

¼ cup olive oil
2 tblsp. oregano
salt and pepper to taste

Peel cucumber and onion, then dice. Add to a mixing bowl. Dice tomatoes and add to bowl. In a separate bowl, mix together balsamic vinegar, olive oil, and oregano. Mix together, then gradually pour in the vinaigrette. Mix final salad and add salt and pepper to taste. Serve, eat, enjoy!

FRUIT SALAD

Bennett John - Age 4
Annabelle Kady - Age 2

2 apples
2 oranges
1 melon
1 pkg. strawberries
1 bunch grapes

2 bananas
1 cup powdered sugar
juice of one lemon
juice of two oranges

Skin or peel fruit and cut into small cubes. Place all cut fruit into a large bowl. In a separate bowl, combine sugar, lemon juice and orange juice. Add this mixture to the fruit mixture and toss lightly. Allow to set in refrigerator.

FRUIT SALAD

Cameron Megan - Age 5 ³⁄₄

1 ctn. French Vanilla Yogurt
1 cup cantaloupe

1 tblsp. grapes
1 apple, chopped

Start with one container of French Vanilla Yogurt. Add cut up cantaloupe, 1 tablespoon of grapes, and chopped up apple. Mix together well. Enjoy!

GOOD SALAD DRESSING

McCall Farrington - Age 13

3 tblsp. olive or vegetable oil
¼ cup white wine vinegar
¼ cup sugar
2 tblsp. soy sauce
2 flavor packets from ramen
  oriental noodle soup packages

(reserve noodles)
romaine lettuce
almond slivers (optional)
poached chicken (optional)

Preheat oven to 350°. Whisk together oil, vinegar, sugar, soy sauce, and flavor ramen packets. Break up noodles and place on cookie sheet---bake for 10 minutes or so---will be crunchy. Chop romaine lettuce, mix in dressing and noodles. Also good to add almonds and poached chicken to make a meal.

ITALIAN SALAD

Elleana Elisabeth - Age 6

1 seedless cucumber
2 medium red ripe tomatoes
1 can small black olives,
  drained

3 tblsp Balsamic Vinegar
3 tblsp Extra Virgin Olive Oil
¼ lb. feta cheese, crumbled
Salt and pepper to taste

Slice cucumber and tomatoes in ¼" thick slices and cut slices in quarters. Combine cucumbers, tomatoes and black olives. Add vinegar, EVOO, salt and pepper and combine together. Gently toss in feta cheese.

Note: You may substitute feta cheese with 3 tablespoons of fresh Parmesan cheese.

KARLI'S SALAD

Karli Jean - Age 10

Arugula
Lettuce
Tomatoes
Fresh Mozzarella
Parmesan Cheese

Pears
Oranges
Sherry Wine Vinegar
Olive Oil

(continued)

98890-09

Rinse the Arugula and lettuce to remove bacteria and put in a large bowl. Mix the Arugula and lettuce, then rinse the tomatoes and add slices of them. Cut slices of fresh Mozzarella and put that in. Rinse and cut slices of pears and add them to the bowl. Add oranges. Put sherry wine vinegar and olive oil in right before serving. Sprinkle Parmesan cheese on the salad before serving.

LIGHT CORN SALAD

Jenna Wing - Age 13

2 pkgs. frozen whole kernel corn, thawed
1 med. tomato chopped
⅓ chopped red onion

2 tsp. homemade pesto (see directions below)
2 tblsp mayonnaise light
2 tblsp lime juice

In a medium bowl, combine all the ingredients listed above. Serve chilled or at room temperature. To make the Pesto you will need: 3 cloves garlic, ½ cup pine nuts, 2 oz. Parmesan cheese, 3 cups basil, and 1 avocado. In a food processor, add all ingredients until it is finely blended. You can store the pesto in a small Tupperware container in the freezer.

MANDARIN ORANGE SALAD

Maxwell George Kavanaugh - Age 8

½ cup Almonds
3 tblsp. sugar
½ romaine lettuce
½ iceberg lettuce
2 whole green onions
1 can (11 oz.) mandarin oranges, drained
Dressing:

½ teaspoon salt
Dash pepper
¼ cup vegetable oil
1 tblsp. parsley
2 tblsp. sugar
2 tblsp. vinegar
Dash Tabasco

In a small pan over medium heat, stir constantly almonds and sugar. Cool and store. Mix other ingredients. Make dressing. Pour over salad before serving or serve on side.

MANDARIN SALAD

Sophie Clark - Age 6
Ian Clark - Age 4

¼ cup sliced almonds
1 T. plus 1 tsp. sugar
¼ head lettuce, torn into bite-size pieces
¼ bunch romaine, torn into bite-size pieces
2 medium stalks celery, chopped (about 1 C.)
2 green onions (with tops), thinly sliced (about 2 T.)
1 can mandarin orange segments, drained

Sweet Sour Dressing:
¼ cup vegetable oil (I use canola or ½ canola ½ vegetable oil
2 tblsp. sugar
2 tblsp. vinegar
1 tblsp. snipped parsley
½ tsp. salt
Dash Pepper
Dash red pepper sauce

Cook almonds and sugar over low heat, stirring constantly, until sugar is melted and almonds are coated. Cool on wax paper and break apart. Store at room temperature. For dressing, shake all ingredients in a tightly covered jar; refrigerate. Place lettuce and romaine in plastic bag; add celery and onions. Pour Sweet-Sour Dressing into bag; add orange segments. Close bag tightly and shake until salad greens and orange segments are well coated. Add almonds and shake. Or just toss all in a large bowl. Before dressing is added, bag of salad greens can be closed tightly and refrigerated no longer than 24 hours.

MARIA SHRIVER'S ORIENTAL CHICKEN SALAD
(Schatzi Recipe, in Famous Friends of Wolf Cookbook)

Maria Shriver
First Lady of California

Chicken Breasts

2 lbs. boneless chicken breasts
¼ - ½ lb. mixed lettuce greens
1 bunch watercress, tops only
1 bunch cilantro

1 bunch mint, leaves only
1 large carrot
1 small cucumber
2 large oranges

To prepare chicken: Combine all marinade ingredients in a baking dish. Add salt and black pepper to taste. Place chicken breasts in the dish, and refrigerate, preferably overnight. Preheat oven to 350°. Pour off and discard marinade. Bake chicken, skin side up, for 30 minutes, or until cooked through. Cool, and remove skin. Shred Chicken. To prepare salad: Clean lettuces, spin dry, and chill for crispness. Mix watercress, mint and cilantro with lettuce. Peel and julienned the carrot and cucumber. Peel and segment the oranges. To prepare vinaigrette: Whisk all ingredients together in a bowl. To assemble salad: Place all ingredients except wonton skins in a large mixing bowl. Dress lightly with vinaigrette

(continued)

98890-09

and toss gently. Add more dressing as required. Garnish with crumbled wonton skins.

Marinade for Chicken

1 cup low sodium soy sauce
3 oz. green onions, chopped
1½ oz. ginger, peeled and
  julienned

2-3 oz. dark sesame oil,
salt and pepper to taste

Sesame Rice Wine Vinaigrette

1 cup rice wine vinegar
½ cup peanut oil
½ cup sugar or to taste
2 tblsp. dark sesame oil
1 tblsp. low-sodium soy sauce

salt and pepper to taste
½ tsp. crushed red chile pepper
½ cup toasted slivered almonds
1 pinch pickled ginger
fried wonton skins for garnish

MARY CATHERINE'S BASIL MOZZARELLA INSALATA

Mary Catherine Schell - Age 5

1 heaping tsp. Gourmet Garden
Basil (Tube in Produce
Section)
⅓ cup Girard's White Balsamic
Vinaigrette
1 (8-oz.) pkg. BelGioioso Fresh
Mozzarella Fresh Ciliegine
Small Balls

1 tsp. Fresh Ground Black
Pepper
1 (2-oz.) pkg. Fresh Basil Leaves
1 (16-oz.) pint Organic Cherry
Tomatoes

Wash & cut tomatoes in half. Set aside. Wash basil leaves and remove stems. Chop basil leaves. Mix with tomatoes. Set aside. Mix Gourmet Garden Basil with Girard's White Balsamic Vinaigrette to make a Basil Dressing. Set aside. Strain BelGioioso Fresh Mozzarella. Pour into a medium bowl. Mix in Tomato & Basil mixture. Pour Basil Dressing over top. Mix well. Grind fresh black pepper over top of mixture. Serve immediately. Makes 4 servings.

MOM'S ANTIPASTO PASTA SALAD

Marc J - Age 8

2 (12-oz.) packages tri-color
  rotini
½ lb. diced salami (turkey or
  no-fat if you can find it)
½ lb. diced provolone cheese
  (low or no fat preferred)
1½ cups cherry tomatoes,
  halved
1 to 2 cups whole, pitted black
  olives
¾ cup green pepper strips
  (diced)

1 bottle Italian salad dressing
  (Good Seasons dry, mixed to
  instructions on pkg)
1 tsp. ground oregano
⅛ tsp. ground basil (or 2 cups
  fresh, chopped basil just prior
  to serving)
⅛ tsp. ground mustard
salt (sea salt is best) and
  pepper to taste

Cook pasta, drain and rinse under cold water. In large bowl, toss pasta with remaining ingredients (except fresh basil if using). Chill and stir (add fresh basil if using) prior to serving.

MY DAD'S ZUCCHINI SOUP
(the only way to eat zucchini)

Lauren Grace - Age 8

4 medium zucchini, shredded (6
  cups)
1 medium onion, chopped
¼ cup butter
2½ cups chicken broth

1 cup milk
¾ tsp. salt
½ tsp. fresh basil, minced
½ tsp. pepper
¼ tsp. ground nutmeg

Sauté zucchini and onion in butter for about 5 minutes. Stir in broth, bring to a boil, turn down heat; cover and simmer for 12-15 minutes. Purée with hand blender. Stir in milk, salt, basil, pepper, and nutmeg. Simmer for a few minutes more. Reheats well. Yield: About 12 servings

PORTARICAN SALAD

Jaime M - Age 12

1 lb. ground meat
1 head lettuce
2-3 tomatoes
1 bottle Wishbone Western
  Salad Dressing

1 bag Doritos
1 onion, chopped

Serves 8-10 people. In a skillet, brown the meat. While doing so, chop lettuce, tomatoes, onions(optional) and put into large bowl. Open the bag of Doritos and crush them. Add the Doritos to the bowl of vegetables. Next, add the cooked ground meat. Pour in Western Salad dressing and mix all together and serve.

 98890-09

RICE SALAD

Cameron Megan - Age 5 ¾

1 cup uncooked organic brown
  rice
8 oz. filet

8 oz. chicken
your favorite vegetables

Measure 1 Cup uncooked organic brown rice. Cook according to instructions (yields about 3 cups cooked). Grill 8 Oz filet (I like mine medium rare). Grill 8 Oz chicken (I prefer mine marinated first in Lawry's Sesame Ginger Marinade). Dice cooked chicken and steak into bite sized pieces Toss with rice. Add any cooked vegetables to taste (I love edamame and peas, my brother likes broccoli- but any of your favorites will do) - mom says green vegetables are the healthiest. Serves 4.

ROASTED RED PEPPER SOUP

Alexandria Marie - Age 10

1 stick unsalted butter
2 large yellow onions, chopped
2 cloves garlic, minced
4 large carrots, peeled, and
  chopped
1 large potato, peeled and
  chopped
6 red peppers, roasted, peeled,
  seeded, and chopped

2 firm pears, peeled, cored and
  chopped
5 cups low sodium chicken
  broth
2 T. fresh parsley, chopped
salt and pepper to taste
sour cream
fresh parsley sprigs

Melt butter in Dutch oven pan. Add onion and garlic, sauté 10 minutes. Add carrots and sauté and additional 10 minutes. Add potato and peppers, sauté 10 minutes. Add pears, chicken broth and 2 T. parsley- bring to a boil. Reduce heat and simmer uncovered 20 minutes or until vegetables are tender. Season with salt and pepper. Use emulsion blender until smooth. Garnish with sour cream and springs of parsley.

Note: I have used jarred roasted bell peppers. Make sure they are drained thoroughly before using.

STRAWBERRY & SPINACH SALAD

Auntie Gina

1 cup salad oil (grapeseed oil or
  olive oil)
½ cup sugar
⅓ cup cider vinegar
1 tblsp. grated onion

1 tblsp. poppy seeds
1 tsp. dry ground mustard
1 tsp. salt
1 bag fresh spinach
1 pint fresh strawberries

In a blender, put all ingredients EXCEPT spinach and strawberries, cover and blend at medium speed until thickened. This dressing can be stored covered in the refrigerator until ready for use. Slice strawber-

(continued)

ries and trim any stems off the spinach. Put strawberries and spinach in a large salad bowl. Just before serving, toss the dressing with the strawberries and spinach, adding the dressing only little by little (a little dressing goes a long way). Enjoy!

TACO SALAD

Jack S - Age 13

1 pkt. small French Onion Dip	**lettuce**
1 cup cream cheese	**tomato**
1 pkt. taco seasoning	**cucumber**
1 lb. ground beef	**shredded cheese**
1 medium onion	

In a skillet, brown ground beef with chopped onion. When cooked, sprinkle taco seasoning mix and stir into ground beef. Let cook about 5 minutes, and drain off grease. Let cool then in small bowl combine cream cheese and onion dip until smooth. Spread the cream cheese mixture on bottom of 9 x 12 dish. On top of that, put the drained beef mixture. Next, add the chopped lettuce and cucumber. Sprinkle the tomatoes and cheese on last.

TACO SOUP

William Michael - Age 3

1½ lbs. ground beef	**1 can kidney beans**
1 onion	**2 pkgs. taco seasoning (total 3**
1 can pinto beans	**oz.)**
1 can red beans	**1 can rotel**
1 can black beans	**2 cups water**

Brown ground beef. Chop onion (I usually use ½ onion.) Pour all ingredients into stock pot and bring to a boil, then simmer 1½ hours. (I usually dump all in the crock pot and cook 4-6 hours on low.) Serve with tortilla chips, sour cream, and shredded cheese.

TAFFY APPLE SALAD

Ava Mary - Age 2

5 cups red delicious apples	**2 tblsp cider vinegar**
1 (8-oz.) can crushed pineapple, drain & save liquid	**1 (8-oz.) ctn. Cool Whip**
	1 cup Spanish peanuts
1 tblsp flour	**½ cup sugar**
1 egg, beaten	

Mix flour, sugar, pineapple juice, egg and vinegar in saucepan over medium heat until thickened, cool in refrigerator. Peel and cube apples, fold into cooled mixture. Fold in Cool Whip and nuts. Sprinkle some nuts on top.

98890-09

THE BEST SALAD IN THE UNIVERSE

Carson Bruce - Age 5

1 bag mixed field greens
1 chopped avocado
1 peeled and diced cucumber
2 lg. diced tomato
1/2 cup shredded cheese

1/2 cup croutons
half dozen crushed Ritz
 crackers
3/4 cup cinnamon pita chips
ranch dressing

Add field greens and chopped vegetables to a large salad bowl. Add the cheese, croutons, crackers and mix. Next, add the secret ingredient responsible for the "best salad in the universe title", cinnamon pita chips. Mix well with as much dressing as you like.

TOMATO ALPHABET SOUP

Anthony Raven - Age 6
Jaydon Mateo - Age 5
Brandon Michael - Age 2

1 (7-oz.) packet Alphabet pasta
2 cloves garlic- sliced (optional)
1 small onion - chopped
1/2 tsp. salt

1 (14-oz.) can sliced tomatoes
 with the juice
1 qt. water
1 tblsp cooking oil

Heat a medium saucepan for 30 seconds and add the cooking oil. Wait another 30 seconds until hot and add the onions, garlic and pasta. On medium heat, stir often until pasta begins to brown. In a blender combine tomatoes with the juice and one cup of water. Blend until completely mixed. Pour the tomato mixture into the saucepan add another quart of water and the salt. You may add more water for a thinner soup or less water for a thicker soup. Mix well and bring to boiling. Reduce heat to low and cover the saucepan leaving a small gap for the steam to escape. Cook for 20 minutes or until the pasta is cooked through. Serve in a bowl and enjoy. P.S., this also works well with fresh tomatoes and if you feel like a heartier soup, skip the blender.

TRI COLOR PASTA SALAD

Jerry & Constance Cosmas

2 (9-oz.) pkgs. tri color cheese
 tortellini - frozen, cooked and
 drained
1 red sweet pepper - sliced fine
1 green pepper - sliced fine
1 small red onion - sliced fine
1/4 cup sliced pitted ripe olives
1/2 cup rice wine vinegar or
 white vinegar

1/2 cup olive oil
3 T. fresh mint - snipped
3 T. lemon juice
2 T. dry sherry
1 1/2 tsp. salt
1 tsp. pepper
1 T. granulated garlic powder
1/4 tsp. crushed red pepper
1/2 cup crumbled feta cheese

(continued)

In a large bowl: Combine pasta, peppers, onions and olives. Make pasta dressing out of the rest - except the feta. Cover and refrigerate 4 to 24 hours. Add feta before serving.

WHITE CHICKEN CHILI

Sophia Brielle - Age 16 months

6-8 boneless chicken breast	2¼ tsp. oregano
1½ lb. onion	2¼ tsp. garlic powder
2 small cans green chilies	1 T. ground red pepper
1 cup salsa	½ cup chopped red pepper
¼ cup oil	1 T. salt
4 cup warm water	1½ oz. chicken bouillon
2 tsp. parsley	2 (48-oz.) cans northern beans

Shred cooked chicken breast. In stockpot, cook onion in oil until tender. Add chicken. Add all other ingredients, except beans. Cook on low for 15 minutes. Add beans and cook on low 2 hours. (I usually just throw everything into the crockpot after. Shredding the chicken and cook on high for 2 hours.) Serve with tortilla chips, sour cream, and shredded cheese.

YUMMY FRUIT SALAD

Carson Bruce - Age 5

1 can peaches	½ cup mini marshmallows
2 apples	1 tube Go-Gurt (we prefer
1 bunch purple grapes	Scooby-Doo Yogurt)
1 cup mandarin oranges	⅓ cup chocolate chips
1 banana	(optional)
⅓ cup sunflower seeds	

Chop all fruit to bite sized pieces and place in large salad bowl. Add the seeds, marshmallows and yogurt. Mix well. Chocolate chips are optional.

YUMMY PASTA SALAD

Allicyn Pearl
Katherine Claudette

1 box Tri - Color Pasta, Cooked	1 Red Pepper, Chopped
1 Cucumber, Peeled and Chopped	½ Bag of Shredded Carrots
1 Tomato, Chopped	1 bottle Wish Bone Italian Dressing
1 Green Pepper, Chopped	8 oz. Mozzarella Cheese, Cubed

Place cold cooked noodles in a large bowl. Add the chopped cucumber, tomato, green and red pepper, ½ bag of shredded carrots and the

(continued)

98890-09

cubed mozzarella cheese. Mix all of the ingredients and pour ½ bottle of the wish bone Italian dressing in and stir. You can then serve right away or you can chill the salad and serve later. If you choose to serve later you will need to add the other ½ of the bottle of dressing as the noodles will soak up the dressing you have already added.

Recipe Favorites

Recipe Favorites

98890-09

Vegetables & Side Dishes

Helpful Hints

- When preparing a casserole, make an additional batch to freeze for when you're short on time. Use within 2 months.

- To keep hot oil from splattering, sprinkle a little salt or flour in the pan before frying.

- To prevent pasta from boiling over, place a wooden spoon or fork across the top of the pot while the pasta is boiling.

- Boil all vegetables that grow above ground without a cover.

- Never soak vegetables after slicing; they will lose much of their nutritional value.

- Green pepper may change the flavor of frozen casseroles. Clove, garlic, and pepper flavors get stronger when frozen, while sage, onion, and salt become more mild.

- For an easy no-mess side dish, grill vegetables along with your meat.

- Store dried pasta, rice (except brown rice), and whole grains in tightly covered containers in a cool, dry place. Refrigerate brown rice, and freeze grains if you will not use them within 5 months.

- A few drops of lemon juice added to simmering rice will keep the grains separated.

- When cooking greens, add a teaspoon of sugar to the water to help vegetables retain their fresh colors.

- To dress up buttered, cooked vegetables, sprinkle them with toasted sesame seeds, toasted chopped nuts, canned french-fried onions, grated cheese, or slightly crushed seasoned croutons.

- Soufflé dishes are designed with straight sides to help your soufflé rise. Ramekins work well for single-serve casseroles.

- A little vinegar or lemon juice added to potatoes before draining will make them extra white when mashed.

- To avoid toughened beans or corn, add salt midway through cooking.

- If your pasta sauce seems a little dry, add a few tablespoons of the pasta's cooking water.

- To prevent cheese from sticking to a grater, spray the grater with cooking spray before beginning.

VEGETABLES & SIDE DISHES

BROCCOLI CASSEROLE

Cassidy Barbara - Age 2½

1 (32-oz.) bag frozen chopped
 broccoli
1 med. chopped onion
1 can mushroom soup

1 small jar cheese whiz
1½ cups cooked white rice
1 cup toasted bread crumbs

Cook broccoli as directed on package and drain, sauté onion in butter. Stir all ingredients except bread crumbs, together in a medium size casserole dish. Top with toasted bread crumbs. Bake at 350° for about 35 minutes or until bubbly.

BUGS ON A LOG
(this is photographed in this book)

Taylor - Age 13
Sarah

2 stalks Celery
¼ cup Peanut Butter
1 tblsp Raisins

1 tblsp Craisins
1 tblsp. Golden Raisins

Cut each celery stalk into three or four sticks. Spread about 1½ teaspoon of peanut butter on each celery stick. Place raisins, craisins and golden raisins on each celery log.

CELERY STICKS TWO WAYS

Cynthia Marie - Age 12

2 sticks celery
1 tblsp peanut butter

1 tblsp cream cheese

Cut and clean 2 sticks of celery. Dry with paper towel. Place peanut butter in groove of one slice and place cream cheese in groove of the other slice. Eat as a quick snack on a hot summer day!

CHEESY BROCCOLI RICE AND TURKEY

Angelina Pascente - Age 12

1 can (14½ oz.) fat-free reduced-
 sodium chicken broth
2 cups chopped cooked turkey
2 cups broccoli florets

2 cups instant white rice,
 uncooked
6 oz. Velveeta Cheese, cut up
 into ½ in. cubes

Combine broth, turkey and broccoli in large skillet. Bring to boil. Reduce heat to low; cover and simmer 5 minutes. Add rice and Velveeta; cover.

(continued)

Remove from heat. Let stand 5 minutes or until rice is tender and Velveeta is melted. Stir until well blended. Substitute: 4 small boneless skinless chicken breast halves (1 lb.) for the chopped cooked turkey. Heat small amount of oil in large nonstick skillet on medium-high heat. Add chicken; cover. Cook 5 minutes on each side or until cooked through (170°). Transfer to plate; cover to keep warm. Bring broth and broccoli to boil in large skillet; continue as directed, returning chicken to skillet along with rice and Velveeta. Prep time: 10 minutes Total Time: 25 minutes Makes 4 servings

CHEESY HASH BROWN POTATOES

Rachel Joyce - Age 10

1 stick butter or margarine
1 (3-oz.) pkg. cream cheese
1 can cream of chicken soup
1 soup can filled with milk

1 (4-oz.) pkg. cheddar cheese
minced onion
1 2-lb. pkg. frozen hash browns
salt and pepper to taste

Butter a 9 x 13 inch pan. Spread frozen hash browns in pan. Sprinkle with salt, pepper, and minced onion. In a saucepan, bring remaining ingredients to a slow boil. Pour over potatoes. Sprinkle with cheese. Bake at 350 degrees for 1½ hours.

CHEESY POTATOES

John Thomas Blanke - Age 12

2 bags hash brown potatoes (in the refrigerator section)
½ stick butter
1 white onion
1 small can of cream of chicken soup

2 cups shredded cheese
16 oz. sour cream
salt and pepper to taste

Sauté onion and butter together in a pan. Mix all other ingredients together in a bowl. Add onions after they are cooked and then put mixture into a greased 9 x 13 inch pan. Cook in 400 degree oven for an hour.

CHEESY POTATOES

Timothy Robert Noland - Age 9

1 stick melted butter
1 (2-lb.) pkg. Southern Hash Browns
1 (8-oz.) container sour cream

8 oz. shredded cheddar cheese
1 can cream of chicken soup
Corn Flake crumbs

Break up potatoes, then drizzle with melted butter. Mix the sour cream, chicken soup and cheddar cheese together. Mix into the hash browns. Place corn flake crumbs on top. Bake at 350° for 1 hour.

46

CREAM COCKTAIL ROUNDUP

Kyle Thomas - Age 8
Brandon Paul - Age 5

1 (8-oz.) pkg. Cream Cheese,
 softened
1 tblsp Mayonnaise
1 (30 oz.) can Fruit Cocktail,
 drained

1 (11-oz.) can Mandarin
 Oranges, drained
small handful of Colored
 Marshmallows

Mix together softened cream cheese and mayonnaise. Then add fruit cocktail, oranges and marshmallows. Chill before serving.

DO AHEAD MACARONI & CHEESE

Sabrina Rose - Age 12

1 (7-oz.) oz. uncooked elbow
 macaroni
2 (8-oz.) cups shredded cheddar
 cheese
1 (10-oz.) can cheddar cheese
 soup

1³/₄ cup milk
³/₄ tsp. salt
1 cup crushed potato chips
 (optional)

Mix the first 5 ingredients together and put in a greased covered 2 qt. casserole dish. Do not boil the elbow macaroni. Refrigerate for up to 24 hours. Bake covered at 350° for 1 hour. Remove cover and sprinkle crushed potato chips over the top (optional) and bake another 20 minutes uncovered. Recipe can be doubled.

EARTH GLOBES
(vegetarian meatballs)

Cynthia Marie - Age 12

1¹/₂ cup uncooked oats
3 eggs
1 tsp. salt
1 cup pecans
1 cup onions

¹/₄ cup Parmesan cheese
¹/₈ cup parsley
¹/₂ tsp. garlic powder
olive oil
(16-20 oz.) jar marinara sauce

Mix oats, salt, garlic powder and chopped parsley in a bowl. Add well beaten eggs, finely chopped onions and chopped pecans and mix well. Let stand at least an hour. Form into meatball size globes. Brown lightly in a little olive oil. Cover with a jar of your favorite marinara sauce and bake in oven at 325 degrees for 20 minutes. Serve with spaghetti!

EMILIA'S VEGGIE RICE

Emilia Anna - Age 3

2 cups Cooked Brown or White
   Rice
1 large Avocado
1 large Tomato

1 small Red Onion
2 tsp. Olive Oil
2 tsp. Bragg Liquid Aminos
1 tsp. Bragg Sprinkle

Add to warm rice a sliced avocado, tomato and red onion. Then stir in olive oil and Bragg Liquid Aminos. Add Bragg Sprinkle to taste.

FROZEN GRAPES

Lucciana Tru - Age 1

1 bunch Purple Grapes   1 Freezer Bag

We learned this tip on vacation and have been doing it for years. After buying grapes, rinse in cold water. Place the grapes in a freezer bag and throw in the freezer. The grapes never spoil, the kids love eating them frozen, and they are more nutritious than popsicles.

FRUIT BUGGY

Carson Bruce - Age 5

2 toothpicks   4 grapes
1 banana   1 orange

Kids will zoom to eat this Fruit Buggy! Peel whole banana. Place one tooth pick through banana as front axle and one in the back for rear axle. Poke each grape on each side of toothpicks for the wheels. Slice a thin piece of orange. Slide it over the banana like a collar to form the steering wheel. Kids will have fun racing this on their plate before eating it.

FRUIT KABOB

Carson Bruce - Age 5

6 skewers   dozen strawberries
1 bunch grapes   2 bananas
2 apples $\frac{1}{2}$ cantaloupe - cubed

Anything on a stick is more fun to eat, even vegetables! Here are some fruit suggestions for the fruit kabob, but you can use any fruit you like. Select fruit, cut into large pieces. Arrange each piece of fruit on the skewer.

98890-09

GARLIC MASHED POTATOES

Cole Steven - Age 9

10 large Yukon Gold potatoes
garlic
milk

½ stick butter
salt & pepper

Peel and bowl potatoes. Also cut garlic cloves top ⅓ off and wrap in aluminum foil and bake in an oven for 45 minutes. Drain potatoes and put in bowl. Add garlic by squeezing and begin to mash potatoes. While mashing add milk and one half stick of butter and continue mashing till smooth. Add salt and pepper to taste.

GRANOLA-STUFFED PEACHES

Mary Rose - Age 10

1 (16-oz.) can halved peaches
2 tblsp butter or margarine
2 tblsp brown sugar

¾ cup granola
1 dollop vanilla yogurt

Preheat oven to 425°. Arrange peaches cut sides up in a microwave safe 8 x 8 inch glass baking dish. Microwave the butter or margarine and brown sugar on high 30 seconds or until melted; stir in the granola. Spoon into peach centers, and bake 10 minutes to heat through. Serve with vanilla yogurt. Serves 4.

HAMBURGER RICE CASSEROLE

Jenna Wing - Age 13

1 lb. hamburger, browned
1 cup celery, chopped
1 small onion, chopped
1 can creamed chicken soup,
  low sodium

1 cup boiling water
½ cup brown rice
dash pepper and oregano

Pre-heat oven to 350 degrees. Mix all of the ingredients together in a casserole dish. Bake in the oven for 1 hour.

HEALTHY LUNCH TIME SNACK WITH APPLES

Alexis Elizabeth - Age 10
Ashley Dianna - Age 8
Nicole Frances - Age 5

Apples, Apples, Apples

Lemon juice

Bringing fruit to school is always a challenge, but this quick tip really works! Slice apple into 8-10 pieces. Put in resealable bag and sprinkle with lemon juice. The fruit will stay fresh until lunch and not turn brown.

(continued)

Red Delicious apples or Granny Smith apples work best. In the fall, we look for Honeycrisp apples for an extra special treat.

HOMEMADE APPLESAUCE

Carson Bruce - Age 5

3 Diced apples
1 tblsp Cinnamon

½ cup Brown Sugar
3 large Marshmallows

Mix apples, cinnamon and sugar together. Place in a baking dish and bake at 375 degrees for 15 - 20 minutes. Place marshmallows on top for last 5 minutes of baking.

HOMEMADE APPLESAUCE

Robert Patrick - Age 6 months

3-4 lbs. peeled, cored and quartered Apples (Fuji or other cooking apple)
4 strips Lemon Peel - use a vegetable peeler to strip 4 lengths

3-4 tblsp. fresh Lemon Juice
3 inches of Cinnamon Stick
¼ cup Dark Brown Sugar
up to ¼ cup White Sugar
1 cup Water
½ tsp. Salt

Put all ingredients into a large pot. Cover. Bring to boil. Lower heat and simmer 20-30 minutes. Remove from heat. Remove cinnamon sticks and lemon peels. Mash with potato masher. Ready to serve hot or refrigerated. Try serving with vanilla ice cream or vanilla yogurt.

HOMEMADE BREAKFAST SAUSAGE

Lindsey Elizabeth - Age 8 months

1 lb. ground pork
2 T. maple syrup
1 T. fresh sage, finely chopped

1 tsp. crushed red pepper flakes
salt and pepper, to taste
1 T. canola oil

Mix all ingredients in a large bowl until thoroughly combined. Using your hands, make individual patties about 2" in diameter and ½" thick. Heat oil in skillet over medium high heat. Place sausage patties in pan and cook about 3 minutes on each side or until cooked through. Do not overcrowd the pan with sausage patties. You may have to do this in batches.

98890-09

HONEY GLAZED CARROTS

Lane - Age 8
Mackenzie - Age 5

1 bag of baby carrots
¼ cup honey
¼ cup water

¼ cup brown sugar
2 tblsp. butter

Place carrots in boiling water, covered for 4-5 minutes. They will be slightly firm. In the meantime, combine honey, water and brown sugar in a saucepan and warm through. Drain carrots well, add to sauce pan with butter mixture and heat uncovered on medium low for an additional 5 minutes. What kid wouldn't want to eat these vegetables!

KENDALL'S (NOT SO MUCH) KRAZY NOODLES

Kendall E. - Age 6

2 c. Elbow Springs Noodles
1 T. Olive Oil

dash Ground Peppercorn
dash Salt to Taste

Cook noodles to desired firmness. Mix cooked noodles with olive oil, pepper and salt. Add a little pasta water to dilute olive oil, if necessary (Kendall says it tastes better if the oil isn't too thick). Enjoy as main meal with cheese slices. Also can serve as a side dish; the noodles go great with veggie patties.

MELON YOGURT BOWLS

Kamren Christopher - Age 5½
Keaten Lawrence - Age 7

whole Cantaloupe or Honeydew
¼ - ½ cup Yogurt per serving

ground Nuts

Wash uncut whole cantaloupe or honeydew melon (or try papaya). Cut cantaloupe in half (lengthwise or width-wise) and reserve the rind shells for later use as bowls. Scoop out seeds. Use melon baller to scoop out balls. Place melon balls into shell bowls with ¼ - ½ cup plain yogurt for each bowl. Sprinkle ground nuts on top. Serve immediately. If the bowls are rolling around and unstable, slice a little piece off the bottom.

MEX CORN CASSEROLE

Johnny Sanfilippo - Age 6

2 cans Mexican Corn
2 cans Creamed Corn
1 cup sour cream
2 eggs
1 box Jiffy Corn Mix

½ cup green onions
1 cup Mexican Shredded
  Cheese
½ stick butter, melted (optional)

(continued)

Spray 13 x 9 inch baking dish. Mix all ingredients together well. Pour into dish and bake for 40-50 minutes in a 350° oven.

MY DADDY'S MASHED POTATOES

Emily Miller - Age 5

5 lbs. Quartered and boiled non-peeled potato's
12 oz. Daisy Sour Cream
8 tblsp Salted Butter
4 tblsp Minced Garlic
4 tblsp Buttermilk Ranch Dressing

4 oz. Parmesano Reggiano Cheese
2 tblsp Cracked Black Pepper
2 tblsp Chopped Parsley

Wash and quarter potato's and place into large pot with boiling water until fork soft. Drain water. Add sour cream and butter and then mash. Add remaining ingredients and adjust to your taste. Tip for leftovers - fry in a frying pan with butter like hash browns the morning after and serve with eggs and bacon.

NOODLE KUGEL

Kayla Tess - Age 7
Hannah Rose - Age 10

½ lb. wide Kosher for Passover egg noodles
½ stick butter
1 lb. cottage cheese
2 cups sour cream

½ cup sugar
6 eggs
1 tsp. ground cinnamon
½ cup raisins

Preheat over to 375 degrees F. Boil noodles in salted water for about 4 minutes. Strain noodles. In a large mixing bowl, combine noodles with remaining ingredients and pour into a greased, approximately 9 x 13 inch baking dish. Bake until custard is set and top is golden brown, about 30 to 45 minutes.

PARTY MEATBALLS

Amber Skulavik

Meatballs

2 lbs. ground chuck
1 cup bread crumbs

1 pkg. Lipton Onion Soup Mix
3 eggs

Mix above ingredients and form into balls. Place in 10 x 13 inch or 11 x 14 inch dish.

(continued)

98890-09

Sauce

1 bottle Heinz Chili Sauce
1 bottle water (use Heinz bottle)
1 cup light brown sugar

1 can drained sauerkraut
(Bavarian)
1 can whole cranberry sauce

Mix all ingredients in a saucepan. Simmer sauce until well mixed. Pour sauce over meatballs. Bake at 350° uncovered for 2 hours (check 10 minutes early).

PITA PIZZA PEOPLE
(these are photographed in this book!)

Taylor - Age 13
Sarah

2 pieces Pita Bread
¼ cup Hummus

Assorted Vegetables

Using a round cookie cutter, cut out two circles from each piece of pita. Spread 1 tablespoon of hummus on each pita circle to make the face base. Use your favorite vegetables and your imagination to decorate each pita pizza with your own funny faces.

PREHISTORIC POTATO BUG
(this is photographed in this book!)

T.J. - Age 12
Sarah

1 Potato
Olive Oil
Salt and Pepper
2 stalks Asparagus
1 Parsnip

1 Zucchini
1 Belgian Endive
Black olives
1 Red Radish, halved and sliced
1 tsp. Sour Cream

Preheat the oven to 400°F. Coat the potato in 1 teaspoon of olive oil, sprinkle with salt and pepper, wrap in tin foil and bake in the oven until tender, about 45 minutes. Remove and allow to cool slightly. Using a toothpick, make two holes at the top of the potato near one end and push in two asparagus tops to make antennae. Using only skinny bottom of the parsnip, make another hole for a nose with the toothpick and place in the parsnip end. Take the zucchini and cut one long ¼ inch thick slice from one side. Turn the zucchini 180° and make an identical slice on the other side. These two pieces are the wings. Attach them to the bug by placing a dollop of sour cream directly behind the antennae and stick the corners of the zucchini slices on top. Layer the sliced radishes between the two wings. For the eyes, cut small rounds from two endive leaves and with the sour cream attach a small diced black olive one each endive circle. Connect the eye to the bug with a dot more of sour cream. Eat him before he eats you!

53

RATATOUILLE

Sarah Denise - Age 11

2 T. olive oil
1 medium onion, chopped
3 cloves garlic, minced
1 medium or large eggplant, diced
4 medium or large tomatoes, diced

2 medium zucchini, diced into large chunks
herbs as desired (Ital. seasoning, oregano, basil)
salt and pepper to taste

Sauté onion and garlic in oil over medium heat until tender. Add the eggplant and tomatoes; reduce heat and simmer, covered, for 10-15 minutes. Add the zucchini, replace cover and simmer for 10 more minutes or until vegetables are soft. Remove from heat; stir in the herbs, salt, and/or pepper. This can be served over rice or pasta if you want and is good topped with grated mozzarella cheese. Also, if you don't have fresh tomatoes you can use a can of stewed tomatoes instead. Serves 4.

RICH AND CREAMY POTATO CASSEROLE

Issac Noah - Age 7

6 med. Potatoes
2 cups Sour Cream
2 cups Shredded Cheddar Cheese
4 tblsp Butter, melted and divided

3 Green Onions, thinly sliced
1 tsp. Salt
1/4 tsp. Pepper

Place potatoes in a large saucepan and cover with water. Bring to a boil. Reduce heat, cover and cook for 15 to 20 minutes or until fork tender. Drain and cool. Peel and grate potatoes. Place in a bowl and add the sour cream, cheddar cheese, and 3 tablespoon of butter, green onions, salt and pepper. Transfer to a greased 2 1/2 qt. baking dish. Drizzle with remaining butter. Bake uncovered at 350 degrees for 30 to 35 minutes or until heated through. Enjoy!

SCALLOPED PINEAPPLE

Mary Beth - Age 13

2 (16-20 oz.) cans crushed pineapple, drained
3 eggs
1 1/2 cups sugar

1 stick margarine
7 slices bread (remove crusts & cube)
1/2 cup milk

Melt margarine. Combine all ingredients in a large casserole dish. Bake at 350° for 1 hour covered. Serve warm. Goes great with ham.

98890-09

SMASHED SWEET POTATOES WITH APPLES

Kathleen Mary - Age 13

6 Large sweet potatoes (about 4 lb.)
½ cup freshly squeezed orange juice
½ cup heavy cream
4 T. unsalted butter
¼ cup light brown sugar
1 tsp. ground nutmeg
½ tsp. ground cinnamon
2 tsp. kosher salt
1 tsp. freshly ground pepper
3 T. unsalted butter
3 Macintosh apples, peeled, cored and cut into ⅛
3 T. light brown sugar

Preheat oven to 350 degrees. Scrub the potatoes, prick them several times with a knife or fork, and bake them for an hour or until soft when pierced with a knife. Remove from the oven and scoop out the insides as soon as they are cool enough to handle. Place the sweet potato meat into the bowl of the electric mixer fitted with the paddle attachment and add the orange juice, cream, butter, brown sugar, nutmeg, cinnamon, salt and pepper. Mix together until combined, but not smooth and pour into a baking dish. For the topping: melt the butter in a skillet over medium - high heat. Add the apple wedges and brown sugar and cook for about 5-10 minutes or until lightly brown on both sides. Place them on top of the sweet potatoes. Bake the potatoes and apples for 20-30 minutes until heated through.

SMISH SMOSH BUTTERNUT SQUASH

William Douglas - Age 3
Mom Andrea

1 cubed butternut squash, seeded/cubed/steamed
¼ cup sugar
1½ cup milk
1 tsp. vanilla
Dash salt
2 tsp. flour
3 eggs or less
¼ cup melted butter
1 tsp. cinnamon
½ pkg. vanilla wafers crushed (We have used various toppings whatever in house)
⅓ cup melted butter
½ cup sugar

Mash steamed squash with masher in a bowl. Add next 8 ingredients to mashed squash in the same bowl. Pour smashed squash into an 8x10 inch glass flat dish. Topping - combine the last 3 ingredients and crumble on top of smashed squash. Bake at 425 degrees for 45 min. This can be served as a side dish or dessert with vanilla ice cream on top.

SPANISH FIESTA RICE

Xavier Mendoza - Age 13

2 cups rice
3 cups chicken broth
4 oz. Spanish style tomato
 sauce
3 cloves garlic, finely chopped

¼ of a medium onion
2 tblsp oil
4 heaping tblsp parsley, finely
 chopped (optional)

In a medium sauce pan, heat oil over medium heat. Add the fresh garlic and onion. Sauté for 1-2 minutes until softened. Add in dry rice. Stir for about 5 minutes until rice becomes a golden brown color. Add in broth and tomato sauce (slowly into rice, not directly onto hot pan!). Add in the parsley if you're using it. Stir it up and bring to a boil. Once it starts boiling, turn the heat to low and cover. Let it simmer for 20 minutes and fluff with a fork.

SUPREME MACARONI & CHEESE
(Grandma Susie's)

Brooke Caroline - Age 6
Gibson "Gibby" Louis - Age 4

1 (7-oz.) box Elbow Macaroni
2 cups cottage cheese
1 cup sour cream
1 slightly beaten egg (optional)
¾ tsp. salt

dash of pepper
8 oz. sharp cheddar cheese
 (shredded)
paprika

Cook macaroni according to directions on the box, drain well. Combine cottage cheese, sour cream, egg (optional), salt, pepper. Add sharp cheese, mixing well. Stir in cooked macaroni. Pour into a greased 9 x 13 inch baking dish. Sprinkle with paprika. Bake at 350 degrees for 45 minutes.

TOMATO DIPPER

Carson Bruce - Age 5

4 Roma Tomato
1 cup Cream Cheese
sprinkles

mini pretzels
dried parsley

Cut off top third of tomato. Scoop out the guts of the tomato. Fill with cream cheese. Garnish the top with sprinkles of your choice (we liked red) and parsley. Serve with the mini pretzels. Kids love dipping into the cream cheese with the pretzels and eating the tomato.

98890-09

TOMATO PIE

Joseph Edward - Age 5

1 unbaked 9" deep dish pie
  crust (like Pillsbury)
5 medium tomatoes, sliced
3 T. chopped fresh basil
1 c. chopped scallions

1½ c. grated cheddar cheese
½ c. mayonnaise
1 tsp. Dijon Mustard
¼ c. grated Parmesan cheese
Salt and Pepper to taste

Preheat oven to 450°. Place pie crust in pie plate and prick holes in bottom of crust with a fork. Bake for 10-15 minutes until golden. Remove from oven and reduce heat to 325°. Lightly salt and pepper tomatoes to taste. Layer ½ the tomatoes on the bottom of the crust. Sprinkle with ½ of the basil and scallions. Repeat layers. Mix cheddar with mayonnaise and mustard. Spread over pie. Sprinkle with Parmesan. Bake 45 minutes until heated through and browned.

TOMATO RINGS
(TOMATO ZIP)

Anne-Marie Kimberly - Age 8

1 Large Beefsteak tomato
1 quarter bottlecap soy sauce

½ teaspoon pepper
½ teaspoon salt

Slice a big tomato into 4 slices. Cut a bottle cap sized pit (not a hole all the way through) in the middle. Then add pepper, salt and soy sauce together in the little pit. Sprinkle some salt on the edges of the tomato slice. Add some tomato juice (left over from the scoop you scooped) back in to the pit. Warning: It is a little spicy . . . but . . .extra good for you!

TURKEY & CHEESE ROLL-UP

Kaleigh - Age 10

turkey slices
white or wheat tortillas

mayonnaise
cheese slices

Get out a white or wheat tortilla, turkey, and american or cheddar cheese. Place the turkey inside the tortilla roll. Put mayonnaise on the top of that. Then, place the cheese on top of that with some extra mayonnaise. Roll the top, cut the middle and enjoy!

YUMMY TUMMY CATERPILLAR
(this is photographed in this book!)

T.J. - Age 12
Sarah

5 pieces Brussels Sprouts
1 tblsp Olive Oil
1 small Onion, sliced
1 Cherry Tomato

1 sprig Chive
2 pieces Peas
1 tsp. Sour Cream

Boil or steam the brussels sprouts until tender and bright green. Heat a sauté pan coated with the olive oil over a low flame. Add the sliced onions and a pinch of salt and cook over low heat, stirring occasionally, until the onions begin to caramelize and are a golden brown, about 25 minutes. To make the body, arrange the brussels sprouts on a plate in a curvy row. Top with caramelized onions. To make the head, use a toothpick to poke a small hole in the top of the cherry tomato. Fold the chive in half and using the toothpick, push the folded end into the hole to make antennae. Place a dot of sour cream on each pea an position on the tomato to make eyes. Place the finished head at the front of the brussels sprout line to complete the caterpillar.

Recipe Favorites

98890-09

Main dishes

Helpful Hints

- Certain meats, like ribs and pot roast, can be parboiled before grilling to reduce the fat content.

- Pound meat lightly with a mallet or rolling pin, pierce with a fork, sprinkle lightly with meat tenderizer, and add marinade. Refrigerate for 20 minutes and cook or grill for a quick and succulent meat.

- Marinating is a cinch if you use a plastic bag. The meat stays in the marinade and it's easy to turn. Cleanup is easy; just toss the bag.

- It's easier to thinly slice meat if it's partially frozen.

- Adding tomatoes to roasts helps to naturally tenderize the meat. Tomatoes contain an acid that works well to break down meats.

- Whenever possible, cut meat across the grain; this will make it easier to eat and also give it a more attractive appearance.

- When frying meat, sprinkle paprika on the meat to turn it golden brown.

- Thaw all meats in the refrigerator for maximum safety.

- Refrigerate poultry promptly after purchasing. Keep it in the coldest part of your refrigerator for up to 2 days. Freeze poultry for longer storage. Never leave poultry at room temperature for over 2 hours.

- When frying chicken, canola oil provides a milder taste, and it contains healthier amounts of saturated and polyunsaturated fats. Do not cover the chicken once it has finished cooking, because covering will cause the coating to loose its crispness.

- One pound of boneless chicken equals approximately 3 cups of cubed chicken.

- Generally, red meats should reach 160° and poultry should reach 180° before serving. If preparing fish, the surface of the fish should flake off with a fork.

- Rub lemon juice on fish before cooking to enhance the flavor and help maintain a good color.

- Scaling a fish is easier if vinegar is rubbed on the scales first.

- When grilling fish, the rule of thumb is to cook 5 minutes on each side per inch of thickness. For example, cook a 2-inch thick fillet for 10 minutes per side. Before grilling, rub with oil to seal in moisture.

MAIN DISHES

AMAZING OVEN BAKED CHICKEN

Ashley Nicole - Age 13

1 tblsp butter or margarine,
  melted
²/₃ cup Bisquick
1¹/₂ tsp. paprika

1¹/₄ tsp. salt
¹/₄ tsp. pepper
2¹/₂ - 3¹/₂ lbs. chicken, cut into
  pieces

Heat oven to 425 degrees. Add melted margarine to a 13 x 9 x 2 baking dish. Mix Bisquick, paprika, salt and pepper; then coat chicken in this mixture. Place chicken skin side down in dish. Bake 35 minutes then turn chicken. Bake about another 15 minutes longer or until juice is no longer pink when center is cut. Enjoy!!!!!

ANNABELLE'S FAVORITE CHICKEN

Gavin Smith - Age 5
Annabelle Smith - Age 7
Gavin and Jennifer Smith

4 Chicken Breasts
4 pieces Sliced Deli Ham

4 slices Swiss Cheese
4 slices Butter

Preheat oven to 400 degrees F. Spray a 9¹/₂ x 13 inch pan with non-stick cooking spray. Flatten chicken breasts with a mallet. Place a flattened chicken breast on a separate plate. Put one piece of ham and one slice of cheese on the chicken. Roll the chicken breast into a small roulade, repeat for each breast and place in pan. Place butter slices on each roulade, sprinkle with salt and pepper to taste. Bake for 30-40 minutes.

ANTHONY AND OLIVIA'S TURKEY SLOPPY JOES

Anthony Feliciani - Age 3
Olivia Feliciani - Age 1

2¹/₂ lb. ground turkey
1 cup Ketchup
6 T. Chili Sauce
1 medium Onion (chopped)
1 T. Sugar
2 T. Yellow mustard

1 tspn Salt
2 T. Apple Cider Vinegar
1-2 T. Celery Seed (depends on
  taste)
1 T. Worcestershire Sauce

Brown the turkey in a pan with the onion. Mix remaining ingredients together and add to browned turkey/onion mix. Stir until distributed evenly. Let simmer on low for 20-30 minutes. Serve on sandwich rolls (potato rolls are great with this)! We love to eat them with homemade sweet potato fries!!!!

ASPARAGUS HAM QUICHE

Sophie Clark - Age 6
Ian Clark - Age 4

2 (10-oz.) Packages frozen cut
asparagus, thawed
1 pound Fully cooked ham,
chopped
2 cups (8 oz.) Shredded
Cheddar Cheese

½ cup Chopped Onion
6 Eggs
2 cups Milk
1½ cups Buttermilk Baking Mix
2 tsp. Dried Vegetable Flakes
¼ tsp. Pepper

In 2 greased 9" pie plates, layer asparagus, ham, cheese and onion. In a bowl, beat eggs. Add remaining ingredients and mix well. Divide in half and pour over asparagus mixture in each pie plate. Bake at 375° for 30 - 45 minutes or until a knife inserted near the center comes out clean. Serves 12.

Variations: Substitute chicken or broccoli in recipe.

ATKINS PARK PORK TENDERLOIN

Timothy Sebastien - Age 5
Sophia Claire - Age 3

¾ c. low sodium chicken stock
½ c. bourbon
½ c. teriyaki sauce
¼ c. teriyaki glaze
½ c. soy sauce

¾ c. brown sugar
5 shallots, sliced
1½ lb. pork tenderloin, cubed
1 T. extra virgin olive oil

In a large bowl, combine broth, bourbon, teriyaki sauce, teriyaki glaze, soy sauce, brown sugar, shallots and rosemary. Reserve half the mixture for the glaze, and use half as marinade. Marinate the pork tenderloin for at least 1 to 2 hours (if making as a freezer meal, freeze meat in the marinade with glaze in a separate Ziploc bag). After marinating, drain meat. In a large skillet over medium-high heat, add oil. Brown meat on both sides. Add reserved marinade and simmer for 5 to 6 minutes, or until meat is just cooked through. If needed, you can remove the meat to a plate and keep warm, while you reduce the glaze a little further. Serve over (or with) rice and any veggie you love!

AUNT ANNETTE'S PB&J ROLLS

Blythe Alise - Age 4
Bailey Lynn - Age 2

1 slice bread
1 T. peanut butter

1 T. jelly

Flatten bread with rolling pin. Remove crusts. Spread with peanut butter and jelly. Roll the bread and cut into four equal pieces. Serve vertically -- sushi style.

98890-09

BAKED BROCCOLI WITH CHICKEN

Jessica Velencia - Age 7

2 small heads of broccoli (cut
  into bite pieces)
4 chicken breasts (stripped)
1 small can cream of mushroom
1 cup low fat mayonnaise

1 big bag of grated cheese
  (Colby Jack)
4 pieces bread (crumbs)
1 regular size aluminum tray
  and spatula

Boil broccoli until cooked, then drain. Boil chicken breasts, then strip into small pieces. Mix cream of mushroom and mayonnaise. Mix broccoli, chicken breast and (½ bag) grated cheese together. Layer them on a tray. Cover evenly with the mixture of cream of mushroom and mayonnaise using spatula. Top with the rest of grated cheese, then with the bread crumbs. Bake at 350 degrees (do not cover), for 30 minutes, or until the bread crumbs and cheese turn brown.

BAKED EGG, HAM & CHEESE QUICHE

Naomi Genevieve - Age 4
Brooke Ashley - Age 2

4 Eggs
¾ cup 2% Milk
¼ cup Unsalted Butter (melted)
2 tblsp. Canola Oil
⅓ cup Flour
⅓ tsp. Salt

Dash Ground Pepper
1 cup Diced Ham
2 cups Shredded Three-Cheese
  (or mix together Cheddar &
  Mozzarella)

Mix eggs, milk, butter, and oil together; Add flour and mix; Add salt & pepper and mix; Add ham and mix; Add cheese and mix; Pour into glass pie baking dish; Cover with foil (cut hole in center); Bake 1 hour at 350°; Cool 5 minutes before cutting

BAKED LASAGNA

Molly Elizabeth - Age 7
Charlie Michel - Age 5

1 jar spaghetti sauce
1 (16-oz.) pkg. lasagna noodles
2 eggs
1 (15-oz.) container ricotta
  cheese

½ cup Parmesan cheese
2 T. parsley flakes
1 lb. thinly sliced mozzarella
  cheese

Boil the lasagna. Combine eggs, ricotta cheese, Parmesan cheese, and parsley flakes together. In a greased 13 X 9 baking dish, arrange layer of lasagna. Next, spread with a layer of ricotta cheese mixture. Then, spread with layer of spaghetti sauce. Last, a layer of mozzarella cheese. Repeat layers until all ingredients are used. Finish with one last layer of mozzarella cheese. Bake at 350 degrees for 30 minutes. Makes 9 servings.

BAKED MACARONI AND CHEESE

Kaleigh - Age 10

Noodles
Flour
Butter

1 cup Milk
Cheese slices
Parmesan cheese

Bring a large saucepan of salted water to a boil. Add pasta, stirring occasionally, cook for 7 to 10 minutes. Pour the macaroni into a colander and drain off the water. Pre-heat oven to 350 degrees. Melt butter in the same saucepan over medium heat and add the flour. Stir Constantly until the mixture starts to bubble. Add ½ cup of milk and stir until smooth. Add the remaining ½ cups of milk and cook, stirring for 10 to 15 minutes or until it comes to a boil. Remove the pan from the heat. Add the american cheese slices and stir until the cheese is completely melted. Add the macaroni and stir gently until is completely coated with cheese. Place the macaroni in a large baking dish and sprinkle with the Parmesan cheese. Bake for 25 to 30 minutes or until the cheese is bubbly.

BAKED ZITI WITH FOUR CHEESES

Riley - Age 7
Ella - Age 6
Matthew - Age 5, Avery - Age 3

1 lb. ziti pasta, uncooked
1 jar pasta sauce
1 cup low fat cottage cheese
¾ cup parsley
(4-oz.) Parmesan cheese, grated

(8-oz.) part skim mozzarella
 cheese
(4-oz.) provolone cheese, cut in
 quarters

Cook the pasta according to the package directions; drain. Coat a 13-by-9-by-2-inch baking dish with cooking spray; set aside. Place a thin layer of sauce in the bottom of the prepared dish. Continue making layers of pasta, cottage cheese, parsley, sauce, pasta, Parmesan cheese, pasta, mozzarella, parsley, pasta, sauce and parsley. Sprinkle provolone on top. Cover and bake in a 375-degree-F oven for about 30 minutes, or until the cheese melts.

BANANA BOAT

Caitlin Elissa - Age 6
Dylan Jacobs - Age 5

1 Banana
3 tblsp Peanut Butter
½ cup Goldfish Crackers

2 tiny pretzel rods
5 Craisins

Peel the banana. Cut off bottom ⅓ of the long side of banana so it will lay flat. Cut out a sliver from the other side (where the people in a boat would sit). Fill the sliver with peanut butter. Put the tiny pretzel rods in

(continued)

peanut butter so they stand up to form the "masts". Put the goldfish on the plates for the "fish in the ocean". Put the Craisins on the peanut butter for "the crew" of the ship. Bon Voyage!

BANANA FANANA PANCAKES

Emelyn Grace Anglebrandt - Age 2
Edyn May Anglebrandt - Age 4

2 cups Jiffy Baking Mix
1¼ cup soy milk or cows milk
2 med. mashed ripe bananas
2 tsp. cinnamon
2 tblsp veg oil or shortening

1 egg, beaten
1 ctn. Cool-Whip, frozen to top
1 bunch fresh strawberries or
  blueberries to top

Mix all ingredients except Cool Whip and berries together until blended. Pour pancake batter on a hot greased griddle to cook, flipping once. Top with cool-whip that is frozen and fresh strawberries or blueberries and syrup. Enjoy~ Serves 15 pancakes.

BANANA ROLL UP

Timothy Sebastien - Age 5
Sophia Claire - Age 3

1 tortilla
¼ c. peanut butter

1 med. banana

Spread peanut butter on the tortilla, leaving a ½ inch gap at one end. Either slice the banana and lay the slices in a line in the middle of the peanut butter or lay the whole banana across the middle of the tortilla. Roll up the tortilla around the banana and enjoy. For a special treat, you can roll the banana in toasted coconut first.

BANANA SPLIT SANDWICH

Candace J. Liu - Age 13

3 bananas
Nutella

2 slices bread

If you like getting sweet, then try this! Spread the Nutella on the pieces of bread. Peel and cut the 3 bananas. Place the slices on the bread; stacked. Eat them together and you have half banana and half chocolate sandwich!

BASIC WAFFLES

Elleana Elisabeth - Age 6

1 cup all-purpose flour
1 cup whole-wheat flour
1/4 cup milled flax seed
1/4 cup wheat germs
1/2 tsp. baking soda
1 tsp. baking powder
1 tsp. salt
3 tblsp sugar

3 whole eggs, beaten
(2-oz.) unsalted butter, melted
(16-oz.) buttermilk, room
  temperature
2-3 mashed bananas (optional)
  you can also add other fruit
  (i.e. blueberries)
Vegetable spray, for waffle iron

Preheat waffle iron according to manufacturer's directions. In a medium bowl, whisk together the flours, soda, baking powder, salt, flax seed, wheat germ and sugar. In another bowl, beat together eggs and melted butter, and then add the buttermilk and bananas. Add the wet ingredients to the dry and stir until combined. Allow to rest for 5 minutes. Ladle the recommended amount of waffle batter onto the iron according to the manufacturer's recommendations. Close iron top and cook until the waffle is golden on both sides and is easily removed from iron. Serve immediately or keep warm in a 200° oven until ready to serve. Once waffles have cooled, place them in zip lock baggies, 2-4 in each bag, and place in freezer. When ready to eat, remove from freezer and microwave for about 30 seconds, turn over then microwave for another 30-60 seconds and enjoy!!!! They are great for breakfast during busy mornings.

BEEF TACO SKILLET

Mary Rose - Age 10

1 lb. ground beef
1 can tomato soup
1/2 cup salsa
1/2 cup water

6 flour tortillas (6") cut into 1"
  pieces
1/2 cup shredded Cheddar
  cheese

Cook beef in a skillet until well browned, stirring to break up meat. Pour off fat. Stir in soup, salsa, water and tortillas. Heat to a boil. Reduce heat to low and cook for 5 min. Stir. Top with cheese. Makes 4 servings.

BON APPETITE SANDWICH

Carson Bruce - Age 5

1 Bagel
1/2 cup shredded cheddar
  cheese
1 tblsp sunflower seeds
2 sesame wafers

2 strips microwavable bacon
1 pretzel rod
4 cheetos
1 clementine orange

(continued)

98890-09

Turn the broiler on in the oven. Slice the bagel and place both halves face up on a cookie sheet. Sprinkle each bagel face with shredded cheese and sunflower seeds. Place bagels on sheet in the broiler for five minutes or until crisp and cheese is melted. Remove and add the sesame wafers, bacon, crushed pretzels and cheetos on bagel. Smush both halves together. Serve with a clementine orange with each piece of the orange placed around the sandwich in a circle. Make sure you have a huge glass of your favorite drink ready for this one!!!

BOOK SANDWICH

Carson Bruce - Age 5

2 slices bread
3 pieces cheese
mayo (optional)

mustard (optional)
edible markers (can be found at
a party store)

We had been working on reading and Carson came up with this for lunch one day. He wanted to create a sandwich that looked like a book. Lay out each piece of bread (the front cover and back cover of the book). Stack three slices of cheese on a piece of bread. With an edible marker, write a word or words on each piece of cheese which are the pages of the book. Carson practiced writing words like cat, dog, and hat. Place the other piece of bread on top and your edible book is now ready to be eaten. Not only edible, but educational!!!

BREAKFAST CASSEROLE

Emilee Anne - Age 9
Lauren Elizabeth - Age 8
Katy Breana - Age 6

2 pkgs. refrigerated crescent
rolls
1 cup Mozzarella Cheese
½ cup chopped onion (optional)
¼ cup butter or margarine
⅓ cup all-purpose flour
¼ tsp. dried thyme, crushed
¼ tsp. pepper

1 cup chicken broth
¾ cup milk
2 cup chopped fully cooked
ham
1-½ cup "Simply Potatoes"
southwestern hash browns
6 hard-cooked eggs chopped or
sliced

For Crust: Separate one package of rolls and press over the bottom and ½-in. up the sides of a 13 x 9 x 2 baking dish. Bake in a 375° oven for 8 to 12 minutes or until golden brown. Remove from oven and sprinkle with cheese, set aside. For filling: cook onion in margarine or butter until tender but not brown. Stir in flour, thyme and pepper. Add broth and milk all at once. Cook and stir over medium heat till thickened and bubbly. Stir in ham, potatoes and eggs; heat through. Pour filling over crust. Separate remaining package of crescent rolls and place triangles across the top of filling. Bake at 375° for 20 to 25 minutes more or till crust is golden brown.

BREAKFAST COOKIES AND MILK

Christopher John - Age 5
Ryan Raymond - Age 3

½ cup butter, softened
⅔ cup packed brown sugar
½ T. baking soda
2 eggs
1 cup whole-wheat flour
¾ cup white flour

3 cup multigrain cereal flakes, crushed
1 cup chocolate chips
1 cup milk (when serving cookies)

Beat butter in electric mixer. Add sugar and baking soda and beat. Add eggs one at a time. Add flour. Use wooden spoon to stir in cereal and then chips. Fill mini muffin cups with dough to the top (cookies will not puff). Flatten dough so it is level with the top of the muffin tin. Makes 3 dozen mini muffins or 14-16 ice cream scoop size cookies. Bake at 350° for 8-10 minutes. Let cool for 2 minutes in muffin tin. Pop cookies out of tin and completely cool cookies on wire rack. Serve with glass of milk for breakfast. Pair with a side of fruit. Be sure to store cookies in a tightly sealed container. (You can double this recipe and freeze the batch. The night before serving, take out cookies you will need for breakfast and place in storage container.)

BREAKFAST PATATIES EGGS

Carson Bruce - Age 5

4 eggs
½ cup milk
½ cup salsa
½ cup shredded cheese

⅓ cup scallions
dollop sour cream
handful of taco chips

Beat the eggs and milk together. Add mixture to a skillet over medium/high heat stirring often. When eggs are almost cooked through, add salsa, scallions and cheese. Cook until cheese has melted. Garnish each serving with a dollop of sour cream and a handful of taco chips.

98890-09

BROCCOLI AND FARFALLE PASTA

Gia Marie - Age 4
Max Peter - Age 2

3-4 bunches broccoli (or 1-2
  bunches asparagus)
1 pound box farfalle pasta
  (bowtie)
4 tblsp extra virgin olive oil
2 shallots (or 1 med. onion)
1 (8-oz.) container heavy
  whipping cream
1 (14-oz.) can college inn
  chicken broth

½ teaspoon salt
parmigiana or romano cheese to
  taste
1 pound fresh shrimp or
  scallops (optional)
1 pound chicken breast
  (optional)

This is a great recipe because it can be called a number of things such as "farfalle with broccoli and chicken" or "farfalle with asparagus and scallops" - you can mix n' match or just leave it alone. Enjoy! Start boiling your water - cut broccoli so you only have the "flower" part remaining - the broccoli will need to be steamed (when water boils add pasta so it's done at the same time as your steamed broccoli flowers). Meanwhile, while waiting for your water to boil: mince shallots (so the kids don't see em') and stir fry in olive oil. Once shallots are translucent, add heavy whipping cream, chicken broth and salt - bring to a gentle boil and reduce sauce stirring constantly until your pasta and broccoli are done (about 10 minutes). Mix pasta, broccoli and sauce in a large pasta bowl and top with parmigiana or romano cheese - be sure to mix dish well before EVERY serving as sauce tends to drain to the bottom of your bowl.

NOTE - if you are adding shrimp, scallops or cut up chicken, cook in sauce about two minutes before your pasta and broccoli are finished. Serves 4-6.

BUTTERED NOODLES

Bennett John - Age 4
Annabelle Kady - Age 2

1 pkg. noodles (any kind)
2 cups unsalted butter

1 pkg. Parmesan cheese

Cook noodles as directed on package. Drain water. Mix in butter and cheese. Bennett then suggests to then top it with more cheese; the more cheese the better!

BUTTERMILK-OATMEAL PANCAKES

Elleana Elisabeth - Age 6

2½ cups buttermilk
¾ cups rolled oats
1 cup all-purpose flour
½ cup whole-wheat flour
¼ cup milled flax seed
¼ cup toasted wheat germ
¼ cup packed light brown
 sugar
2 tsp. baking powder
1 tsp. baking soda

1 tsp. ground cinnamon
½ tsp. salt
1 large egg
2 large egg whites
2 tsp. teaspoons canola oil,
 divided
3 mashed bananas (optional)
 you can also add other fruit
 (i.e. blueberries)
Maple syrup (optional)

Combine buttermilk and rolled oats in a small bowl; let stand for 20 to 30 minutes to soften oats. Stir together flours, wheat germ, milled flax seed, brown sugar, baking powder, baking soda, cinnamon and salt in a medium bowl. Mix together egg, egg whites and 1 teaspoon oil in another bowl with a whisk or fork. Add the oat mixture and the flour mixture and bananas (optional) stir with a wooden spoon until combined.

Note: If batter is too thick add a little more buttermilk. Lightly brush a large nonstick skillet with a little of the remaining 1 teaspoon oil and place over medium heat. Using ¼ cup batter for each pancake, pour batter onto the pan and cook until the underside is browned and the bubbles on top remain open, 2 to 3 minutes. Turn the pancakes over and cook until the underside is browned, about 1 to 2 minutes. Transfer to a platter and keep warm in a 200°F oven. Repeat with remaining batter, brushing the pan with a little of the remaining oil as needed. Serve hot, topping with maple syrup if desired. Frozen pancakes - Once pancakes have cooled place them in zip lock (for freezer) baggies in the freezer, 2-4 in each bag. When ready to eat, take out from freezer and microwave for about 30 seconds, turn over then microwave for another 30-60 seconds and enjoy!!!! They are great for breakfast during busy mornings.

CADE'S CRISPY COCONUT CHICKEN

Cade Thomas Murphy - Age 3

1 cup Baker's Angel Flake
 Coconut
1 cup Flour
¼ tsp. garlic salt

Dash pepper
1 med. egg, beaten
1½ lbs. boneless skinless
 chicken breasts

Preheat oven to 420 degrees. Mix the following ingredients in a medium, shallow bowl: flour, coconut, garlic salt, pepper. Cut chicken into 1-inch strips, add to egg mixture, shake access and dredge in flour mixture. Put strips on a lightly greased baking sheet and cook for 20-25 minutes, until slightly browned. Serve with honey mustard sauce!

98890-09

CARYN BURKHARDT'S GRANDMOTHER'S SLOPPY JOES

Sean Hayes, Actor

1½ - 2 lbs. ground beef
½ onion, chopped
½ green pepper, chopped
1 can tomato soup
1 sm. can tomato paste
¼ cup chili sauce

¼ cup brown sugar
½ tsp. salt
¼ tsp. pepper
2-3 tblsp. dark molasses
1 tblsp. vinegar

Brown 1½ - 2 lbs. ground beef, drain and set aside. Sauté chopped onion with chopped green pepper for a few minutes and add ground beef back to pan with onion and pepper. Add the can of tomato soup, can tomato paste, chili sauce, brown sugar, salt, pepper, dark molasses, and vinegar. Heat together and simmer until flavors combine. Add Sloppy Joe mixture to your favorite hamburger buns. I call this Caryn Burkhardt's grandmother's Sloppy Joes. Cause they're not mine. They're Caryn Burkhardt's grandmother's Sloppy Joes. Tastes best with a glass of Caryn Burkhardt's grandmother's milk. Go nuts! Sean Hayes

CATE & DADDY'S PIZZA

Catherine Ann - Age 3

1 frozen cheese pizza
2 (4-oz.) cans sliced mushrooms
1 (6-oz.) can sliced black olives
¼ (6-oz.) can sliced green
    olives (optional)

2 cups shredded mozzarella
    cheese

Unwrap frozen pizza. Thoroughly drain mushrooms and olives. Sprinkle mushrooms, black olives and cheese on top. (Add green olives to ¼ of the pizza ONLY if Julia is eating with you.) Cook an additional 3-5 minutes according to package directions.

CHEESY NOODLES

Ally - Age 13

1 box spaghetti noodles (or any
    kind of pasta)

1 handful of shredded cheddar
    cheese per serving

Cook pasta according to directions on the box. Drain and put serving size in a microwavable bowl. Toss with shredded cheddar cheese and microwave for 30 seconds.

CHICAGO STYLE HOT DOG

Shane

1 all beef hot dog	4 tomato wedges
1 poppy seed hot dog bun	1 dill pickle spear
1 tblsp yellow mustard	2 sport peppers
1 tblsp sweet green pickle relish	1 dash celery salt
1 tblsp chopped onion	

Bring a pot of water to a boil. Reduce heat to low, place hot dog in water, and cook 5 minutes or until done. Remove hot dog and set aside. Carefully place a steamer basket into the pot and steam the hot dog bun 2 minutes or until warm. Place hot dog in the steamed bun. Pile on the toppings in this order: yellow mustard, sweet green pickle relish, onion, tomato wedges, pickle spear, sport peppers, and celery salt. The tomatoes should be nestled between the hot dog and the top of the bun. Place the pickle between the hot dog and the bottom of the bun. Don't even think about ketchup!

CHICKEN A LA KING

Maggie Mae - Age 7
Abby Lynn - Age 5

2 tblsp melted butter	1 tsp. sugar
mushrooms (optional)	2 tblsp chopped onion
1 can Cream of Chicken soup	2 cups cooked, cubed chicken
1 tblsp Worcestershire sauce	breast
1 tsp. salt	

Brown mushrooms and onion in butter. Add remaining ingredients. Heat thoroughly. Serve on Pepperidge Farm patty, shells or toast.

CHICKEN BROCCOLI PIE

Sophia Emma

1 Rotisserie Chicken	1 pkg. Buehler's Pie Crusts
1 Large head Broccoli	
2 cans Cream of Mushroom	
Soup	

This is another of my absolute favorite meals and it is so easy to do! Steam the broccoli to al dente while you cut the chicken up into chunks and put into a bowl. Add the al dente broccoli into the bowl with the chicken. Add the two cans of cream of mushroom soup to the chicken and broccoli (do not add any milk - just the soup!). Put one of the Buehler's pie crusts into the bottom of a 9 inch pie plate. Add in the chicken, broccoli and soup mixture. Top with the second pastry crust. Bake on 375° F for approximately 45 minutes or until the pie crust is

(continued)

98890-09

golden. Serve with boiled potatoes and your favorite vegetables. You'll love this hearty meat dish - much better than the store bought pies!!

CHICKEN CURRY

Markus Victor - Age 9

½ lb. cubed chicken
1 diced onion
salt and pepper
3 cups water
½ box Vermont Curry paste

1 T. vegetable oil
3 cloves garlic
3 chopped carrots
3 large potatoes

Brown chicken with oil, onion, garlic, salt & pepper. Add water, carrots, and potatoes - bring to boil. Lower temperature and simmer for 20 minutes (until potatoes are cooked). Add curry paste, stir until gravy like. Ready to eat with white rice.

CHICKEN NUGGETS

Anna - Age 7
Luke - Age 5
Ashley - Age 3, Jake - Age 2

2 lbs. skinless boneless chicken
  breast halves
¾ cup cornflakes
½ cup all-purpose flour
1 tsp. paprika

¾ tsp. salt
½ tsp. pepper
⅓ cup low-fat buttermilk
½ cup barbecue sauce
½ cup sweet-and-sour sauce

Heat oven to 400 degrees. Line jelly roll pan, 15½ x 10½ x 1 inch, with aluminum foil. Trim fat from chicken. Cut chicken into 2-inch pieces. Place cornflakes, flour, paprika, sat and pepper in blender. Cover and blend on medium speed until cornflakes are reduced to crumbs; pour into bowl. Place chicken and buttermilk in heavy resealable plastic bag; seal bag and let stand 5 minutes, turning once. Dip chicken into cornflake mixture to coat. Place in pan. Spray chicken with nonstick cooking spray. Bake about 30 minutes or until crisp and chicken is no longer pink in center. Serve with barbecue sauce and sweet-and-sour sauce.

CHICKEN POT PIE

Eddie - Age 10

2 (10¾-oz.) cans Campbell's
  Cream of Broccoli Soup
1 c. milk
¼ tsp. pepper
1 (16-oz.) bag frozen vegetable
  combination, cooked and
  drained

1 c. potato, peeled, cubed, and
  cooked
2 c. cooked chicken, cubed
1 (10-oz.) can refrigerated flaky
  biscuits

(continued)

In a 3 quart oblong baking dish, combine soup, milk, and pepper. Stir in vegetables and chicken. Bake at 400° for 15 minutes or until mixture begins to bubble. Meanwhile, cut each biscuit into quarters. Remove dish from oven; stir. Arrange biscuit pieces over hot chicken mixture. Bake 15 minutes or until biscuits are golden brown. Serves 5.

CHICKEN POT PIE OVER A BISCUIT

Billy O'Donnell
Patrick O'Donnell

1 sm. green pepper, chopped
4-6 oz. fresh mushrooms, chopped & sautéed
1/2 cup butter
1/4 cup flour
1 tsp. salt
1/4 tsp. pepper
1 1/2 cup milk

1 1/4 cup chicken broth
2 cups cooked chicken (cut into chunks)
1 (2 oz.) jar pimentos
1 bag frozen peas and carrots
1 pkg. frozen Pepperidge Farm Puffed Pastries or can of Pillsbury Biscuits

In a large saucepan, cook and stir green peppers, sliced mushrooms and butter over medium heat about 5 minutes. Stir in flour, salt and pepper to make a paste - until bubbly. Stir in milk and chicken broth. Heat until boiling, stirring constantly. Add cut-up chicken, peas, carrots and pimentos. Serve warm over heated puffed pastry or biscuits. Enjoy!

CHICKEN RIBBONS SATAY

Jose Hernandez - Age 12

1/2 cup Creamy peanut butter
1/2 cup Water
1/4 cup Soy Sauce
4 cloves Garlic, pressed
3 tblsp Lemon juice
2 tblsp Firmly packed brown sugar

3/4 tsp. Ground ginger
1/2 tsp. Crushed red pepper flakes
4 Boneless skinless chicken breast halves
Sliced green onion tops for garnish

Makes 4 servings. Combine peanut butter, water, soy sauce, garlic, lemon juice, brown sugar, ginger and red pepper flakes in small saucepan. Cook over medium heat 1 minute or until smooth; cool. Remove garlic from sauce; discard. Reserve half of sauce for dipping. Cut chicken lengthwise into 1-inch-wide strips. Thread onto 8 metal or bamboo skewers. (Soak bamboo skewers in water a least 20 minute to keep them from burning.) Oil hot grill to help prevent sticking. Grill chicken, on a covered grill, over medium-hot Kingsford briquets, 6 to 8 minutes until chicken is cooked through, turning once. Baste with sauce once or twice during cooking. Serve with reserved sauce garnished with sliced green onion tops.

98890-09

CHICKEN SATAY WITH PEANUT SAUCE

Freida - Age 6
Beata - Age 5

1½ lbs. skinless, boneless
chicken breasts, cut into strips
20 skewers, soaked in water for
30 minutes
vegetable oil, for grilling
Butter lettuce leaves
fresh cilantro leaves
Marinade Ingredients:
1 cup plain yogurt
1 tsp. freshly grated ginger
1 tsp. minced garlic

1 tblsp. curry powder
Peanut Sauce Ingredients:
1 cup smooth peanut butter
¼ cup low-sodium soy sauce
2 tsp. red chili paste, such as
samba
2 tblsp. dark brown sugar
2 limes, juiced
½ cup hot water
¼ cup chopped peanuts, for
garnish

Combine the yogurt, ginger, garlic and curry powder in a shallow mixing bowl, stir to combine. Place the chicken strips in the yogurt marinade and gently toss until well coated. Cover and let the chicken marinate in the refrigerator for up to 2 hours. Thread the chicken pieces onto the soaked skewers working the skewer in and out of the meat, down the middle of the piece, so that it stays in place during grilling. Place a grill pan over medium heat and brush it with oil to prevent the meat from sticking. Grill the chicken satays for 3-5 minutes on each side, until nicely seared and cooked through. Serve the satays on a platter lined with lettuce leaves and cilantro; accompanied by a small bowl of peanut sauce on the side. For the Peanut Sauce, combine the peanut butter, soy sauce, red chili paste, brown sugar, and lime juice in a food processor or blender. Purée to combine. While the motor is running, drizzle in the hot water to thin out the sauce, you may not need all of it. Pour the sauce into a nice serving bowl and garnish with the chopped peanuts. Serve with chicken satay.

CHICKEN TETRAZZINI

Madalynn Victoria - Age 7

1½ cup raw spaghetti, broken
1 boiled chicken, boned, in large
chunks
½ cup diced onion
½ cup chopped celery

1 can cream of mushroom soup
½ cup broth
½ tsp. salt
⅛ tsp. pepper
1¾ cup grated cheddar cheese

Boil chicken, cool, skin, and debone. Reserve broth. Set aside ½ c. broth. Boil spaghetti in reserved broth until ½ done. Meanwhile, mix all other ingredients together (including ½ c. broth). Pour into greased 9 x 13 pan. Bake at 350 for 45 minutes uncovered. Be sure casserole is very moist or the pasta will not cook completely.

CHILI

Tiffany - Age 10

2 lbs. hamburger meat
1 can tomato sauce
1 can tomato soup
1 can tomato and chili peppers,
  optional
1 can Busch kidney beans

2 pkgs. McCormick mild chili
  mix
1 pkg. McCormick hot chili mix
1-2 cans water
1 small sour cream
1 pkg. shredded cheese

Brown hamburger meat and drain the grease. Once that is done, put the meat, sauce, soup, tomato and chili peppers, beans, chili mix, and water in a large pot. Make sure you drain the kidney beans first. Cook for 1 hour over medium heat. Top it off with shredded cheese and a spoonful of sour cream. And enjoy!

CHIP AND DALE'S CHIPMUNK WHOLE WHEAT PANCAKES

Connor Nathaniel - Age 5

½ cup sifted all-purpose flour
½ cup unsifted whole-wheat
  flour
½ tsp. salt
2 tblsp sugar

2 tsp. baking powder
1 egg lightly beaten
1 cup milk
2 tblsp apple sauce, cooking oil,
  melted butter or margarine

Preheat griddle over moderate heat while you mix batter. Sift flour, sugar, salt and baking powder into a bowl or wide mouth pitcher. Combine egg, milk and oil, slowly stir into dry ingredients, and mix until dampened, batter should be lumpy. When a drop of cold water will dance on the griddle, begin cooking pancakes, using about 1 tablespoon batter for each (size of a silver dollar), allowing plenty of space between them. Cook until bubbles form over surface, turn gently and brown flip side. Stack on plate and serve with plenty of maple syrup.

CHUCK ROAST AU GRATIN
(Grandma's Best!)

Hannah B. Meyer
Kendra R. Meyer
Jamie K. Horsman

3-4 pounds Boneless Chuck
  Roast
2 cans Cream of Mushroom
  Soup

6 med. Potatoes
½ cup Grated Cheddar Cheese
1 tsp. Paprika (optional)

Place meat in a large baking pan. Roast at 350 degrees for 1 hour. Spoon off fat. Arrange potatoes around roast. Combine soup, chives, and 1 soup can of water. Pour over meat and potatoes. Cover and cook

(continued)

98890-09

2 more hours or until meat is tender. Sprinkle with cheese and paprika. Return to oven just until the cheese melts. Approximately 5 minutes. Makes 6 servings. RECIPE CAN BE COMPLETED IN A SLOW COOKER. Brown both sides of roast. Arrange potatoes in bottom of slow cooker. Place meat on top. Pour one can of soup and ½ can of water over meat and potatoes. Cover and cook on low for 8 hours. Sprinkle with cheese and paprika.

CILANTRO CHICKEN

Emma Delaney - Age 8

2 chicken breasts
1 large clove garlic
¼ cup extra virgin olive oil

¼ cup fresh cilantro (chopped)
½ tsp. kosher salt
1 small lime

Pound chicken breasts out evenly to around ½ inch thickness. To prepare marinade, combine garlic (finely chopped), extra virgin olive oil, cilantro (chopped) and the juice from one small lime. Cover chicken on both sides with marinade. Place chicken in container and sprinkle with kosher salt. (Salt can be reduced or omitted from recipe.) Allow chicken to marinate in the refrigerator for at least 30 minutes. Heat grill pan or outside grill. Place chicken on grill and cook thoroughly on both sides.

CINNAMON OATMEAL PANCAKES

Travis James - Age 12
Jakob Daniel - Age 10
Trey Vincent - Age 7

1 c. Oats or quick oats
1⅔ c. Milk
1½ c. Pancake mix (Bisquick)

2 tsp. Cinnamon
1 Egg

Pour oats into milk. Let soak for 2 minutes. Add Pancake mix, cinnamon and egg and beat until smooth. Pour by ¼ cupfuls onto hot griddle (350 degree electric griddle). Cook until edges are dry. Turn, cook until golden brown. About 18 (4 inch) pancakes. The boys favorite type of pancakes.

CINNAMON PANCAKES

Jessica Lynn - Age 6
Ryan Robert - Age 4

1 box whole-wheat pancake mix
1 tsp. cinnamon

1 tsp. vanilla

Follow directions from the pancake mix box. Make pancake batter. Add cinnamon and vanilla for extra tastiness! Make pancakes as directed. Enjoy!

CLASSIC HOT DOG
(Best Hot Dog Ever)

Nathan Christopher - Age 21 months

1 Hot dog

1 squirt of Ketchup

Steam 1 hot dog (or as many as you want), allow to cool then cut into small pieces. Add enough Ketchup to coat the hot dog pieces and stir. Serve with milk and pretzels.

CROCKPOT PORK ROAST

Grant Kenneth - Age 6
Jacob "Jake" Dennis - Age 4

4-5 lbs. boneless pork loin roast
½ tsp. salt
¼ tsp. ground black pepper
1-2 cloves garlic, slivered
4 medium onions, sliced

2 bay leaves
1 whole garlic clove
½ cup water
2 tblsp. soy sauce

Trim pork roast off fat (if roast is thick, I cut it into 2 long roasts). Rub roast with salt and pepper. Make tiny slits in meat and insert slivers of garlic. Place 2 sliced onions in bottom of stoneware. Add pork roast, remaining onion, and other ingredients (I like to add a little extra soy sauce). Cover and cook on LOW 10 to 12 hours, or HIGH 5-6 hours. Great with your favorite rice and vegetable on the side!

CROISSANT SANDWICHES

Andrew Tyler

1 can Buttery Croissants
12 slices Favorite lunch meat
6 slices Favorite cheese

1 dollop mustard
1 can green chilies

Preheat oven to 375° degrees. Roll out the croissants on a cookie sheet and spread the mustard and green chilies on. Put two slices of your favorite lunch meat and a slice of cheese and roll it up and then press and seal edges of each pocket. Place cookie sheet in oven for 17-21 minutes. (till golden brown). Cut up and serve! Be careful, may be hot! Enjoy~

CRUNCHY, MUNCHY SANDWICH

Alexandra Lee - Age 7

2 slices bread
mayo
turkey slices

1 slice American cheese
handful of Doritos

(continued)

98890-09

Put mayo on bread slices. Add turkey slices and cheese slice. Take handful of Doritos and put on top of turkey and cheese. Place bread slice on top and smash down with your hand. Take a bite and eat your crunchy sandwich!

DAD'S EGG AND CHEESE SCRAMBLER

Billy Grogan

6 eggs
2 slices american cheese

2 tblsp. milk
olive oil cooking spray

Heat a large non-stick frying pan to a setting just above medium. Whisk together eggs and milk for about 2 minutes. Spray frying pan with olive oil spray and add egg & milk mixture. Cook eggs until they are almost complete. Put slices of cheese on half of the eggs. Place the other half of eggs on top of the cheese and continue cooking until the cheese melts in between the eggs. Yummy--great for any time of day.

DAVE'S DAGWOOD SANDWICH

David Bruce - Age 12

2 slices bread
1 slice bologna
1 slice Velveeta cheese
1 slice tomato
1 rounded tsp. peanut butter

1 rounded tsp. strawberry jam
1 tsp. mustard
1 tsp. mayonnaise
2 lettuce leaves

Between two slices of your favorite kind of bread place bologna, cheese, tomato, peanut butter, strawberry jam, mustard, mayo and lettuce. Serve with chips and milk.

DOUBLE BUTTER AND JELLY

Kamren Christopher - Age 5½
Keaten Lawrence - Age 7

3 slices bread
Peanut Butter

Raspberry Preserves

Make a regular peanut butter and jelly sandwich. Next spread peanut butter on top of the sandwich. Finally take a third slice and spread raspberry preserves. Place the raspberry slice on top of the peanut butter and you have a Double Butter and Jelly.

EASY CINNAMON SWIRL FRENCH TOAST

Alexis Hughes - Age 11

Oil
3 Eggs
½ cup Milk

8 slices Cinnamon bread
pinch Powdered Sugar
pinch Cinnamon

Heat skillet or griddle to 350°F. Grease lightly with oil. In pie pan, combine eggs and milk; beat well. Dip bread in egg mixture, turning to coat both sides. Cook in skillet about 2 to 3 minutes on each side or until golden brown. Sprinkle with powdered sugar and cinnamon. Serve with syrup, if desired. 8 slices.

EASY SCRAMBLED EGGS

Ethan Koertje

6 Eggs
1 handful of Spinach
3 tblsp Chopped Fresh Basil
1 handful of your favorite
  shredded cheese

2 shakes Sea Salt
3 shakes Cracked Black Pepper

Spray a large skillet with olive oil, and warm to low/medium heat. Meanwhile, combine all ingredients in a large bowl, whisking everything together. Then pour the egg mixture into the pre-heated skillet and cook for approximately 10 minutes. Stir occasionally to ensure the eggs are scrambled and mixture does not turn into an omelet. Once cooked thoroughly, season with additional salt and pepper to taste, and serve!

EDDIE'S SPAGHETTI

Eddie James - Age 1

1 box Barilla Spaghetti Noodles   1 jar Prego Spaghetti Sauce

Bring water to boil. Add noodles. Cook noodles for about 8-10 minutes. Drain. In a sauce pan heat sauce. In large bowl combine noodles and sauce. Enjoy!

EGG & SAUSAGE BREAKFAST PIZZA

Lauren - Age 9
Claire - Age 5
Evan - Age 2

5 eggs, lightly beaten
1 tblsp. butter
1 tblsp. extra-virgin olive oil
2 pizza crusts 8-inch (pre-made
  is ok)
2 cups shredded jack cheese

4-5 fully cooked sausage
  patties, crumbled
¼ cup shredded Parmesan
1-2 medium tomato, diced
1-1½ tsp. Italian seasoning

(continued)

Preheat oven to 450 degrees F. In a medium pan over medium heat, scramble eggs in butter, set aside. Lay out pizza crusts and brush with oil. Top with eggs, cheese, crumbled sausage, Parmesan, tomatoes, and Italian seasoning. Bake in preheated oven for 8 to 10 minutes or until cheese is melted and begins to bubble.

EGG IN THE HOLE

Grace Margaret - Age 3
Olivia McNaghten

4 slices whole-wheat bread   **1 T. butter or margarine**
4 eggs

Select your favorite cookie cutter (we like stars, flowers, hearts and butterflies) and cut out the shape from the center of each piece of bread. In a skillet, melt butter over medium heat. Tilt skillet so butter coats pan. Place slices of bread in pan (include the cut-out shapes if you can fit them, or cook in batches). Crack eggs, one at a time, into the center of each piece of bread. After about 3 minutes, flip bread over and continue to cook until egg is set. We like to eat the cut-out shapes with jelly. Serves 4.

EGG SURPRISE

Christian Luke - Age 6

1 slice white or wheat bread   **favorite cookie cutter**
1 T. butter   **salt and pepper to taste**
1 egg

Place bread on hard surface and cut out favorite shape in center with a cookie cutter. Melt butter in pan and add bread cut out. Crack egg on top (in cut out area) and fry on both sides. Salt and pepper to taste. Enjoy!

EGGO SANDWICH

Caitlin Elissa - Age 6
Dylan Jacobs - Age 5

2 Eggo Waffles   **maple syrup**
2 tblsp peanut butter

Toast the Eggo waffles in the toaster. Spread the peanut butter on one waffle. Pour syrup on the other waffle. Put them together for a tasty breakfast sandwich.

ENGLISH COTTAGE PIE

Sophia Emma

1-lb. Ground Beef
2 Medium Onions
2 Large Carrots
½ tsp. Ground Cinnamon
½ tsp. Italian Herbs
1 tblsp. Parsley

1 tblsp. Flour
1 tblsp. Tomato Paste
(10-oz.) Beef Stock
Salt and Pepper
Shredded Cheddar Cheese - as
   much as you like!

This is one of my most favorite meals! I hope you will try it. I would like to clarify that in England, Cottage Pie is made with ground beef and Shepherd's Pie is made with ground lamb. You can use either meat with this recipe. If you make Shepherd's Pie, add a ½ tsp. of mint to the recipe. Preheat Oven to 400°F. Fry onions until soft, then add chopped carrot and ground beef, continuing to cook for about 10 minutes until the meat has browned. Season with salt, pepper, cinnamon, Italian herbs and parsley. Mix the hot beef stock and tomato paste together. Then stir flour into the meat and herb mixture. Now add the beef stock to the meat, herbs and flour. Make creamy mashed potatoes for the topping. Put the meat mixture into a baking dish. We use a round Pyrex dish. Top the entire meat mixture with the mashed potatoes and sprinkle with grated cheddar cheese. Bake for 25 minutes until top is crusty and golden. Serve with your favorite vegetables.

FAJITAS

Martin - Age 7

1 lb. Chicken
1 Green Pepper
1 Onion
1 Lemon
8 Tortillas

Salt
Pepper
Tomatoes
Lettuce
1 cup Red Beans

Cut pepper. Stir fry pepper. Mix onion in. Add salt, pepper. Cut chicken and add to peppers and onions. Squeeze lemon juice into stir fry. Remove from heat. Warm tortillas. Serve with tomatoes, lettuce and red beans. Eat!

FILIPINO ROLL

Ce-Ce

1 green pepper, chopped
1 small onion
1 lb. ground beef
2 c. bread crumbs
2 tsp. salt
¼ T. pepper
1 egg, beaten

1 T. ketchup
¼ c. milk
bacon slices
1 can tomato soup
½ can water
1 T. sugar
2 T. flour

(continued)

Mix together green pepper, onion, beef, bread crumbs, salt, pepper, egg, ketchup, and milk. Form into roll and place into baking pan. Lay slices of bacon over top and bake 45 minutes at 350°. Remove from pan and to liquid add ½ cup water and 1 can tomato soup, 1 T. sugar, salt, and 2 T. flour. Boil till thick, pour around roll and serve.

FIREMAN HATS WITH SCRAMBLED EGGS

Lucciana Tru - Age 1

2 Hot Dogs
½ cup Your Favorite Shredded
  Cheese

2 Eggs
splash of Water or Milk
Salt and Pepper to taste

Scramble two eggs in a bowl with a splash of water or milk, set aside. Slice hot dogs on a slant (the "fireman hats"). Brown hot dogs to your liking in small frying pan then add egg mixture. Scramble the eggs together with the fireman hats until eggs are cooked. Add shredded cheese and mix until melted. Add salt and pepper to taste. Serve on a plate and you now have "Fireman Hats with Scrambled Eggs". Enjoy!

FIREMAN SANDWICH

Travis James - Age 12

2 slices Your favorite bread
2 slices American Cheese
2 slices Ham

2 slices Swiss Cheese
2 slices Turkey
2 slices Salami

Open 2 slices of bread, put one slice of each item in the above order, then the remaining slices again in that order. Close sandwich with remaining piece of bread. Travis created this sandwich when he was 5 years old, shortly after 9/11, because he felt that firemen would need this size sandwich for all the energy they would need to save people and put out fires, and he makes this to eat when he is really hungry so that he will grow up big and strong like them!

FISH WITH SHRIMP SAUCE

Sophie Clark - Age 6
Ian Clark - Age 4

1½ - 2 lbs. Haddock (or any
  thick white fish)
1 can Cream of Shrimp soup
Cracker Crumb Mix:
½ stick melted butter (in sauce
  pan)

Add:
½ tsp. Worcestershire sauce
½ tsp. Onion Powder
¼ tsp. Garlic Powder
15-20 crushed Ritz Crackers

Place fish in baking dish (skin side down). Salt lightly and cover with can of Cream of Shrimp soup. Bake at 375° for 20 minutes. Remove

(continued)

from oven, cover with cracker crumb mix. Bake again until browned - another 20 minutes or so.

FIT FOR A PRINCESS PASTA

Rocco Napoli - Age 9
Isabella Napoli - Age 5

1 (12-oz.) box pasta bows
1 tblsp olive oil
5 slices bacon
2 onions, chopped
2 cloves garlic, crushed

1 (12-oz.) pkg. frozen peas
½ cup prepared pesto sauce
dash black pepper
handful of fresh chopped basil

Cook pasta in a pot of boiling water for 10 minutes. While pasta is cooking, in a large frying pan heat oil on medium until hot. Add bacon and fry for 5 minutes until browned. Remove bacon from pan and set aside. Add onions for 5 minutes until soft. Add garlic and fry for 1 minute. Then add peas and cook, stirring frequently, until tender. Stir in pesto sauce and black pepper. Drain pasta and then add to sauce. Lastly, sprinkle chopped basil over and serve.

FLOUR TORTILLA PIZZA

Connor John - Age 11
Stirling James - Age 6

large flour tortilla
⅔ tablespoons tomato pasta
** sauce**

shredded cheese
pepperoni or other topping

Spread sauce evenly over flour tortilla. Sprinkle shredded cheese evenly on top of sauce. Add other toppings if desired. Bake in an oven at 375° for 8-10 minutes, until cheese is melted and tortilla is crispy. Cut into wedges.

FRENCH TOAST

Andrew Michael - Age 10

4 large eggs
few shakes of cinnamon
pinch of nutmeg

pinch of salt
6-8 slices bread (thick bread is
** best)**

Crack your eggs into a flat bowl or you can use a glass pie pan. Use a fork to beat the eggs. Add the cinnamon, nutmeg and salt. Beat eggs some more. Heat a flat frying pan - you can put oil in the pan to make the French Toast a little crispier. Dip both sides of the bread in the eggs and let the extra drip off so the bread isn't too soggy. Put bread on hot frying pan. You can put 4 pieces on at one time. Fry each side until they are just starting to get brown, maybe 2-3 minutes. Stack the slices

(continued)

on a plate and pour syrup over the stack. You can also put powdered sugar or whipped cream on them, but syrup is the best and easiest.

FRENCH TOAST

Ross Richard - Age 7
Cassidy Rae - Age 10

2 Egg	1 shake Sugar
2 cups Milk	1 tsp. Vanilla
1 tblsp. Cinnamon	1 loaf Texas Toast

Mix all ingredients except toast. Dip Texas toast in mixture and place on a hot flat griddle pan. Cook until browned on both sides. Cover with syrup or fruit and enjoy!

FRENCH TOAST CASSEROLE
(It's like dessert for breakfast!)

Olivia Mitchell - Age 2

1 cup Light Brown Sugar	5 Eggs
½ cup Butter	½ cup Low fat (2%) milk
2 tblsp. Light Corn Syrup	1 tsp. Vanilla extract
1 loaf French Bread- cut into ¾" slices	Powdered sugar and cinnamon to garnish

Cook butter, brown sugar and corn syrup over low heat until bubbly. Pour into a greased 9 X 13" pan. Place bread slices on top of mixture. Pour egg, milk, and vanilla mixture onto and refrigerate overnight or at least 6 hours. Cook at 350 degrees for 30 minutes or until egg mixture is set and not runny. Garnish with powdered sugar and cinnamon. Enjoy. Then enjoy again!

FRENCH TOAST CASSEROLE

Summer Stitt - Age 13

1 loaf French bread	½ tsp. cinnamon
8 eggs	½ cup brown sugar
1-½ cups milk	¼ cup butter
3 tblsp sugar	½ cup pecans optional

Slice French bread into ¾ inch slices and arrange in a 13 x 9 inch baking pan. Whisk eggs, milk, sugar and cinnamon together and pour on top of bread. Refrigerate for two hours or overnight. Before baking, preheat oven to 375 degrees. Blend brown sugar and butter and spread on top of bread. Optional, sprinkle with pecans. Cook for 35-40 minutes. Serve with warm maple syrup. Our family enjoys this breakfast French toast casserole on Easter morning.

FRIED EGG AND CHEESE SANDWICH WITH RED SAUCE

Camille Arianne - Age 5

2 eggs
splash of milk
handful of grated cheese

English Muffins
ketchup

Combine eggs, milk and cheese in a small bowl and whisk. Pour into a small frying pan prepped with non-stick spray. Allow to cook into pancake form. When finished cooking, cut in half or quarters and put on top of toasted English muffin. Top with ketchup/red sauce.

FRITTATA

Elleana Elisabeth - Age 6

6 egg whites
3 whole eggs
½ cup milk
⅓ lb. chopped Canadian bacon
1 pkg. frozen spinach, thawed
and drained

1 cup chopped mushrooms
1½ cups shredded cheese
(cheddar or other favorite
cheese)
1 pinch salt and pepper to taste
2-3 tblsp hot sauce (optional)

Preheat oven to 350°. In a medium bowl, combine and whisk together eggs, egg whites, and milk. Add Canadian bacon, spinach, mushrooms, 1 cup of cheese, salt and pepper and hot sauce. Mix well. Spray non-stick oil in cup cake tins (options - (1) use paper liners or (2) pour into 9 inch pie dish - cooking time may take longer). Pour egg mixture into cupcake tin, about ¾ full. Top with remaining cheese. Bake at 350° for 30-40 minutes until centers are cooked and not runny. Enjoy while hot with extra hot sauce on top. Refrigerate leftovers. Microwave for 30-60 seconds and enjoy!!!! They are great for breakfast during busy mornings.

GAVIN'S FAVORITE CHICKEN

Gavin Smith - Age 5
Annabelle Smith - Age 7
Gavin and Jennifer Smith

4 Chicken Breasts
1 cup Ranch Dressing
1 cup Barbecue Sauce

1½ cups Shredded Monterey
Jack Cheese
4 pieces Canadian Bacon

Preheat oven to 350 degrees F. Spray 9½ x 13 inch Pyrex cooking pan with non-stick spray. Place flattened chicken breasts at the bottom of the pan. Combine Ranch dressing and Barbecue sauce in a small bowl. Pour mixture over the top of the chicken. Sprinkle shredded cheese over the top of the chicken. With cooking sheers, cut small strips of Canadian Bacon over the top of the chicken dish, spreading

(continued)

98890-09

evenly. Cover with foil and bake for 30-40 minutes, removing foil for the last 5-10 minutes.

GERMAN BABY

Emily Kathryn

3 eggs
¾ c. milk
¾ c. all-purpose flour
¼ c. butter

2 T. powdered sugar
maple syrup
lemon wedges

Preheat oven to 425°. Place butter in a 10 inch cast iron skillet and heat the skillet in the oven. Beat eggs at high speed with electric mixer. Slowly add the milk and flour. Pour batter into hot skillet. Return skillet to oven and bake for 20 minutes. It will rise like a soufflé, and then fall when taken out of the oven. Lightly dust with powdered sugar and serve with lemon wedges and warm maple syrup (if desired).

GRAMMA & ETHAN'S SUNDAY MORNING PANCAKES

Ethan - Age 3

1 cup Krusteaz Pancake Mix   ¾ cup water

Blend the pancake mix and cold water together. Pour batter onto lightly greased griddle. Cook pancakes until golden brown. We love to use fun pancake cutouts. We have Santa and a reindeer for Christmas and a bat and witch hat for Halloween.

GRAMMIE AND NANA'S HOMEMADE MAC N' CHEESE

Abby Wynne - Age 6

1 pkg. macaroni noodles
3 tblsp. butter
1 cup sharp shredded cheddar
   cheese

3 tblsp. Wondra (do not use
   flour)
2 cups Milk
dash Pepper

Pre-Heat Oven to 350 Degrees. Boil macaroni noodles until cooked and then drain. After draining the noodles, set aside. Melt butter, sharp cheddar cheese, wondra, and milk in a sauce pan. Once the sauce is melted add the cooked noodles and stir until the noodles are well covered in the sauce. If the sauce is too thin, add more wondra before adding the noodles. Spray a casserole dish with Pam. Put cooked macaroni noodles in casserole dish. Optional: Melt some additional butter with some bread crumbs and toss on top of the macaroni. Bake covered for 45 minutes in 350 degree oven. Recipe given to Nana Cutshall from Grammie Cutshall on 2/21/67.

GRANDMA BETH'S MEXICAN LASAGNA
(A Family Favorite!)

Ethan Richard - Age 5 months

1 1-lb. jar Spaghetti Sauce
1 1-lb. pkg. Italian Sausage
1 (15-oz.) pkg. Ricotta Cheese
1 large Egg

½ cup Shredded Parmesan
Cheese
1 pkg. 10 inch Flour Tortillas
2 cups Mozzarella Cheese

Spread small amount of spaghetti sauce on bottom of 9 x 13 inch pan. Cook, drain and crumble sausage. Combine remaining sauce with sausage in a bowl. In another bowl, combine ricotta, egg, Parmesan, and one cup of Mozzarella. Spread equal amounts of cheese mixture on all of the tortillas. Roll up tortillas and arrange snugly (width-wise) on top of sauce in bottom of pan. Pour remaining sauce mixture over tortillas. Sprinkle remaining Mozzarella over top. Cover with Aluminum foil and bake for 50 minutes at 350 degrees. Let stand for 15 minutes before serving. Amply serves 12.

GRANDMA HOPWOOD'S MEATBALLS

Andrew John - Age 6
Elizabeth Lyn - Age 5
William John - Age 1

Meatballs

1½ lbs. Ground Beef
⅔ cup oats
1 cup milk

⅓ cup chopped onion
1 tsp. salt
dash pepper

Combine (uncooked) ground beef, oats, milk, onion, salt and pepper. Form into 2 inch meatballs. Place in 9x13 greased pan.

Sauce

1 cup ketchup
½ cup water

3 T. sugar
3 T. white vinegar

Mix ketchup, water, sugar, white vinegar. Spoon sauce over meatballs. Bake uncovered at 350 degrees for 45 minutes - 1 hour.

GRANDMA'S PANCAKES

Nicholas Butera - Age 11
Joshua Butera - Age 8

1½ cups all-purpose flour
3½ tsp. baking powder
1 tsp. salt
1 tblsp white sugar

1¼ cups milk
3 tblsp. butter, melted
1 egg
any fruit topping of your choice

In a large bowl, sift together the flour, baking powder, salt and sugar. Make a well in the center and pour in the milk, egg and melted butter;

(continued)

98890-09

mix until smooth. Heat a lightly oiled griddle or frying pan over medium-high heat. Pour or scoop the batter on the griddle, using approximately ¼ cup for each pancake. Brown on both sides. Top with your favorite fruit and enjoy!

GRANDMA'S TASTIEST CHICKEN AND PASTA
(Grilled Chicken with Pasta and Mexican Pesto)

James Henry - Age 12

1½ cup fresh cilantro
½ cup Parmesan cheese
3 T. toasted pecan halves
1 tsp. kosher salt
2 garlic cloves
1 Serrano Chile, seeded and sliced
2 T. olive oil
2 tsp. wine vinegar
⅛ tsp. black pepper
¾ lb. boneless, skinless chicken breast
6 cups cooked pasta (about 3 cups uncooked)
2 cups cherry tomatoes, halved

Place cilantro and next six ingredients (through chili) in a food processor, process until well blended. With processor on, slowly pour oil through the food chute, process until well blended. Place pesto in large bowl, stir in vinegar and black pepper. If the pesto sauce is too thick you can thin it out with a little hot cooking water from the pasta. Coat chicken with cooked spray. Cook on grill pan over medium heat, 5 minutes per side or until done. Cut chicken into bite size pieces. Add chicken, pasta and tomatoes to the pesto, toss to combine. This recipe is from Cooking Light so that may not satisfy hearty appetites. You might want to double the pasta.

GREEN NOODLES

Andy Gates - Age 12

Basil Pesto - any kind you like
Shell or Bow Tie Pasta
½ lb. Parmesan Cheese

Cook the shell noodles according to the package and mix with the basil pesto. Sprinkle with the Parmesan cheese and serve warm or cold as a salad.

GRILLED BULL'S-EYE

Josh Soukup - Age 13

2 eggs
2 pieces of bread
1 slice cheese
butter

Cut a hole in the center of each piece of bread using a glass, glass jar, or cookie cutter. Butter pan. Turn stove on low at first then move to medium once eggs are in. Place both pieces of bread on the pan. Crack

(continued)

each egg and drop one into each hole in the center of the bread. Cook egg to your liking, take two pieces of bread off pan and let cool. Put cheese slice in-between slices of bread. Place in microwave for 30 seconds or under the grill to melt cheese. Enjoy!

GRILLED LEMON CHICKEN KEBABS

Timothy Sebastien - Age 5

3 Chicken breasts
2 Lemons
3 cloves Garlic
1/3 c. Olive oil

1 pint Grape tomatoes
1 Pepper (red, orange or yellow)
1 Spanish onion
Salt and pepper, to taste

Trim the chicken breasts, and cut them into chunks for the skewers. Don't make them too large, or they won't cook fast enough, but you don't want them tiny either. In a Ziploc or other container, zest one lemon and then squeeze the juice of the lemons. Peel and chop the garlic into the container. Add the olive oil and salt and pepper. You'll want more pepper and less salt than you'd expect. Mix this well, and then add the chicken. Marinate for at least two hours but no more than four or so. You want the flavor to get into the chicken, but you don't want chicken cerviche! While it's marinating, cut the peppers and onion into large pieces. I typically keep three onion pieces "together" vs separating them entirely. If you are using wooden skewers, soak them for a good hour or longer to ensure that you have skewers remaining when you're finished grilling. If I'm doing this for company, I'll do chicken, pepper, chicken, onion, chicken, tomato, chicken, onion, chicken, pepper, chicken on the skewer -- and yes, I have long skewers. It looks pretty that way. If I'm just doing it at home, I'll put all the veggies on a skewer, with the chicken on separate skewers. This way I can better monitor the cooking time. I usually grill this on medium (I have a pretty hot grill) for five to eight minutes, turning after 4 minutes.

GRILLED PINEAPPLE-GLAZED CHICKEN

Christopher Rosenberg - Age 14

1 tblsp. Brown Sugar
1/4 tsp. Ginger
1 tblsp. Soy Sauce
1 can Pineapple Rings in it's own juice, drained, reserving juice

2 small Whole Chicken Breasts, skinned, halved, boned
4 Kaiser Rolls
Spinach Leaves
Sweet-Tangy Mustard Sauce

Marinade: In shallow dish, combine brown sugar, ginger, soy sauce, and reserved pineapple juice; mix well. Chicken: Place 1 chicken breast half boned side up between 2 pieces of plastic wrap or waxed paper. Working from center, gently pound chicken with rolling pin or flat side of meat mallet with about 1/4 inch thick. Repeat with remaining chicken breasts. Place chicken breasts in marinade, turning to coat all sides.

(continued)

98890-09

Cover; refrigerate for 45 minutes. Meanwhile, prepare charcoal fire for grilling. Drain Chicken breasts, reserving marinade. When ready top barbeque, place chicken on grill about 8 inches from medium coals. Cook 8 to 10 minutes or until chicken is fork tender and juices run clear, turning once and brushing with marinade. Place pineapple rings on grill when turning chicken; cook until thoroughly heated, turning once and brushing with marinade. Cut rolls in half. On bottom half of each roll, layer spinach leaves, chicken breast half, and pineapple ring; replace top half of roll. Repeat for remaining sandwiches. Serve with sweet tangy mustard sauce. 4 sandwiches.

HAM AND CHEESE MACARONI BAKE WITH PEAS
(Adapted from Cooking Light)

Jessica Lindberg
Ethan Lindberg - Age 3

1 1-lb. uncooked medium elbow macaroni
1 1½ cups chopped lean ham
1 1½ cups frozen peas
cooking spray
1½ cups finely chopped onion
3 1 cups 2% milk
1 1 cup Shredded Cheddar Cheese
1 1 cup Shredded Swiss Cheese
1¾ tsp. salt
1¼ tsp. ground pepper
1½ cup bread crumbs
1 2 tblsp melted butter

Preheat oven to 400°. Cook pasta in boiling water for 6 minutes. Drain and rinse with cold water; drain. Combine pasta, ham and peas in large bowl. Heat medium saucepan over medium heat. Coat pan with cooking spray. Add onion and cook for 4 minutes. Add milk; bring to simmer. Remove from heat; stir in cheeses, salt and pepper. Pour cheese mixture over pasta mixture; stir to coat. Spoon past mixture into a 13 x 9 inch baking dish coated with cooking spray. Combine bread crumbs and butter in bowl. Spread bread crumb mixture over pasta mixture. Bake at 400° for 20 minutes. Sometimes I double the cheese sauce portion to make it even more cheesier!

HASH BROWN CASSEROLE

Adreanna Buster - Age 18

3 (4-oz.) ctn. cholesterol-free egg product or 6 large eggs, well beaten
1 (12-oz.) can Nestle Carnation Evaporated Milk
1 tsp. salt
½ tsp. ground black pepper
1 (30 oz.) package frozen shredded hash brown potatoes
2 (8-oz.) cups shredded cheddar cheese
1 med. onion, chopped
1 small green bell pepper, chopped
1 cup diced ham (optional)

(continued)

Preheat oven to 350°F. Grease 13 x 9 inch baking dish. Combine egg product, evaporated milk, salt and black pepper in large bowl. Add potatoes, cheese, onion, bell pepper and ham; mix well. Pour mixture into prepared baking dish. Bake for 60 to 65 minutes or until set. Makes 12 servings

HEAVENLY HASH

Jack S - Age 13

1 lb. ground hamburger
1 onion
salt and pepper to taste

1 pkg. egg noodles
1 can vegetable soup
1 can whole kernel corn

In a skillet, brown the hamburger meat. Add the onion and salt and pepper. In a baking dish, add egg noodles, soup and corn and mix. Pour the hamburger mixture over the noodles. Bake at 350 degrees for 45 minutes.

HOLIDAY PANCAKES

Carson Bruce - Age 5

1 box Pancake Mix
Assorted Food Markers

Sprinkles
Syrup

Carson loves to do this. Its breakfast and an art project in one! Make pancakes as indicated on the box. Before serving, draw holiday symbols or messages on the pancakes. Suggested designs: hearts, Christmas trees, shamrocks, pumpkins, birthday hats, etc. Edible markers can be found at a craft or party store. Enhance this project with festive sprinkles and of course serve with syrup.

JUNE'S SWEDISH PANCAKES

Grant Woodward - Age 12

5 Eggs
2 cups Milk
1 cup Flour

4 tblsp Sugar
½ tsp. Salt
½ stick Butter

In a bowl, combine all ingredients. Cook on stove top. When pancakes bubble flip and cook for an additional 2 minutes. Remove and serve immediately.

98890-09

KATIE JOEL'S MEAT LOAF

Sophie Clark - Age 6
Ian Clark - Age 4

1 tblsp. olive oil
½ medium yellow onion, diced (about ¾ cup)
1 clove garlic, minced
1 medium red pepper, finely diced (about 1 cup)
1 bay leaf
2 tblsp. chopped, fresh flat-leaf parsley
2 tsp. chopped, fresh thyme

2 pounds lean ground beef
2 large eggs, lightly beaten
¾ cup dry bread crumbs
1 cup ketchup, divided (half will go in meat loaf, half on top)
1 tblsp. Worcestershire sauce
2 tsp. kosher salt
1 tsp. freshly ground black pepper

Heat oven to 350°. Line a baking sheet with parchment paper. Spray lightly with oil. Heat the olive oil in a medium skillet over medium heat. Sauté the onions, garlic and bay leaf until the onions are tender, about 3 minutes. Add the red pepper and cook until the red pepper is tender, about 5 minutes. Stir in the parsley and thyme and cook for another 2 minutes. Remove the pan from the heat and let the onion mixture cool. Discard the bay leaf. In a large bowl, combine the beef, egg, bread crumbs, ½ cup ketchup, the Worcestershire sauce, salt, pepper and the cooled vegetables. Use your hands to mix everything together. Transfer the mixture to the center of the baking sheet and form into a loaf. Coat the meat loaf with the remaining ½ cup ketchup. Bake for 1 to 1½ hours (depending on the shape of your loaf), until the meat loaf is firm. Let set for about 5 minutes before slicing.

KETCHUP-COLA CHICKEN

Ryan Matthew - Age 6
Clayton Anthony - Age 11

1 cup ketchup
1 cup Coke, Pepsi or other cola

3½ lb. chicken, quartered

Preheat the oven to 350 degrees. In a large bowl, whisk together the ketchup and cola until thoroughly mixed. Wash the chicken and pat dry with paper towels. Remove the wings from the chicken breast quarters. Put all chicken pieces in a bowl and toss so that the chicken is coated with the ketchup-cola mixture. Let sit for 30 minutes or, refrigerated, up to 8 hours. Remove the chicken, reserving the marinade. Place the chicken, skin side up, on a rimmed baking sheet. Sprinkle with salt and pepper. Bake for 1 hour. Meanwhile, put the marinade in a small saucepan and bring to a boil. Reduce the heat to medium and cook until the marinade is reduced to 1 cup, about 15 minutes. During baking, baste the chicken with reduced marinade several times, using a pastry brush. After 30 minutes, have an adult help you transfer the chicken to a plate, pour off the fat and return chicken to the pan. Continue cooking for 30 minutes. When the chicken is done, transfer it to a warm platter.

(continued)

Drizzle with a little more warm marinade, serving any extra on the side.
Serves 4

LETTUCE WRAP SANDWICHES

Alexis Elizabeth - Age 10
Ashley Dianna - Age 8
Nicole Frances - Age 5

1 head Lettuce (either Iceberg or
  Romaine)
1 cup Shredded Cheese
½ cup Sliced Olives
4 slices Favorite Lunch Meat -
  sliced

2 cups Shaved Carrots OR
  Broccoli Coleslaw
Favorite Salad Dressing

We came up with this one day when we noticed we ran out of bread
at lunchtime. My sisters and I loved it! Wash large leaves of lettuce. In
a bowl, mix together the shredded cheese, sliced olives, and sliced
Julian lunch meat and shaved carrots (or bag of Broccoli Coleslaw for
added vitamins). Place a large scoop of the mixture into each large leaf
of lettuce. Add ranch dressing. Fold the lettuce into a wrap and enjoy.
This is a great way to get kids to eat their veggies!

M&M MICKEY MOUSE PANCAKES

Cole Robert - Age 4
Ella Grace - Age 2

Box of Pancake Mix
M&M's

Syrup

Simply mix up a batch of your favorite pancakes. Next, drop 3 pancakes
onto your skillet (one larger for Mickey's face and 2 smaller ones for
ears.) Then gently put some M&M's onto the top of each pancake. Cook
until golden brown. May need to flip pancake to other side for a short
time. Add syrup if you would like. Enjoy!

MACARONI & CHEESE

Leanna Smith

6 cups water
4 tblsp. margarine
¼ cup milk

1 slice cheese
cheese sauce mix
cup macaroni, uncooked

Boil water, stir in macaroni. Cook for 7-8 minutes or until macaroni is
tender, stirring occasionally. Drain, add margarine, milk and cheese
sauce mix, mix well. Add cheese slice and mix well. Enjoy!

92

MACARONI AND CHEESE

Anna - Age 7
Luke - Age 5
Ashley - Age 3, Jake - Age 2

1 (8-oz.) pkg. elbow macaroni
(about 2 cups uncooked
macaroni)
2 cups milk
¼ cup all-purpose flour
2 (10-oz.) blocks sharp cheddar
cheese, shredded (about 4½
cups) and divided

1 cup soft bread crumbs (4
slices, crusts removed)
¼ cup butter or margarine,
melted
1 tsp. onion salt

Cook macaroni according to package directions; drain well. Set aside.
Place milk, flour, and onion salt in a bowl and whisk for 1 minute. Stir
together flour mixture, 3½ cups cheese, and macaroni. Pour macaroni
mixture into a lightly greased 13 x 9 inch baking dish or 2 (11 inch) oval
baking dishes. Sprinkle evenly with bread crumbs and remaining 1 cup
cheese; drizzle evenly with melted butter. Bake at 350 degrees for 45
minutes or until golden brown.

MACARONI AND CHEESE

Sarah Denise - Age 11
Benjamin Daniel - Age 7

2 cups dry elbow macaroni
16 oz. shredded Mexican cheese
blend
1 (12-oz.) can evaporated milk

½ c. grated Parmesan cheese,
divided
½ tsp. ground black pepper
2 T. bread crumbs

Preheat oven to 350°. Lightly butter 2½ qt. casserole dish. Cook macaroni in large sauce pan according to package directions; drain. Combine
cooked pasta, Mexican cheese, ¼ c. Parmesan cheese, evaporated
milk and black pepper in large bowl. Pour into prepared casserole dish.
Combine remaining Parmesan cheese and bread crumbs; sprinkle over
mixture. Cover tightly with aluminum foil. Bake covered for 20 minutes.
Remove foil and bake for an additional 10 minutes or until lightly brown.
Serves 8.

MACARONI AND CHEESE WITH SPINACH

Lauren - Age 10

1 (8-oz.) box Creamette elbow
macaroni
3 T. butter
3 T. all-purpose flour
2½ c. milk

1 tsp. ground mustard
½ tsp. salt
1 tsp. pepper
1 can Glory spinach
2 c. shredded cheddar cheese

(continued)

Preheat oven to 350°. Boil 3 quarts of water to a rapid boil. Add salt for flavor and to reduce stickiness. Add pasta and stir; return to rapid boil. Cook uncovered, stirring occasionally. Cooking time 6 - 8 minutes. Drain well. Heat spinach in medium saucepan, melt butter and stir in flour. Gradually stir in milk. Cook, stirring constantly over medium heat, until sauce thickens. Stir in ground mustard, salt, and pepper. Add cheese. Stir until cheese melts. Stir cheese sauce into cooked pasta. Spoon into greased 2 quart baking dish. Serves 4 - 6.

MCKENZIE FAVORITE TATER TOT CASSEROLE
(Casserole)

McKenzie Belle - Age 6

1 pound Lean Ground Beef
1 (10³/₄-oz.) can Cream of
  Mushroom Soup
1 cup Milk

2 cups Cheddar Jack Cheese
1 bag Frozen Tater Tots
Salt
Pepper

Preheat oven to 350 degrees, Spray a 8¹/₂ by 11 inch pan with non stick spray. Brown the ground beef and drain. Mix soup and milk and pour on the bottom of pan add salt and pepper to taste. Add beef on top of soup and add cheese. Place tater tots on top of cheese. Put aluminum foil on top and bake for 45 mins. Take off foil and bake till tots are crispy. Enjoy.

MEAT LOAF

Reina Hershner - Age 6
Reed Hershner - Age 3

2 lbs. Ground chuck
1 cup Bread crumbs
1 egg, slightly beaten
2 T. minced onion

¹/₂ cup ketchup
¹/₂ cup water
¹/₂ cup shredded cheese
Ketchup for the top

Combine ground beef, bread crumbs, egg, minced onion, ketchup, water and shredded cheese. Press into a loaf pan. Top with ketchup. Bake at 350° for 1 hour.

MEATBALL SUB

Anna Marie - Age 11

4 beef or turkey precooked
  meatballs
2 heaping tblsp. pizza sauce
¹/₄ cup shredded mozzarella
  cheese

1 medium submarine sandwich
  bun

(continued)

98890-09

Heat the meatballs and pizza sauce together. When heated through, spoon them into a submarine sandwich bun. Sprinkle the mozzarella cheese on and enjoy.

MEATBALLS IN TOMATO SAUCE
(Turkish dish called Sulu Kofte)

Ryan Logan
Erin Logan

400 gr ground beef
½ cup rice
1 egg
salt & pepper
½ cup flour
1 onion, grated

4-5 tblsp. crushed tomatoes, in
  a can
3 tblsp. olive oil
2 cups water
salt & pepper

Place flour on a large plate. Knead all the kofte ingredients in a bowl. Break off small pieces and give a small ball shape with your palms and place them in the flour. Meanwhile, sauté the onion with olive oil for a couple minutes in a medium sized pot. Add crushed tomatoes, water, salt & pepper, then bring to a boil over medium heat. Flour all the little kofte and gently drop into the pot and stir slowly. Cook for about 20 min over a little bit under medium heat.

MEAT LOAF

Amber - Age 10

1 lb. chopped meat
1 egg
1 c. bread crumbs

½ c. barbeque sauce
1 pinch salt

Preheat oven to 400°. In a bowl, put the chopped meat, egg, bread crumbs, barbeque sauce, and salt. Mix together in the bowl with your hands. Get a cookie sheet and mold the meat into a square. Cook for one hour. Serves 4 people.

MEXICAN CASSEROLE

Emma Elizabeth - Age 11
Jacob James - Age 8

5 Flour Tortillas
1 (16-oz.) Lean Ground Beef
1/2 cup Diced Green Pepper
1/2 cup Diced Onion
1 (1.4-oz.) pkg. Taco Seasoning Mix
1 (8-oz.) can Tomato Sauce
1 (6-oz.) can Tomato Paste
1/2 cup Sliced Pitted Black Olives

1/4 cup Water
1/2 tsp. Chili Powder
1 cup Sour Cream
2 Large Eggs
1/4 tsp. Black Pepper
2 cups Broken Tortilla Chips
2 cups Shredded Monterey Jack Cheese

Cook the ground beef in a skillet over medium heat. Drain if necessary. Add green pepper and onions and sauté until vegetables are tender crisp. Mix in taco seasoning, tomato sauce, tomato paste, water, olives, and chili powder. Simmer until thickened. Blend sour cream, eggs and black pepper together in a small bowl. Place 2 tortillas on the bottom of a 12" X 8" dish sprayed with cooking spray. Top with half of the meat mixture followed by half the sour cream mixture. Top with 1 cup cheese. Repeat layers with remaining ingredients. Sprinkle with chips and cheese. Cook for 15 minutes in a 350° oven. Let stand 5 minutes before serving.

MEXICAN TAQUITOS

Trevor Michael - Age 7
Morgan Kate - Age 4
Elise Nicole - Age 1

1 pound Ground Beef
1 pkg. Taco Mix
1 tblsp. Vegetable Oil

Flour Tortillas
1 cup Mild Cheddar

Heat oven to 400°. Brown ground beef in pan. Drain meat and stir in taco mix. Place tortillas on a plate and cover them with damp paper towels. Microwave until pliable, about 40 seconds. Top each tortilla with 1/4 beef mixture, spreading it to an inch from the edges. Sprinkle cheese evenly over beef. Roll up tortillas and place them on foil-lined baking sheet with seam side down. Brush taquitos lightly with veggie oil, then bake them until filling is heated through and the tortillas are lightly browned, about 8-12 minutes. Serve them hot with sour cream and/ or salsa.

MINI MEAT LOAVES

Nina Lynn - Age 6

1 Egg
¾ cup Milk
1 cup Shredded cheddar cheese
½ cup Quick-cooking oats
½ cup Chopped onion

1 lb. Ground beef
⅔ cup Ketchup
½ cup Packed brown sugar
1½ tspn yellow mustard

Beat the egg and milk in bowl. Stir in cheese, oats and onion. Mix in the beef. Shape into eight mini loaves. Place them on a greased baking dish. Combine ketchup, brown sugar and yellow mustard and spread over the mini loaves. Bake at 350° for 45 minutes uncovered.

MISO GLAZED CHICKEN

Timothy Sebastien - Age 5
Sophia Claire - Age 3

½ c. white or yellow miso paste
¼ c. sugar (scant)
1 T. soy sauce
¼ c. chicken stock

3 T. oil
1 T. ginger, grated
4-6 boneless, skinless chicken
   breasts

Put all the marinade ingredients into a bag, and squish the bag until it's all nicely combined. Then add chicken. I prefer to let it marinate overnight in the fridge and cook it for dinner the next day. After you've marinated it, heat the grill to medium and cook 4-5 minutes per side. Let cool a moment, and then slice into ½ inch slices. Serve with rice.

MOM'S RED PEPPER ZITI

Molly Ann - Age 6
Cooper Goodall - Age 5
Tallulah Marie - Age 3

1 tblsp. Minced garlic
1 medium Vidalia onion, minced
1 large Red Pepper, minced
1-2 lbs. Ground turkey, browned

(16-oz.) Mostaccioli pasta
   noodles, cooked and drained
1 cup Water from cooked pasta
2 cups Parmesan cheese

Sauté garlic, onion and red pepper in olive oil until soft. Brown ground turkey. Cook pasta and drain, keep 1 cup of water. Combine sautéed vegetables, turkey, pasta, sauce, 1 ½ cups Parmesan cheese and the pasta water. Spray 9 x 13 inch baking dish with non-stick spray. Pour pasta mixture into 9 X 13 inch baking dish. Top with remaining Parmesan cheese. Bake cover for 20 minutes at 375°; uncover and bake 10 minutes. Serve with salad and breadsticks.

MOMMY'S HOMEMADE CHICKEN FINGERS

Timothy Sebastien - Age 5
Sophia Claire - Age 3

1 egg, lightly beaten
1 T. honey
1 tsp. yellow mustard
1 c. corn flake cereal, finely
  crushed

1/4 tsp. salt
dash pepper
12 oz. boneless, skinless
  chicken breast halves

Heat oven to 450°. Cut chicken into 3/4 inch strips. In a shallow dish, combine the egg, honey, and mustard. In another shallow dish, stir together corn flake crumbs, salt, and pepper. Dip the chicken into the egg mixture, then roll them in the crumb mixture to coat evenly. Arrange chicken strips on a baking sheet. Bake 12 to 15 minutes, or until chicken is cooked through.

MY FAVORITE BEEF STEW
(that my mom likes because it is easy)

Andy Gates - Age 12

3 lbs. cubed stew meat
2 cans Campbell's Golden
  Mushroom Soup

1 pkg. dry onion soup mix
1/2 cup cream sherry

Mix above and put in covered casserole dish. Bake 3 hours at 325 degrees. Serve over noodles or rice.

NANA'S MEATBALLS

Aidan Thomas - Age 6

2 lbs. ground beef
1 egg
1/2 cup spaghetti sauce
1/4 cup Italian salad dressing
1/4 cup grated cheese
  (Parmesan, Romano, etc.)

3 T. dried basil
1/4 cup Italian bread crumbs
  (optional)

Preheat oven to 375°. Mix ground beef and all other ingredients into a large bowl - mix well. Shape into meatballs - should yield 10 to 15 meatballs depending on size. Line 9 X 13 inch baking dish with aluminum foil. Place meatballs into baking dish. Bake uncovered for approximately 45 minutes. Turn meatballs over once during baking. When done baking, drain meatballs on paper towels. Place cooked and drained meatballs into hot spaghetti sauce and serve.

98890-09

NOODLE PUDDING

Sean - Age 5
Meghan - Age 3

1 tblsp sugar
1 tsp. cinnamon
pasta noodles

1 slice of butter
1 cup cottage cheese
1 handful raisins

Mix sugar and cinnamon in a bowl. Cook pasta noodles. Drain noodles and add butter, cottage cheese, raisins and stir. Sprinkle with cinnamon sugar. Ready to Eat.

NOODLELINI

Jack B - Age 7

4 cups egg noodles
1 cup hot water
3 tblsp olive oil

salt and pepper to taste
1 tspn garlic powder

Bring pot of water to a boil. Add egg noodles and cook until soft. Drain. Return noodles to pot. Add hot water, olive oil and garlic powder. Salt and pepper to taste. Mmmmm tasty!

NOODLES AND TREES

Becca Kylie - Age 2

1 lb. broccoli tops
pinch salt
1 lb. your favorite pasta

1 T. extra-virgin olive oil
2 T. butter
1 cup grated Parmesan cheese

Place the broccoli tops (trees) in a pot with just enough water to cover the tops. Add a pinch of salt and boil for 5 minutes. Drain. At the same time, boil the noodles according to package directions. Drain. Place the olive oil and butter in a big bowl. Add cheese, cooked noodles and broccoli. Stir until the cheese and butter are melted. Serve hot.

OCTOPUS HOT DOGS

John Miller - Age 4
Thomas Merritt - Age 1

1 Hot Dog

Ketchup or Mustard

Cut the hot dog in half crosswise. With each half, slice lengthwise from a mid-point to the cut end to form 2 "arms," leaving the "head" intact. Further slice each arm lengthwise into 4 arms, forming a total of 8 arms. Place the octopus on a microwave-safe plate with the arms spread out beneath the head. Microwave on high for 20 seconds or less, until the arms curl upwards. Put 2 dots of ketchup or mustard on the head to form eyes.

OLIVIA'S VEGGIE WRAP

Olivia Clare - Age 1

1 large Sprouted Tortilla
1/4 small Ripe Avocado
2 Lettuce Leaves
1/4 small Tomato
1/4 small Red Pepper

1/4 small Red Onion
1 tsp. Olive Oil
1 tsp. Braggs Aminos
1 tsp. Braggs Spice

Lay out your Tortilla and spread on avocado with butter knife. Then add diced lettuce, tomato, red pepper and onion. Drizzle the Braggs Aminos and olive oil over the top. Sprinkle Braggs Spice to taste. Then roll up the wrap and secure tightly in saran wrap.

OMELETS IN A BAG

Patricia Ann

2 eggs
handful of chopped ham
handful of diced onions
handful of chopped green
  peppers

handful of chopped tomato
dollop salsa
handful of sliced mushrooms
handful of hash browns

Crack 2 eggs (large or extra large) into a one quart size freezer bag and shake to combine them. Put out a variety of ingredients such as cheese, ham, onion, green pepper, tomato, hash browns, salsa, mushrooms, etc. Each person adds prepared ingredients of choice to their bag. Zip and shake! (Make sure to get the air out!!!!!!!!!!!!!! of the bag and zip it up tightly!) Place the bags into rolling, boiling water for exactly 13 minutes. You can usually cook 6-8 omelets in a large pot. For more, make another pot of boiling water. Open the bags and the omelet will roll out easily. Be very careful taking the bags out of the boiling water. Place on a dish or paper towels. Be prepared for everyone to be amazed. Nice to serve with fresh fruit and toast. It is so much fun!

ONE SKILLET SPAGHETTI

Parker Joseph - Age 15

1 pound hamburger
2 med. onions, chopped about 1
  cup
2 (14-oz.) canned diced
  tomatoes
1/2 cup water
1 (4-oz.) mushrooms stems,
  drained (optional)

2 tsp. salt
1 tsp. sugar
1 tblsp. chili powder
3/4 cup chopped green peppers
7 ounce uncooked spaghetti,
  broken into pieces
1 cup shredded cheddar cheese

Cook and stir hamburger and onions in Dutch oven until hamburger is light brown, drain. Stir in tomatoes (with liquid), green pepper, water,

(continued)

98890-09

mushrooms, salt, sugar, chili powder and spaghetti. Heat to boiling, reduce heat. Cover and simmer, stirring occasionally, until spaghetti is tender about 30 minutes. (Add water during cooking if necessary). Sprinkle with cheese. Cover until cheese is melted. 7 servings. Enjoy!!!

OUR FAMILY CHILI

Ethan Parker - 5 weeks
Matthew Edward - 11 years
Christopher James - 9 years

1 lb. ground beef
3/4 cup chopped onion
1 clove garlic minced
1 tblsp. chili powder
1 tblsp. flour
1 tsp. salt

1/2 tsp. cumin (can double)
1/2 tsp. sugar
1 (8-oz.) can tomato sauce
1 (8-oz.) can water
1 Large can light red kidney beans

(Optional Ingredient: Can of tomatoes.) Brown meat. Add onions and cook till tender. Mix dry ingredients and stir into meat mixture. Add sauce, water and drained beans. Simmer 1 hour or bake (250° for 5 - 6 hours) or (350° for 3-4 hours). Crock pot on low for 6 hours, but sauté meat and onions first.

NOTES: Three recipes, can use: (Two 8 oz. sauce: 2 cans tomatoes, no water) + 4 cans (15.5 oz.) beans: 2 # of meat. Two recipes, can use: (1 can sauce: 2 cans tomatoes).

OVERNIGHT FRENCH TOAST

Tatum Elizabeth - Age 3

1 c. brown sugar
1/2 c. butter
2 T. light corn syrup
12 slices of bread or 6 slices of
  Texas toast

1/4 c. sugar
1 tsp. ground cinnamon
6 eggs
1 1/2 c. milk
1 tsp. vanilla

In a saucepan over medium heat bring brown sugar, butter and corn syrup to a boil, stirring constantly. Pour into a greased 9x13 pan. Lay slices of bread in pan. Combine cinnamon and sugar and sprinkle over the bread. Beat eggs, milk and vanilla and pour over bread. Refrigerate overnight. Remove from refrigerator 30 minutes before baking. Bake at 350 degrees for 30-35 minutes.

PAPA'S MEATBALLS AND SPAGHETTI

Abby Wynne - Age 6

½ lb. lean ground beef
½ lb. ground Italian Sausage
1 large egg
1 med. onion chopped
¼ cup Italian Seasoned Bread
  Crumbs
1 tsp. oregano

¼ tsp. red pepper
1 dash pepper
2 tblsp. Shredded Parmigiana
  Reggiano Cheese
1 jar Prego Tomato/Basil Sauce
  for Pasta
1 lb. Barilla Spaghetti Noodles

Mix the all the ingredients (except for the Pasta Sauce and the Noodles) in a large mixing bowl. Use your hands to make sure that everything gets mixed in really well. Then roll meatballs about two inches in size. Set aside. Heat a large pot over medium heat lined with a little bit of olive oil. Add the meatballs. Brown the meatballs on all sides (takes about five minutes). Once the meatballs are brown on all sides, slowly pour the pasta sauce over them. Put a lid on the pot and simmer for 45 minutes. Meanwhile prepare the spaghetti noodles according to the package. Try to time them so that the spaghetti noodles are finished about the same time the meatballs will be finished. Pour the meatballs and sauce over the pasta and enjoy.

PARMESAN CRUSTED CHICKEN

Anna - Age 7
Luke - Age 5
Ashley - Age 3, Jake - Age 2

2 boneless, skinless chicken
  breast halves
2 egg whites
2 tsp. cornstarch
juice of 1 lemon
1 cup dry bread crumbs
1 T. chopped fresh parsley
1 tsp. kosher salt
¼ tsp. ground black pepper
½ cup Parmesan cheese

1 zest of a lemon
3 T. shallot, minced
½ cup dry white wine
½ cup heavy cream
½ cup low sodium chicken
  broth
1 tsp. fresh lemon juice
4 T. butter
2 tsp. fresh sage, minced
taste of salt, pepper, cayenne

Preheat oven to 450 degrees. Prepare chicken breast by halving and pounding. Whisk egg whites, cornstarch and lemon juice in shallow dish; set aside. Combine bread crumbs, parsley, salt, pepper, Parmesan cheese and zest in second wide shallow dish. Dip chicken breast into egg mixture, then into bread crust mixture, crusting may not adhere right away, just scoop handfuls onto chicken, then transfer to rack set over a baking sheet. Let air dry to 20-30 minutes. Sauté chicken in oil in a large nonstick ovenproof skillet over medium high heat for 3 min or until golden brown. Turn and transfer skillet to oven to finish cooking, about 8 min. Serve chicken with sage butter sauce. Sage butter sauce: Sauté in 1 T. unsalted butter shallot until soft 2-3 min. Add wine, cream,

(continued)

98890-09

broth, and lemon juice. Simmer until reduced by half, 8-10 mins. Whisk in butter, 1 T. at a time, stirring constantly. Do not add more butter until previous addition is melted. Finish sauce with sage and seasonings, keep warm in water bath until ready to serve. Makes 4 servings.

PASGETTI CASSEROLE
(When regular spaghetti just won't do)

Owen & Lyla Joy Ruff

1 lb. spaghetti noodles, boiled
1 lb. ground beef
1 medium onion, chopped
1 jar favorite spaghetti sauce
8 oz. cream cheese
16 oz. sour cream
1 small container cottage cheese
1 small container ricotta cheese
1 pkg. shredded mozzarella cheese

Brown ground beef and onion over medium heat. Add spaghetti sauce and set aside. Combine cream cheese, sour cream, cottage cheese and ricotta cheese. Layer 9x13 inch pan with sauce, then spaghetti, then cheese mixture; repeat layering twice. Finish with sauce and then top with mozzarella cheese. Cover with foil. Bake at 350 degrees for 45 minutes.

PASTA WITH TOMATOES

Riley Ferraresi Williams

(8-oz.) pasta
4-5 medium plum tomatoes
1/3 cup extra virgin olive oil
1 tsp. sea salt
1 tsp. dry basil or 1 tblsp. fresh basil
freshly ground pepper to taste
freshly grated Parmesan (optional)

Prepare the pasta according the the instructions. In the meantime, dice tomatoes and put them (and their juice) in a large serving bowl. Mix the remaining ingredients together (except optional Parmesan cheese) with the tomatoes. Drain pasta and toss into the tomato mixture. Top with Parmesan if desired and serve. Serves 2-4.

PEANUT BUTTER & BANANA SANDWICHES

William Michael - Age 3

Whole Wheat Bread
Skippy's Natural Peanut Butter
Banana slices

Will can't have jelly or jam, so we experimented and found bananas to be a great substitute. Enjoy!

PEANUT BUTTER & JELLY SANDWICH

Ellie - Age 5

peanut butter
black berry jelly

wheat bread

Spread peanut butter on the wheat bread. Put the black berry jelly on top of the peanut butter. Put another piece of bread on top. Enjoy!

PEANUT BUTTER JELLY SANDWICH

Kaleigh - Age 10

bread
peanut butter

jelly

Take out two pieces of bread. Place jelly on one piece (not too thick) and peanut butter on the other. Place them both together. Cut in half. Enjoy!

PEANUT BUTTER OATMEAL

Caitlin Elissa - Age 6
Dylan Jacobs - Age 5

1 packet Instant Oatmeal
1 tspn Peanut Butter

1 tspn Brown Sugar

Follow the instructions on the instant oatmeal packet. Add the peanut butter and brown sugar and stir. Perfect on a cold winter's day!

PEANUT BUTTER QUESADILLAS

Jessica Lynn - Age 6
Ryan Robert - Age 4

1 bag wheat tortillas

1 tblsp peanut butter

Take a tortilla and spread peanut butter onto it. Fold in half. Cut into triangles and enjoy!

PEANUT BUTTER, PINEAPPLE AND JELLY SANDWICH

Jessica Lynn - Age 6
Ryan Robert - Age 4

2 slices wheat bread
1 tblsp peanut butter

1 tblsp strawberry jelly
1 small can crushed pineapple

Take your slices of bread and place on a plate. Spread the peanut butter and jelly onto 1 slice of bread. Open the can of pineapples and place some pineapples onto the jelly. Place other slice of bread on top. Cut into 4 pieces and enjoy this interesting combo of flavors!!

98890-09

PEANUTBUTTERFLUFFERNUTTER

Ally - Age 13

2 slices bread
Peanut Butter
Marshmallow Fluff

Banana slices (optional)
Chocolate chips (optional)

Spread peanut butter on 1 slice of bread. Spread marshmallow fluff on the other slice of bread. Put together and enjoy. You can also add sliced bananas and or chocolate chips in the middle.

PENNIES IN A CLOUD

Zac Edward - Age 8

1 Hot dog

1 box Instant mashed potatoes

Make 2 servings of mashed potatoes according to the box directions. Microwave 1 hot dog. Cut the hot dog up and mix it into the mashed potatoes. The potatoes are the clouds and the hot dogs are the pennies.

PEPPERONI PIZZA CASSEROLE

Austin Tyler - Age 13
Amy Margaret (Maggie) - Age 8

8 oz. Spaghetti Noodles
2 tblsp. Butter
2 Eggs, beaten
1 lb. Ground Beef
1 (32-oz.) jar Ragu Sauce

4 cups Shredded Mozzarella
Cheese
1 (3.5 oz.) pkg. Sliced Pepperoni
1 tsp. Olive Oil

Preheat oven to 350 degrees. Cook spaghetti noodles. Drain well. Brown Ground Beef and drain well. Grease a 9 x 13 inch pan. In large bowl, combine noodles, butter, 1/3 cup of the mozzarella cheese and eggs. Spread the mixture in the pan. Spoon ground beef over the spaghetti mixture. Spread Ragu over the meat layer and then cover with all the remaining mozzarella cheese. Arrange slices of pepperoni on top. Drizzle with olive oil. Bake for about 30 minutes.

PERFECT PORK TENDERLOIN

Timothy Sebastien - Age 5
Sophia Claire - Age 3

2 pork tenderloins
1 T. olive oil
1/2 c. cornstarch
1 T. powdered sugar

2 tsp. salt
1 tsp. pepper
1/2 c. barbeque sauce

Preheat your oven for 400°. Heat the tablespoon of olive oil in a heavy skillet over medium high heat. Mix the cornstarch, sugar, salt and pepper

(continued)

in a bag. Dredge the pork tenderloins in the mixture. When the oil is hot, pop the tenderloins in and quickly brown on all sides. Baste the tenderloin with the barbeque sauce on each side after being browned. After thorough browning, place the whole skillet in the oven and bake for 20 minutes (when internal temp reaches 145). Baste the tenderloin periodically during baking. Remove from the oven and tent the skillet. Let the tenderloin rest for 5 minutes then slice and serve. You can also grill this on medium heat.

PINEAPPLE SHRIMP RICE BAKE

Amy Podborny - Age 12

2 cups Chicken Broth
1 cup Uncooked long grain rice
1 Garlic clove, minced
1 Medium onion, chopped
1 Medium green pepper,
  julienned
2 tblsp Vegetable oil

2 tsp. Soy sauce
1/4 tsp. Ground ginger
1 1/2 pounds Cooked medium
  shrimp, peeled and deveined
1 1/2 cups Cubed fully cooked
  ham
3/4 cup Pineapple tidbits, drained

Yield: 8 servings. In a large saucepan, bring broth to a boil. Stir in rice. Reduce heat; cover and simmer for 25 minutes or until tender. Meanwhile, in a large skillet, sauté the garlic, onion and green pepper in oil until tender. Stir in rice. Transfer to a greased 2-qt baking dish. Baked, uncovered, at 350°F for 15-20 minutes or until heated through. Stir before serving.

PIRATE SANDWICH

Caitlin Elissa - Age 6
Dylan Jacobs - Age 5

1 cup Pirate Booty
2 tblsp Peanut Butter

1 tblsp Jelly
2 slices Bread

Spread peanut butter on one slice of bread. Spread jelly on other slice of bread. Sprinkle the Pirate Booty on top of jelly. Smush two pieces of bread together and enjoy your Pirate Sandwich.

PITA PIZZA

Shaylan - Age 5
Simryn - Age 4
Karina - Age 1

Whole Wheat Pita Bread
Pizza Sauce
Low Fat Mozzarella Cheese
  shredded

Chicken or Turkey Sausage
  sliced

(continued)

98890-09

Preheat oven to 350 Degrees. Have kids spread pizza sauce on their own pita bread. They can top pizza sauce with slices of sausage (or any other favorite toppings). Sprinkle shredded cheese on top. Place pizzas on a baking sheet and bake until cheese melts (5 to 10 minutes). Cool, Cut & Serve!

PIZZA CASSEROLE

Isabella Audrey - Age 3

1 (1-lb.) pkg. Ground Beef or
  Turkey
1 (16-oz.) can Pizza Sauce
1 (4-oz.) can Sliced Mushrooms
1 tblsp. Dried Oregano, crushed
1 tsp. Garlic Salt

2 cups Rotini or any curly
  noodle, cooked & drained
2/3 cup Milk
2 cups Shredded Mozzarella
  Cheese

In a skillet, brown ground meat: drain off fat. Stir in pizza sauce, un-drained mushrooms, oregano, and garlic salt. Combine cooked rotini and milk. In a 2-quart casserole dish layer half each of the meat sauce, rotini mixture and cheese. Repeat layers. Bake, covered, in a 350° oven for 25-30 minutes. Garnish with salami slices, cherry tomatoes and parsley, if desired. Serves 6.

POPPY SEED CHICKEN

Sam P

3 cups Cooked, cubed chicken
1 can Cream of Chicken soup
1 small tub Sour Cream

1 tblsp poppy seeds
1 env. Town House Crackers
2 tblsp melted butter

Combine chicken, soup, sour cream and poppy seeds in large bowl. Spoon into glass baking dish. Crush 1 sleeve of Townhouse crackers and put into a bowl. Pour melted butter over crackers and stir. Spoon cracker/butter mixture on top of chicken mixture. Bake at 350° for 30 min.

PRIMO EGG OMELETTE SANDWICH

Michael Vitale - Age 5
Matthew Vitale - Age 3

5 Eggs
1/2 cup Milk
2 Slices of Cheese
2 Slices of Turkey

1 Slice of Ham
2 Slices of Wheat Bread
Touch of Salt and Pepper

Crack eggs and place in bowl, add milk and mix. Add a touch of salt and pepper. Pour into skillet to make omelette. Add cheese, turkey and ham and fold in half. Place the omelette on slice of bread and cover with other slice of bread. Cut sandwich in half. Enjoy!

PUFF PANCAKE

Katia Rose Horn - Age 5

½ cup milk
½ cup flour
¼ cup sugar

2 large eggs, at room
 temperature
½ stick unsalted butter

Preheated oven to 425°. Whisk all ingredients except butter together until smooth. Melt butter in 10 inch ovenproof skillet (cast iron is best) over medium heat. Coat all sides of the pan with butter. Pour in egg mixture into skillet. Cook for 1 minute. Place skillet in oven and bake 12 - 15 minutes. Serve immediately.

QUESADILLAS

Xavier Espino

Tortillas
Mozzarella Cheese
Cabbage/Lettuce

Tomatoes
Hot Sauce

Warm a tortilla on the stove in a pan. Add the mozzarella cheese on top of tortilla. Put another tortilla on top when the cheese starts to melt. Flip the tortillas over and allow cheese to melt. Then take off of the stove and top with chopped cabbage or lettuce, chopped tomatos, and some hot sauce. Serve!

QUESADILLAS

Erin Risser - Age 5

1 Tortilla
½ cup Shredded 4 cheese
 Mexican blend

¼ cup cubed pre-cooked
 chicken (optional)

Place tortilla on a cutting board. Sprinkle the cheese on one half of the tortilla. Fold over the tortilla. Place tortilla in a non-stick frying pan. Heat on the stove over a medium-low flame until the tortilla starts to brown. Flip the tortilla over and brown the second side. Take out the tortilla and use a pizza cutter the slice into wedges. Serve warm for lunch or dinner. Optional Chicken: Sprinkle only half the cheese on the tortilla. Add the chicken and cover with the remaining cheese. Finish cooking as you would with only cheese.

98890-09

QUICK TACO SNACK

Nikolas Southard

1¼ lbs. ground beef
1¼ oz. pkg. taco mix
½ cup water
⅓ cup sliced olives
1 cup sour cream

1 cup shredded cheese
1 (8 oz.) can crescent rolls
2 cups crushed fritos
shredded lettuce
guacamole

Brown ground beef and drain. Stir in taco seasoning, water, and olives. Simmer about 5 minutes. Place crescent roll triangles in an ungreased 9 or 10 inch pie pan. Press over bottom and sides to form a crust. Sprinkle 1 cup of crushed corn chips over bottom. Spoon meat mixture on top. Spread sour cream on meat mixture. Cover with cheese and sprinkle remaining crushed corn chips. Bake at 375° for 20-25 minutes. Top with lettuce and guacamole (optional).

RATATOUILLE STEW

Nathan - Age 10

1 red or green pepper, chopped
1 med. zucchini, chopped
½ med. eggplant, peeled, cut into ½ to ¾ inch cubes (about 2½ cups)
1 (29-oz.) can whole tomatoes, undrained, cut up

1 c. water
3 cloves garlic, minced
1 tsp. dried Italian seasoning
¼ tsp. pepper
3 oz. orzo or rosamarina

In a large nonstick saucepan or Dutch oven combine all ingredients except for orzo. Bring to a boil over medium heat. Reduce heat to medium low; cover and cook for 15 minutes. Add orzo; cover and cook 10 to 15 minutes until orzo and vegetables are tender, stirring frequently. Makes 4 servings.

RED EYE BURGER

Kiki S. - Age 9

1 (2-oz.) hamburger
1 tblsp mayonnaise
1 hamburger bun

1 tsp. salt
4 pimento stuffed olives

Form hamburger into shape. Sprinkle salt in bottom of skillet. Place hamburger patty on salted skillet. Flip over. When done, remove from pan and place in bun. Put mayonnaise on burger. Place sliced olives on burger. The name comes from the red pimento in the olives that make them look like eyes!

RELIGION RECIPE PIZZA

Steven Allen - Age 12

pizza dough
tomato sauce

cheese
(toppings of your choice)

Take a big piece of dough and roll it with your hands to flatten it. Spread tomato sauce with a big spoon. Add cheese and your favorite toppings. Cook the pizza for about 20 to 25 minutes in the oven. Eat it, enjoy!

RICE WRAPS

Daniel Kim

1 cup cooked rice
3 slices cotto salami, bologna,
** or hard salami**

Boil rice in water until cooked (set aside). Fry lunch meat on both sides in a pan until the edges curl up. Remove lunch meat from pan and top with cooked rice. Roll up and eat like a soft shell burrito.

ROASTED CHICKEN DRUMSTICKS

Devina - Age 7

10 chicken drumsticks
1 sm. can tomato paste
2 spoonfuls ketchup
6 garlic cloves, crushed

salt to taste
1 tsp. lemon pepper
1 tsp. basil
1 tsp. cumin powder

Wash and take skin off of drumsticks. Make paste; mix tomato paste, ketchup, garlic, salt, lemon pepper, basil and cumin powder. Then, marinate chicken with this paste for 2-4 hours and keep refrigerated. Put it on baking sheet and bake for 45 minutes or until done. Serve hot with ketchup or favorite sauce.

ROCKIN' MEATBALLS

Timothy Sebastien - Age 5
Sophia Claire - Age 3

1½ lbs. ground chuck
½ lb. ground pork
2 eggs
1 c. Panko flakes
1 c. Parmesan, grated (not from
** the can!)**

1 T. salt
½ c. fresh parsley, chopped
pepper, to taste

Preheat the oven to 375 degrees. Put all ingredients in a bowl. Very gently mix the ingredients together until you can no longer see the egg.

(continued)

Don't squish and overwork the meat, or you'll end up with dry meatballs. Shape into small ping pong sized balls. This makes about 24 meatballs. Place meatballs on a parchment or silpat lined baking sheet. Bake about 15 or so minutes until nicely browned.

ROGANJOSH

Arjun Varma - Age 12

800 grams lamb
4 tblsp. oil
1¼ tsp. asafetida
2 (1 inch) pieces of cinnamon
6-8 cloves
5-6 black peppercorns
4 large cardamoms

1 tblsp. Kashmiri Red chili
   powder
2 tsp. fennel powder
1 tblsp. ginger powder
1 tblsp. coriander powder
1 cup yogurt

Clean, wash and cut lamb into medium sized pieces. Heat oil in a thin-bottomed pan. Add asafetida, cinnamon sticks, cloves, black peppercorns and large cardamoms. Sauté for half a minute. Add lamb pieces and cook on a medium flame, stirring constantly till lamb pieces get a nice reddish brown color. This may take twelve to fifteen minutes. Sprinkle a little water and repeat cooking of meat for twelve to fifteen minutes on a low flame. Make sure to stir constantly and scrape all the sediments from the bottom of the pan. Add red chili powder, fennel powder, ginger powder, coriander powder and salt. Add the beaten yogurt and two cups of water. Cook covered until meat is tender. Stir occasionally.

RYAN'S WHOLE GRAIN CHOCOLATE CHIP PANCAKES

Christopher John - Age 5
Ryan Raymond - Age 3

1¾ cups white flour
1¾ cups wheat flour
¼ cup wheat germ
¼ cup flax seed meal
2 tspn baking soda
2 tspn baking powder
¼ cup ground cinnamon

4 eggs
½ cup brown sugar
¼ cup vegetable oil
4 cups skim milk
1-2 cups chocolate chips (or
   blueberries, banana slices,
   etc.)

In a large bowl, mix the dry ingredients: flours, wheat germ, flax seed meal, baking soda, baking powder, and ground cinnamon then put aside. In a medium size bowl, beat eggs. Add brown sugar and mix until eggs and sugar are blended well. Pour in vegetable oil and skim milk and mix. Pour egg mixture into dry ingredients and mix. Do not over mix - it's okay if the batter is lumpy. Warm a large nonstick skillet on low-medium heat. (A square skillet if more desirable for cooking a larger amount of pancakes at once.) Place chocolate chips in a small

(continued)

bowl, and put them on the counter close to the stove. Using an ice cream scooper, drop pancake mix onto skillet. Repeat until you have skillet full. Add 4-6 chocolate chips per pancake right after pouring the last pancake on the skillet. With your fingertip, push the chips down as far as they can be pushed. Cook 3-5 minutes. (It is ok to peak underneath to see if they are a light brown color on the bottom side.) Once you start to see bubbles forming on the pancakes, flip the pancakes and cook another 1-2 minutes. (Again, it is ok to peak and look underneath to see how well the pancakes are cooked.) After pancakes are fully cooked, serve immediately. Since this makes a HUGE batch of pancakes, you could cool them completely on wire racks and then freeze them in storage containers or large freezer bags. The night before serving the pancakes, put the pancakes you will need into a storage container. Keep them in the fridge to thaw overnight. In the morning warm them in the oven or toaster oven at 350° for 4-5 minutes. You could also warm them in the microwave for 30-60 seconds depending on how many pancakes you put in the microwave at once.

SALSA MAC-N-CHEESE

Robin Krc - Age 16

1 lb. ground beef
1 jar (16 oz.) salsa
1¾ cup water
2 cups elbow macaroni, uncooked

¾ pound (12 oz.) Velveeta Cheese, cut up

Brown meat in large skillet; drain. Stir in salsa and water. Bring to a boil. Stir in macaroni. Reduce heat to medium-low heat; cover. Simmer 8-10 minutes or until macaroni is tender. Add Velveeta Cheese and stir until melted. Makes 4-6 servings.

SAUSAGE & PEPPERS

John Thomas Blanke - Age 12

2 green peppers
2 red peppers
1 orange pepper
1 yellow pepper
1 tsp. lime juice

oregano
salt and pepper to taste
olive oil
6 Italian sausages
1 box penne pasta

Cut up the peppers into strips and mix them with lime juice, olive oil, oregano and salt & pepper. Put the peppers into the oven and broil them for about 20 minutes turning them every 6-7 minutes. After this, move them into a 400° oven and continue cooking for another 15-20 minutes. Cook the sausage and pasta - then mix together and serve warm.

98890-09

SCALLOPS
(Grown-ups will love these too!)

Chloe Elizabeth - Age 9

1 lb. sea scallops, cut in half
 horizontally
kosher salt
black pepper

all-purpose flour
unsalted butter
lemon, optional

Sprinkle the scallops with salt and pepper, then dredge them in flour, shaking off the excess. In a large pan, heat 2 tablespoons of butter over high heat until it sizzles. Add the scallops. Lower the heat to medium and let the scallops brown lightly without moving them. Turn them over and brown the other side. This takes 4 minutes, total. Serve hot and try with a lemon. You can use bay scallops, but keep them whole.

SCRAMBLED EGGS

Nina - Age 10

eggs
Parmesan cheese

pepper

Crack the eggs. Put the eggs in a bowl (make sure no shells go in the bowl). Put the Parmesan cheese in the bowl (cut into little pieces). Then put the pepper in the bowl (not a lot). Stir the eggs around with a fork. Put the eggs in the skillet. Make sure to get the eggs on the side of the skillet to get all the eggs in. Enjoy!

SEAFOOD KABOBS

Heaven Gordon - Age 11

24 large sea scallops
12 medium shrimp, shelled and
 deveined
1 (8.5 oz.) can whole small
 artichoke hearts, drained and
 cut into halves

2 red or yellow peppers, cut into
 2-inch pieces
1/4 cup olive or vegetable oil
1/4 cup lime juice
lime slices and sage sprigs for
 garnish

Thread scallops, shrimp, artichoke hearts and peppers alternately on metal or bamboo skewers. (Soak bamboo skewers in water at least 20 minutes to keep them from burning). Combine oil and lime juice in a small bowl; brush kabobs with lime mixture. Oil hot grill to help prevent sticking. Grill kabobs, on an uncovered grill over low Kingsford briquets, 6 to 8 minutes. Halfway through cooking time, baste top with lime mixture, then turn kabobs and continue grilling until scallops and shrimp firm up and turn opaque throughout. Remove kabobs from grill; baste with lime mixture. Garnish with lime slices and sage sprigs. Makes 6 servings.

SHOOTING STAR SANDWICH

Carson Bruce - Age 5

2 slices bread
2 slices cheese
butter

1 slice salami
2 slices cucumber

Spread butter on one slice of bread. Layer the cheese, salami, and cucumber on the bread. Top with the other slice of bread. Take your favorite cookie cutter, like a Star, and press down firmly in the middle of the sandwich to make your shape. In this case, we have a Shooting Star Sandwich!

SHRIMP PASTA

Anais - Age 10

1 lb. pasta, cooked
1 lb. shrimp
1 lb. mixed frozen vegetables
2 T. olive oil

garlic
1 c. chicken broth
red pepper flakes

Put olive oil in a pan. Sauté the garlic in the oil. Put the shrimp in the pan and cook. Put the frozen vegetables in the pan. Add pasta and chicken broth. Last add red pepper flakes. Serves 6 people.

SIR ROC'S A LOT PASTA

Rocco Napoli - Age 9
Isabella Napoli - Age 5

1 (12-oz.) box spiral pasta
2 cups broccoli florets
1 tblsp. olive oil
1 small onion, chopped
1 clove fresh garlic

8 oz. cooked and cubed
  boneless chicken breast
4 tblsp. sour cream
1 tblsp. Dijon mustard

Cook the pasta in a large pot of boiling water for about 10 minutes. While pasta is cooking, place a steamer over pasta and cook broccoli until tender. In frying pan, heat oil on medium until hot, then add onions for 5 minutes or until browned. Add garlic for 1 more minute. Then, add chicken, sour cream and Dijon mustard. Heat through and continue to stir. Drain pasta and stir into sauce. Finally, add broccoli florets.

98890-09

SLOPPY JOE SQUARES

Logan Joseph - Age 7
Jackson William - Age 4

1 pound ground beef or turkey
1 (8-oz.) can tomato sauce
1 cup water
1 1½ ounce envelope sloppy joe mix
1 tsp. instant minced onion

2 (8-oz.) packages refrigerated crescent dinner rolls
1 cup shredded Cheddar Cheese
1 tblsp. milk
1 tblsp sesame seeds

Brown ground beef or turkey in a large skillet over medium high heat, stirring until it crumbles. Drain and return to skillet. Stir in tomato sauce and next 3 ingredients; bring to a boil. Reduce heat, and simmer 10 minutes. Unroll 1 package dinner rolls, pressing seams together; fit into bottom of a lightly greased 13 x 9 inch baking dish. Spread ground beef mixture over dough; sprinkle with cheese. Unroll remaining package of dinner rolls, pressing seams together; place over cheese. Brush dough with milk, and sprinkle with sesame seeds. Bake at 425 degrees for 15 minutes or until top is golden brown. Yum! Serves 6.

SLOPPY JOE'S
(Gibby Style)

Brooke Caroline - Age 6
Gibson "Gibby" Louis - Age 4

1 lb. ground beef
¼ cup apple cider vinegar

¼ cup brown sugar
1 cup ketchup

Brown ground beef. Drain off grease. Return to a low heat. Add the apple cider, brown sugar and ketchup. If you feel like adding a little more ketchup go for it. Serve on a bun. Also can be served with cheese and/or a pickle. YUMMY, but sloppy!

SLOW COOKER MAC N CHEESE

Jordan Johann Janke - Age 6

2 cups uncooked elbow macaroni (an 8 oz. box isn't quite 2 cups)
4 tblsp. (½ stick) butter, cut into pieces
2½ cups (about 10 oz.) grated sharp cheddar cheese
3 eggs, beaten

½ cup sour cream
1 10¾ oz. can condensed cheddar cheese soup
½ teaspoon salt
1 cup whole milk
½ teaspoon dry mustard
½ teaspoon black pepper

Boil the macaroni in a 2 quart saucepan in plenty of water until tender, about 7 minutes. Drain. In a medium saucepan, mix butter and cheese. Stir until the cheese melts. In a slow cooker, combine cheese/butter

(continued)

mixture and add the eggs, sour cream, soup, salt, milk, mustard and pepper and stir well. Then add drained macaroni and stir again. Set the slow cooker on low setting and cook for 3 hours stirring occasionally.

SMILEY FACE M&M AND BANANA PANCAKES

Shaylan - Age 5
Simryn - Age 4
Karina - Age 1

Pancake Mix
1/2 Mashed banana
M&M's

Maple Syrup
1 tsp. Vanilla Extract
1 tsp. Powdered Cinnamon

In a large mixing bowl, make pancake batter (follow directions on the box). Add mashed banana, vanilla extract, and cinnamon to pancake batter. Cook pancakes on hot griddle. Before flipping pancakes, add M&Ms in a smiley face pattern. Serve with Syrup.

SPAGHETTI A CACIO E PEPE

Timothy Sebastien - Age 5
Sophia Claire - Age 3

8 oz. dried spaghetti
2 T. olive oil
2 cloves garlic
2 T. butter

1 T. freshly ground black pepper
1-2 c. grated pecorino romano
  cheese
salt to taste

In a large saucepan or stock pot, bring 4 quarts salted water to a boil, add the spaghetti, and cook the pasta until al dente. Reserve at least 1 c. of the cooking liquid, then drain the pasta but do not rinse. Heat a small skillet over medium heat, add the olive oil, and when hot, add the garlic and sauté until golden but not brown. Remove the garlic, as it will continue to cook and burn. Add the butter and pepper to the pan. Return 1/2 to 1 c. of the cooking water to the saucepan, add the olive oil mixture and 1 c. of the cheese. Stir and heat over medium heat. Add the pasta, and toss for about three minutes, until the cheese melts and the sauce coats the pasta, adding more reserved cooking liquid if dry. Taste and season with salt. Place the pasta in a large bowl, top with the reserved garlic, and serve with extra cheese on the side. Serves two as an entree, four as a first course.

SPAGHETTI AND MEATBALLS

Marissa Nicole - Age 7

1/3 bag Kirkland Meatballs
1 jar Spaghetti Sauce

1 box Spaghetti Noodles

Place meatballs into a crock pot (1/3 of a bag serves our family of 5). Pour entire jar of spaghetti sauce in pot, covering meatballs. Leave on

(continued)

low heat for 3 to 4 hours (can be longer as long as it's on low heat). If you don't have that much time, leave on high heat for an hour or two (meatballs need to be 165 degrees inside before eating). Have your mom or dad drive you to soccer practice, baseball, gymnastics, swimming or wherever you need to be after school. Come home to a meal that's almost done. All you need to do is boil water and cook the spaghetti noodles for 8 minutes. Drain noodles, pour meatballs and sauce over pasta, and enjoy!!

SPAGHETTI WITH RAISINS!

Kaylianna Jane - Age 2.5

lots of spaghetti   **lots of raisins**

When mom's regular spaghetti just isn't exciting anymore, you can make it fun with raisins! Just have mom prepare her normal recipe, with or without meat. Then sprinkle or dump in a bunch of raisins for added sweetness and fun. as many as you want!! Even mom will think it's surprisingly yummy!

SPEEDY TRIPLE-DECKER CLUB

Joseph

2 tblsp. Miracle Whip dressing
6 slices whole-wheat bread, toasted
8 slices Oscar Mayer Deli Fresh Shaved Rotisserie Seasoned Chicken Breast

4 slices Oscar Mayer Center Cut Bacon, crisply cooked, drained
1 tomato, cut into 4 slices
1 cup shredded lettuce

Spread 1 tblsp. of the dressing evenly onto 2 toast slices; top with chicken. Cover each with second toast slice. Layer bacon, tomatoes, and lettuce on top. Place remaining toast slice on top and spread with 1 tblsp. of dressing. Cut each sandwich into four triangles. Secure with a wooden toothpick. Shortcuts: Substitute 4 slices Oscar Mayer Fully Cooked Bacon for the cooked bacon slices. For a rich deli taste, prepare as directed, adding a Kraft Singles Select to each sandwich.

SUMMER STUFFED PERFECT BURGERS

Logan Joseph - Age 7
Jackson William - Age 4

2 eggs
½ cup finely chopped celery
½ cup finely chopped onion
1 tomato, peeled and chopped
1 tsp. chili powder

1 tblsp Worcestershire sauce
1 tsp. Dijon style mustard
salt and pepper to taste
2 pounds lean ground beef

(continued)

Combine all ingredients. Shape into patties. Squeeze out excess liquids from patties. Grill for 14 to 18 minutes or until well done. Add hamburger buns, lettuce, tomatoes and cheeses. Enjoy! Makes about 10 patties.

SUPER CHICKEN

Brooke Ashley - Age 6

8-10 pcs. chicken
2 cups uncooked rice
1 can cream of mushroom or
  cream of chicken soup

1 can cream of celery soup
1 can mushrooms (optional)
1 env. onion soup mix
1½ cups milk

Place chicken in 9x13 pan and bake at 350 degrees for 1 hour. Mix together rice, soups, mushrooms (optional), and milk. Move chicken pieces to one side of the pan, pour in rice mixture, and place chicken parts on top. Cover with foil. Bake at 350 degrees for 1 hour. Yield: 8 servings

Notes: We prepare this recipe using only chicken legs. We also remove the skin before baking the chicken.

SUPER SPIEGEL SANDWICH

Justin Spiegel

2 slices Turkey Breast
2 slices Hard Salami
1 tblsp Mayonnaise

1 tblsp Butter
2 slices Rye Bread

First, you take 2 pieces of rye bread and put them on a plate. Next, you spread butter on one piece of bread and mayonnaise on the other piece. Then, you place 2 slices of turkey on the mayonnaise side and 2 pieces of hard salami on the butter side. A slice of your favorite cheese can be added. Lastly, you put the two slices together and you have yourself a Super Spiegel Sandwich!

SUPER STEAK ON THE GRILL

Reese Michael - Age 7

4 sirloin steaks
4 tsp. soybean oil
8 large mushrooms sliced

1 tsp. salt
1 tsp. pepper

Preheat grill. Grill steaks until rare. Heat a skillet and add oil. Remove steaks from grill and cut into bit size cubes. Place steak pieces and mushrooms in hot skillet. Season with salt and pepper. Toss and serve.

118

SWEDISH PANCAKES

Cassidy Rae - Age 10
Ross Richard - Age 7

1½ cups Flour
½ cup Sugar
3 Eggs

¼ cup Butter (melted)
1 pinch Salt

Mix all ingredients until all lumps are gone. Heat a non-stick omelet pan. Pour spoon-full of batter and swirl until very thin. Let cook until bubbles form, then flip. Cook for a short time on this side and slide out of pan. Roll hot pancake (like you would a crepe). Cover with syrup or fruit and enjoy!

SWEET CHEESE SANDWICH

Alex Ray - Age 8
Robert Anthony - Age 7
Kayli Grace - Age 2

2 slices bread
1 tspn butter / margarine
½ tspn sugar

½ tspn ground cinnamon
1 slice American cheese

Spread butter or margarine on each slice of bread. Sprinkle both sides with the cinnamon and the sugar. Place the cheese on one slice of bread. Place prepared slices of bread in a toaster oven for a light toast, enough to melt the cheese. Once cheese is melted, remove bread from the toaster oven, place slices together like a sandwich, and cut into four pieces or fun shapes! Enjoy!

SYDNEY'S MEAT LOAF

Sydney L - Age 9

1½ lbs. ground beef (we use 1 lb. beef and ½ lb. turkey breast)
¾ cup oatmeal
½ cup chopped onions (optional)

½ cup tomato sauce
1 egg, slightly beaten
½ tsp. salt
¼ tsp. pepper

Heat: Oven 350°. Combine all ingredients. Mix well. Bake 60 minutes; drain.

TACO FILLED PEPPERS

Sophia Brielle - Age 16 months

1 lb. Ground Beef
1 pkg. Taco Seasoning
1 can Kidney Beans, rinsed and
  drained

1 cup Salsa
4 med. Green Peppers

Brown ground beef, drain. Stir in taco seasoning, kidney beans and salsa. Bring to a boil, simmer for 5 minutes. Remove and discard seeds and stern from green peppers. Immerse in boiling water for 3 minutes, drain. Spoon meat mixture into peppers. Place in ungreased baking dish. Cover and bake at 350° for 15-20 minutes. Top with tomatoes, cheese, and a dollop of sour cream.

TACO PANCAKES

Grace Gersch

1 Pancake

Chocolate Chips

Using your favorite recipe or frozen pancake, cook pancake according to the directions. After cooking, place chocolate chips in a line across the center of the pancake. Fold into the shape of a taco. You are done! Any flavor chips or small chocolate candies may be used.

TACOS

Zachary Luke - Age 7

1 lb. ground beef
¾ c. hot water
favorite taco seasonings

favorite taco toppings
taco shells

Cook the ground beef on stove til no longer pink. Add favorite taco seasonings and hot water. Let simmer for 10 minutes. Warm up some taco shells. Then add on the shells your favorite toppings. Enjoy!

TANDOORI CHICKEN

Arjun Varma - Age 12

800 grams chicken
1 tsp. Kashmiri red chili powder
1 tblsp lemon juice
salt to taste
Following ingredients for
  marinade:
100 grams yogurt

1 tsp. Kashmir red chili powder
salt to taste
2 tblsp ginger paste
2 tblsp garlic paste
2 tblsp lemon juice
½ tsp. garam masala powder
2 tblsp mustard oil

Skin, wash and clean the chicken. Make incisions with a sharp knife on breast and leg pieces. Apply a mixture of Kashmir red chili powder,

(continued)

98890-09

lemon juice and salt to the chicken and keep it aside for half an hour. Remove whey of yogurt by hanging it in a muslin cloth for fifteen to twenty minutes. Mix Kashmiri red chili powder, salt, ginger-garlic paste, lemon juice, garam masala powder and mustard oil to the yogurt. Apply this marinade onto the chicken pieces and refrigerate for three to four hours. Put the chicken onto the skewers and cook in a moderately hot tandooror a pre-heated oven (400 degrees Fahrenheit) for ten to twelve minutes or until almost done. Baste it with butter and cook for another four minutes. Garnish with onion rings and lemon wedges.

TASTY BEEF SANDWICHES

Sabrina Rose - Age 12

2½ lb. Boneless Chuck Roast, thawed
2 pkg. Hidden Valley Ranch Dressing Mix

1 cup Water

Put all of the above into a crock pot sprayed with non-stick cooking spray. Cook on high for 6-8 hours until meat is falling apart. Take 2 forks and pull meat apart so it is shredded for sandwiches. Serve on semi-hard rolls or French bread.

TASTY TUNA MELT

Rachel Sue - Age 5

4 English muffins
2 (9-oz.) cans tuna in water (well-drained)
5 rounded tblsp sweet pickle relish

2 ribs celery, finely chopped
½ cup mayonnaise
4 slices american cheese
salt & pepper to taste

Preheat broiler. Place English muffins on a cookie sheet; lightly toast, then remove from oven. Leave broiler on. Mix tuna with relish, celery and mayo. Season with salt & pepper. Place a large scoop evenly on top of the 8 muffin halves. Top each mound with cheese slices and place the open-faced sandwiches under the broiler to melt the cheese. Serve immediately.

TERIYAKI NOODLES

Jay Torres - Age 15

8 oz. Multigrain or whole-wheat spaghetti
4 tsp. Canola or olive oil
½ tsp. Crushed red pepper flakes
1 lb. Boneless beef chuck or shoulder blade steak, trimmed, thinly sliced
3 cups Green Giant frozen broccoli florets

2 cups Cascadian Farm organic shelled edamame
¼ cup Water
⅔ cup Reduced-sodium teriyaki sauce
1 cup Shredded Carrots
6 Green onions, thinly sliced
1 tblsp Finely chopped gingerroot

Prep time: 30 Minutes. Start to finish: 30 Minutes. 6 Servings (½ cups each). Cook spaghetti without salt as directed on package; drain. Place in large serving bowl; toss with 2 teaspoons of the oil and the pepper flakes. Meanwhile, in 12-inch skillet, heat remaining 2 teaspoons oil over medium-high heat. Add beef and gingerroot: cook 3 to 5 minutes, turning frequently, until beef is no longer pink. Add to spaghetti; toss to mix. In same skillet, place broccoli, edamane and water. Cover and cook over medium-high heat 2 minutes, stirring once. Uncover, add teriyaki sauce, carrots and onions; cook and stir 2 minutes. Add to beef-spaghetti mixture; toss to mix.

TERIYAKI ROAST CHICKEN

Shaun Gereno - Age 12

1 3-lb. Broiler-fryer
1 small Onion, quartered

⅓ tsp. Garlic-Pepper seasoning
Cooking Spray

Preheat oven to 350°. Remove giblets from chicken. Reserve for another use. Rinse and drain chicken; pat dry. Place onion in cavity of chicken. Brush chicken on all sides with teriyaki sauce. Sprinkle with garlic-pepper seasoning. Place chicken, breast up, on rack of a roasting pan coated with cooking spray. Insert meat thermometer into meaty part of thigh, making sure it does not touch the bone. Pour remaining teriyaki sauce over chicken. Bake, uncovered, at 375° for 1½ hours or until meat thermometer registers 185°. Remove skin before serving. 6 servings.

98890-09

TERIYAKI SALMON FOIL

Aleia Foster - Age 14

¾ cup A.1. Steakhouse
  Marinade for Seafood Ginger
  Teriyaki with Orange, divided
4 Salmon fillets
2 cups Instant white rice,
  uncooked

2 cups Hot water
2 cups Shredded carrots
1 bag Snow peas

Pour ½ cup of the marinade over salmon in resealable plastic bag. Seal bag; turn to evenly coat salmon with marinade. Refrigerate 30 minutes to marinate. Preheat grill to medium-high heat. Remove salmon from marinade; discard marinade. Place 1 salmon fillet on center of each of four 18x12 inch sheets of heavy-duty foil. Combine remaining ¼ cup marinade, rice, water and vegetables; spoon evenly over salmon. Bring up foil sides. Double fold top and ends to seal packet, leaving room for heat circulation inside. Grill 15 min. or until salmon flakes easily with fork. Cut slits in foil to release steam before opening each packet. Or use your oven. Assemble packets as directed. Preheat oven to 350°F. Place packets in single layer in 15x10x1 inch baking pan. Bake 20 min. or until salmon flakes easily with fork. Continue as directed.

TERRIFIC TURKEY TACOS

Chris O'Donnell & Family
Caroline, Lily, Chip, Charlie
Finn, and Maeve

1 pkg. Lawry's Taco Seasoning
1 tblsp. olive oil
2 garlic cloves, finely chopped
¼ cup onion, finely chopped
1 lb. ground turkey

taco shells
shredded cheddar cheese
shredded lettuce
diced tomatoes

Sauté onions, olive oil, and garlic. Remove from pan and set aside. Brown ground turkey in the same pan. Add taco seasoning (and water as directed on package). Stir in onion mixture until blended. Serve with taco shells and your favorite taco fixin's! Enjoy!

THE CHEESE SMASH SANDWICH

Carson Bruce - Age 5

2 slices bread
butter
cream cheese
2 Nutter Butter Cookies

1 individual pkg. mozzarella
  string cheese
1 tblsp sunflower seeds

Spread butter and cream cheese on each slice of bread. Add the cookies and string cheese torn into pieces. Sprinkle the seeds in the sandwich. Smash it together and eat it up!

THE GIO-FOUR-O BREAKFAST SANDWICH

Stephanie Joy - 8
Jessica Grace - 6
Allison Hope - 5, Cassidy Faith - 2

1 tube croissants
3 eggs
½ cup asiago cheese (or your
  choice)

salt to taste

Grease an 8 x 8 inch pan. Preheat oven to 350°. Unroll ½ of the croissants and lay on bottom of pan. Pat down to spread. Sprinkle the asiago cheese over the layer of croissants. Mix eggs together with salt and pepper. Pour the mixture over the croissants in pan. Unroll the rest of the croissants from the tube. Lay them as the top layer in the pan. Sprinkle the rest of the asiago cheese on top. Bake at 350° for 12 minutes or until the croissant is fluffy and brown. P.S. Don't forget to blow on it!

THE STICKWICH

Mrs. Dionesotes Fourth Grade Class
Countryside School

2 slices ham or turkey
3 pieces cheddar cheese (in
  cubes)
2 slices of pickles
1 slice bread

lettuce, in small pieces
1 tomato, cut into 4 pieces
1 skewer (stick)
1 tblsp. mayonnaise

Cut each slice of meat in half and roll each half. Spread mayonnaise on slice of bread. Cut bread into 4 pieces. Place one piece of bread on stick. Place one rolled up piece of meat next to bread. Place one cube of cheese next to meat. Place lettuce next to cheese. Place one piece of tomato next to lettuce. Place one slice of pickle next to tomato. Repeat steps, ending with a piece of bread. Enjoy!

TIMOTHY'S FAVORITE MARINATED STEAK

Timothy Sebastien - Age 5

¾ c. Soy sauce
¼ c. Worcestershire sauce
2 tsp. dry mustard
1½ tsp. pepper

½ c. vinegar
2 cloves garlic (or more)
⅓ c. lemon juice
¾ c. vegetable oil

Get out your blender. Pop in the soy, Wresters, mustard powder, pepper (ground), vinegar, garlic, and lemon juice. Blend it up until it's well mixed. Slowly add the vegetable oil while blending until emulsified. Put your steaks in a Ziploc bag or container, and pour the marinade over them. Store in the fridge to marinate. Turn them periodically. For the

(continued)

last hour, take them out of the fridge to finish. Steaks cook better when close to room temperature, and I promise that an hour out of the fridge isn't going to make the meat go bad. Save the marinade after you take out the steaks. Put it in a saucepan and boil. Boil, boil, boil for at least ten minutes. Grill the steaks to your preferred doneness (if you're using tenderloin, don't go past medium rare or a light medium). I sometimes save some of the marinade to baste the steaks, as well, but it isn't necessary. Serve the steaks with the reduced marinade sauce as an accompaniment.

TINFOIL SANDWICHES
(Hot Ham and Cheese)

Noah Matthew - Age 5
Nicholas Lawrence - Age 8
Jack Patrick - Age 8

1 stick butter
¼ c. yellow mustard
¼ c. chopped onion
1 T. poppy seeds

1 lb. ham
1 lb. swiss cheese
hard rolls or buns

Mix softened butter, mustard, onions and poppy seeds together. Spread both sides of a hard roll or bun with the mixture. Place slices of ham and swiss cheese on the bun. Wrap in tinfoil. Bake at 350 degrees for 15-20 minutes or until cheese melts. Can be made ahead of time. Great with soup!

TURKEY RANCH ROLL UP

Millie Claire - Age 13

1½ cup shredded lettuce
1 medium sized whole-wheat
  tortilla
2 tblsp shredded cheddar
  cheese

2 tblsp ranch dressing
4 slices turkey lunch meat

Heat the tortilla for 15 seconds in the microwave. Place the tortilla on a large plate and lay turkey slices across the top ⅔ of the tortilla. In a bowl, mix the lettuce, cheese, and ranch dressing together and spoon it on top of the turkey. Fold the bottom third of the tortilla up over the turkey and lettuce and roll the rest of the tortilla into a wrap. Enjoy!

TURKEY SLOPPY JOES

Michael Knighton - Age 11

1½ lbs. Ground Turkey
1 Green Pepper, chopped fine
1 medium Onion, chopped fine
2 tblsp. Prepared Mustard

2 tblsp. Sugar
2 tblsp. Vinegar
¾ cup Catsup
¼ tsp. Salt (or salt substitute)

Brown and drain ground turkey. Add remaining ingredients and simmer all together for 30 to 45 minutes. If you prefer, you can simmer in a crock pot for two hours. Serve on buns or rolls.

TURKEY STICKS

Christian Robert - Age 10

4 tblsp. cream cheese
1 tsp. honey mustard

12 slices turkey
4 unsalted bread sticks

Combine cream cheese and honey mustard in small bowl and mix well. Take 3 turkey slices and place on a plate or wax paper, overlapping the turkey slices. Spread ¼ of your cream cheese mixture evenly onto the turkey slices. Make sure to cover all around the turkey. Place a breadstick by the bottom of the turkey slices and roll. Make sure the turkey slices stay all together. Repeat step 2 with remaining ingredients to make a total of 4 servings.

TURKEYLOAF

Ellie - Age 3

1 lb. Ground Turkey
1 cup Italian bread crumbs
½ cup BBQ sauce
2 heaping splashes Worcester
  sauce

1 Egg
1 heaping dash Red Pepper
  Flakes
½ cup Chopped Onion
Ketchup

Mix everything in a bowl by hand. Mold into a loaf and place in a loaf pan. Bake at 400 degrees for 1+ hour, until fully cooked. Top with ketchup. Slice and serve.

UNCLE STEVE'S WORLD FAMOUS WAFFLES

Natalie Barbara - Age 3
Allison Hope - Age 5

2 cups flour
3 tsp. baking powder
½ tsp. salt
3 eggs, separated

1¾ cups milk
4 tblsp. butter, melted
3 tblsp. sugar

(continued)

98890-09

Combine flour, baking powder and salt in a bowl and set aside. In another bowl, beat yolks, milk and butter with a hand mixer. Combine flour mixture with egg mixture and beat until smooth. In a clean bowl, beat egg whites until stiff, but not dry (they should make peaks). Slowly add the sugar to the egg whites, beating constantly. Mix 1/3 of the egg whites into the batter. Fold in the remaining egg whites gently with a spatula. Cook in a waffle maker and enjoy them while they are hot!

VAN'S TUMMY YUMMY TACO CASSEROLE

Van - Age 6

1-lb. ground turkey, browned and drained
1 (16-oz.) can refried beans
1 cup low fat sour cream
6-8 corn tortillas

1 (11-oz.) can corn niblets (drained)
1+ cups mild salsa (to taste)
3 cups cheddar cheese

Brown and drain ground turkey and add one or more cups salsa to meat. In a 9 x 13 inch casserole dish, layer evenly like a lasagna; refried beans, sour cream, sprinkle one cup cheese, one layer corn tortillas to fill dish (3-4), ground turkey/salsa, sprinkle corn, last layer of tortillas (3-4), and remaining cheese to cover top of dish. Bake at 350 degrees until warm and bubbly. Optional: garnish with black olives. Scoop with baked tortilla chips.

VEGGIE BURRITO

Issac Noah - Age 7

2 (16-oz.) cans Enchilada Sauce
1/2 cup Uncooked Rice
1 (15-oz.) can Black Beans - rinsed and drained
1 (10-oz.) packet Frozen chopped spinach, thawed

1 1/2 cups Shredded Cheddar cheese
6 Flour tortillas (9 inch)

Preheat the oven to 375 degrees. In a 13 x 9 inch baking dish, spread 1/2 cup enchilada sauce. In a pot, mix rice, beans and 1 1/2 cups water. Cover and cook over high heat, bring to boil. Reduce heat to low and simmer until water is absorbed and rice is tender. About 25 minutes. Squeeze spinach dry and stir into rice mixture with 1 cup of the enchilada sauce and 3/4 cup cheese. Cook for 5 more minutes. Spoon mixture down the center of the tortillas. Roll up and place in the dish. Top with the remaining sauce and cheese. Bake until bubbly, 15 minutes. Enjoy!

VEGGIE INFUSED GRILLED CHEESE SANDWICH

Natalie Barbara - Age 3
Allison Hope - Age 5

sliced bread
cheese

puréed vegetables
butter or margarine

In advance of preparing the sandwich, steam and purée some vegetables, such as sweet potatoes, butternut squash or cauliflower. Spread the purée on one side of each slice of bread (decide how much based on how observant your child is!). Spread butter or margarine on top of the purée as you normally would prepare the sandwich. Build the sandwich and fry in a pan until golden brown. This trick is great for upping the nutritional content of a grilled cheese sandwich for kids who don't eat enough vegetables. The same idea can be applied to many recipes by adding or substituting for some of the wet ingredients. Purées can be made in advance and frozen until needed.

WALKING TACOS

Rebecca Nicole Neises - Age 10

1 bag Doritos
Taco meat
Cheese (any kind)

Lettuce
Sour Cream

Crunch the Doritos when they are still in the bag. Cut off top of the bag. Add the lettuce, taco meat, cheese and sour cream in and mix it. Then you eat it right out of the bag!

WISCONSIN TUNA CAKE WITH LEMON-DILL SAUCE

Aleia Foster - Age 14

1 (12.5 oz.) can StarKist Tuna,
   drained and finely flaked
3/4 cup Seasoned bread crumbs
1/4 cup Minced green onions
2 tblsp. Chopped drained
   pimiento

1 Egg
1/2 cup Low-fat milk
1/2 tsp. Grated lemon peel
2 tblsp. butter or margarine

In a large bowl, toss together tuna, bread crumbs, onions and pimiento. In a small bowl, beat together egg and milk; stir in lemon peel. Stir into tuna mixture; toss until moistened. With lightly floured hands, shape mixture into eight 4-inch patties. In a large nonstick skillet melt butter. Fry patties, a few at a time, until golden brown on both sides, about 3 minutes per side. Place on an ovenproof platter in 300°F oven until ready to service.

Lemon-Dill Sauce

1/4 cup Chicken Broth
1 tblsp Lemon Juice

1/4 tsp. Dill weed

(continued)

128

98890-09

For sauce, in a small saucepan heat broth, lemon juice and dill. For each serving, spoon shredded carrots and zucchini onto each plate; top with 2 tuna cakes. Top each cake with a half-slice lemon; spoon sauce over. Makes 4 servings.

WORMS & EYEBALLS

Camille Erin - Age 9

1 lb. bucatini pasta (hallow spaghetti)
1 sm. red bell pepper
1½ lbs. ground chicken breast
2 cloves garlic, chopped
2 tblsp. ginger, chopped
2 scallions, finely chopped
2 tblsp. hoiser sauce (Chinese BBQ)

salt & freshly ground black pepper to taste
3 tblsp. vegetable oil
1 cup preshredded carrots
1 cup bean sprouts
1 cup snow pea pods (cut into pieces with scissor knife)
½ cup tamari

Preheat oven to 400°. Put a large pot of water to boil for the pasta. Cut off a quarter of the bell pepper and have your grown-up helper (GH) chop it finely. Slice the rest of the pepper yourself. Combine chicken, garlic, ginger, scallions, finely chopped pepper, hoisin sauce, salt and pepper in a bowl. Roll the mixture into meatballs the size of chicken eyeballs and place balls on a nonstick cookie sheet, coated lightly with 1 tblsp. vegetable oil. Roast the chicken eyeballs for 10-12 minutes. When the past water comes to a boil, cook pasta according to directions. When the pasta is almost cooked through and the eyeballs are about 5 minutes away from coming out of the oven, start stir-frying the veggies. Heat a large nonstick skillet over high heat and add remaining 2 tblsp. of vegetable oil. Stir the veggies for 1 minute. Have your GH drain the noodles and add the worms to the veggies. Pour in the tamari while the GH tosses the worms and veggies to coat. Transfer noodles to serving platter. Remove the eyeballs from the oven, roll them on top of the worms, then serve.

YOGURT PANCAKES

William Stephen

1 Egg
⅔ cup Full-fat plain yogurt
⅔ cup Milk
1¼ cups Self-raising flour

¼ tsp. Salt
Vegetable Oil (for frying)
Maple Syrup
Fruit topping of your choice

Lightly beat egg. Mix beaten egg and yogurt, then stir in milk, flour and salt. Mix until batter is smooth. Heat a little oil in frying pan until hot. Drop tablespoons of batter into the pan and flatten with spatula. Cook 1- 2 minutes until lightly browned, then flip and cook on the other side. Drizzle with maple syrup and add some fruit topping.

YUMMY CHICKEN SALAD

Erick R Leska - Age 6

2 cups cubed cooked chicken breast
1 cup red, seedless grapes
½ cup chopped celery

¼ cup poppy seed salad dressing
¼ cup mayonnaise

Toss everything together and serve on croissant, pita or lettuce.

YUMMY PANCAKES

Sophie Grace - Age 7

2 eggs
1¼ cups milk
1 tsp. vanilla
3 tblsp. butter or vegetable oil

1½ cups all-purpose flour
¾ tsp. salt
2 tsp. baking powder
1 tblsp. sugar, optional

Blend the eggs, milk and vanilla in a blender or food processor for about 3 minutes. Mix dry ingredients together (flour, salt, baking powder, sugar) in a large bowl. Gently fold in egg mixture and quickly (and gently) stir until completely mixed. Let the batter rest while the griddle is heating (batter will thicken upon standing). Grease the preheated griddle and pour ¼ cupfuls of batter on the lightly greased griddle. Cook on one side until bubbles begin to form and break. Then turn the pancakes and cook on the other side until brown (turn only once). Healthy tip: Toddlers and kids are usually happy to eat pancakes with a yogurt or applesauce spread, rather than maple syrup. You can also omit the sugar.

98890-09

BREADS & ROLLS

Helpful Hints

- When baking bread, a small dish of water in the oven will help keep the crust from getting too hard or brown.

- Use shortening, not margarine or oil, to grease pans when baking bread. Margarine and oil absorb more readily into the dough.

- To make self-rising flour, mix 4 cups flour, 2 teaspoons salt, and 2 tablespoons baking powder. Store in a tightly covered container.

- One scant tablespoon of bulk yeast is equal to one packet of yeast.

- Hot water kills yeast. One way to tell the correct temperature is to pour the water over your forearm. If you cannot feel hot or cold, the temperature is just right.

- When in doubt, always sift flour before measuring.

- Use bread flour for baking heavier breads, such as mixed grain, pizza doughs, bagels, etc.

- When baking in a glass pan, reduce the oven temperature by 25°.

- When baking bread, you can achieve a finer texture if you use milk. Water makes a coarser bread.

- Nuts, shelled or unshelled, keep best and longest when stored in the freezer. Unshelled nuts crack more easily when frozen. Nuts can be used directly from the freezer.

- Enhance the flavor of nuts, such as almonds, walnuts, and pecans, by toasting them before using in recipes. Place nuts on a baking sheet and bake at 300° for 5−8 minutes or until slightly browned.

- Dust a bread pan or work surface with flour by filling an empty salt shaker with flour.

- For successful quick breads, do not overmix the dough. Mix only until combined. An overmixed batter creates tough and rubbery muffins, biscuits, and quick breads.

- Muffins can be eaten warm. Most other quick breads taste better the next day. Nut breads are better if stored 24 hours before serving.

- Over-ripe bananas can be frozen until it's time to bake. Store them unpeeled in a plastic bag.

- The freshness of eggs can be tested by placing them in a large bowl of cold water; if they float, do not use them.

BREADS & ROLLS

APPLE BREAD

Issac Noah - Age 7

1½ cups Vegetable oil
3 Eggs
2 tsp. Vanilla
3 cups Flour
1 tsp. Baking Soda
2 tsp. Cinnamon

½ tsp. Salt
1 cup Chopped Walnuts
2 cups Peeled and chopped apples
2 cups Sugar

Grease and flour two 8 inch loaf pans. In a large bowl, mix sugar, oil, eggs and vanilla. Mix well. Add in dry ingredients. Stir well. Add the apples and nuts. Pour into the prepared pans. Bake for 1 hour in a 350 degree oven. Enjoy!

BACON CRESCENTS

Meagan Reigh - Age 12

1 (8-oz.) pkg. cream cheese, softened
8 slices bacon, crisply cooked and crumbled
⅓ c. grated Parmesan cheese
1 egg beaten with 1 tsp. of cold water

2 tsp. fresh parsley, chopped
1 T. milk
2 (8-oz.) cans refrigerated crescent dinner rolls

Preheat oven to 375 degrees. Beat cream cheese, bacon, Parmesan cheese, parsley and milk in a mixing bowl at medium speed with electric mixer until well blended. This mixture can be refrigerated over night or frozen. Separate dinner rolls into four large rectangles. With each rectangle cut along the perforations, and make additional cuts in the opposite direction to create 8 triangles from each of the four large rectangles. Put a dab of filling in each triangle and roll up, starting at the short end. Place on greased cookie sheet. Brush with egg and water mixture. Bake 12 to 15 minutes or until browned. Makes about 5-6 dozen.

BAGUETTE

Timothy Sebastien - Age 5
Sophia Claire - Age 3

1½ c. water (110° to 115°)
1 tsp. yeast
1 tsp. sugar

2½ c. flour
2 c. bread flour
2 tsp. salt

(continued)

Place water into a large bowl and sprinkle with the yeast on top. Add the sugar and stir to dissolve the yeast. Stir in half the flour, then add the salt and the remaining flour. Knead until smooth, 7 to 10 minutes. Allow to rise in a covered container until doubled, about 1 1/2 hours at room temperature or 12 hours in the refrigerator. Punch down the dough, divide in half and shape into two long loaves. To shape, press with fingertips, pushing out to make a rectangle; lift occasionally to keep from sticking. Roll both sides to the middle, then pinch closed at the seam. Use the side of your hand to push down on the seam, then pinch the edges together again. Roll over so seam is on the bottom. Taper ends by rolling gently with your hands. Place in lightly oiled baguette pans or on parchment-lined baking sheets and allow to rise until puffy, about one hour. Slash the loaves with a sharp knife. Bake in a preheated 400° oven, adding water to the oven in 1/2 c increments (NOT on the bread) three or four times in the first seven minutes of baking. Bake until golden, about 25 to 30 minutes. Allow to cool before slicing.

BAKED FRENCH TOAST

Connor - Age 6 1/2

1 loaf stiff bread
10 eggs
1 1/2 cups half & half

1/4 cup maple syrup
8 T. melted butter

Tear up the bread in an 8 x 13 pan. Whisk up the rest of the ingredients. Pour over the bread and push the bread down so it all gets soaked. Put in the fridge overnight. Bake at 350° for 40-50 minutes. It will rise in the oven, then fall back down.

BANANA BREAD

John "Jack" Raymond - Age 7

2/3 cup sugar
1/4 cup margarine, softened
1 egg
2 egg whites
1 cup mashed, ripe bananas
  (about 2 bananas)

1/4 cup water
1-2/3 cup flour
1 tsp. baking soda
1/2 tsp. salt
1/4 tsp. baking powder

Heat oven to 350 degrees. Spray loaf pan with nonstick cooking spray. Beat sugar and margarine in medium bowl on medium speed, scraping bowl constantly until light and fluffy, about 30 seconds. Mix in remaining ingredients just until moistened. Pour into loaf pan. Bake at 350 degrees, on middle rack in oven, until wooden pick inserted in center comes out clean. 8-inch loaf, approx. 60 minutes; 9-inch loaf, approx. 45-55 minutes. Cool 5 minutes. Loosen sides of loaf from pan; remove from pan. Cool completely before slicing.

98890-09

BANANA BREAD

Jackson Lee

1¾ cup flour
2 tsp. baking powder
¼ tsp. baking soda
½ tsp. salt
⅔ cup sugar

2 large Brown Bananas
⅓ cup Crisco shortening stick
2 large eggs, unbeaten
½ cup chopped nuts (optional)

Mix together: flour, baking powder, baking soda, salt and sugar. Add in: bananas, shortening, eggs and nuts. Beat until blended. Pour into greased bread pan. Bake at 350° for 1 hour. Makes 1 loaf.

(Note: the browner and mushier the bananas, the better flavor the bread will have.)

BANANA BREAD

Andrew John - Age 6
Elizabeth Lyn - Age 5
William John - Age 1

1 stick Butter
1 cup sugar
2 eggs
2 cups flour

1 tsp. baking soda
¼ tsp. salt
4 ripe bananas

Mix butter, sugar, eggs, flour, baking soda, and salt. Mix in mashed bananas. Spoon into greased loaf pan or 4 mini-loaf pans. Bake 1 hour at 300 degrees.

BANANA BREAD

Mackenzie Marie - Age 9
Mason Michael - Age 7

3 overripe bananas
1½ cup whole-wheat flour
1 cup sugar
½ tsp. baking soda

dash salt
¼ cup butter
1 egg
4 tblsp chocolate chips

Preheat oven to 325 degrees. Mash bananas in a large bowl. Add flour, sugar, baking soda, salt and egg. Melt butter in microwave and add to bowl...stir until blended. Pour into greased loaf pan. Sprinkle with chocolate chips. Bake for 70 minutes or until a toothpick inserted in middle comes out clean.

BANANA BREAD

Lucas William - Age 7
Ryan Thomas - Age 4
Tyler McCarty - Age 2

1 stick butter	1 tsp. baking soda
1 c. sugar	1 tsp. salt
2 eggs	1 c. (about 3) mashed bananas
1½ c. flour	1 tsp. vanilla

Cream butter, sugar, and eggs. Add flour, baking soda, salt, bananas, and vanilla. Pour in greased 9 x 5 inch loaf pan. Cook at 350° for 1 hour.

BANANA BREAD

Reina Hershner - Age 6
Reed Hershner - Age 3

1¾ cups flour	⅓ cup shortening
2 tsp. baking powder	⅔ cup sugar
¼ tsp. baking soda	2 eggs
¾ tsp. salt	1 cup very ripe mashed bananas

Sift flour. Measure and resift 3 times with baking powder, baking soda, and salt - set aside. Cream shortening (can use oil too) and sugar until light and fluffy. Add eggs, 1 at a time and beat well after each addition. Add mashed bananas and mix. Add flour mixture in 3 to 4 portions and beat until smooth after each portion. Turn into a well greased loaf pan and bake at 350° for 50 minutes. Cool on rack.

BANANA BREAD

Meghan Sclafani

½ cup Sugar	2 cups flour
1 stick Butter	½ cup Milk
2 Eggs	1 tsp. Vanilla
1 tsp. salt	1 cup nuts
1 tsp. soda	cinnamon
3 med. bananas (mashed)	

Cream sugar and butter, add eggs. Mix soda, salt and flour. Add milk and flour mixture. Pour in baking pan and back at 350 degrees for 15 minutes. Reduce heat to 325 degrees and cook for an additional 45 minutes.

98890-09

BANANA BREAD

Emma Olson - Age 6

1½ c. sugar
½ c. butter or margarine
2 eggs
½ tsp. salt, if desired
1 tsp. vinegar

1 tsp. baking soda
2 c. flour
½ c. milk
3-4 med. brown bananas,
 mashed

Cream sugar and margarine. Add the eggs, salt, vinegar and baking soda. Alternate flour with milk. Beat well. Stir in mashed bananas. Grease 2 loaf pans and bake together for 1 hour to 1 hour and 20 minutes at 300 degrees. (Depending on your oven, check every 5-10 minutes after the first hour) Brown, "bad" bananas work best. Eat one loaf and freeze the other! Freezes well! This is an all time favorite!

BANANA CHOCOLATE CHIP MUFFINS

Allyson Paige

1¾ c. all-purpose flour
¾ c. sugar
1 tsp. baking powder
1 tsp. baking soda
½ tsp. salt
1 egg

¾ c. vegetable oil
½ c. plain yogurt
1 tsp. vanilla extract
1 c. ripe bananas, mashed
¾ c. semi-sweet chocolate
 chips

Preheat oven to 350°. In a large bowl, combine flour, sugar, baking powder, baking soda and salt. In another bowl, combine egg, oil, yogurt and vanilla. Stir wet mixture into dry ingredients until just moistened. Be careful not to over mix. Fold in bananas and chocolate chips. Fill greased or paper-lined muffin cups ⅔ full. Bake for 22 to 25 minutes or until a toothpick inserted into the middle of muffin comes out clean. Allow to cool for 5 minutes before removing to wire racks. Makes 18 muffins

BANANA CHOCOLATE CHIP MUFFINS
(a muffin a day keeps the doctor away)

Kendall Blair - Age 12

½ cup butter, softened
1 cup packed light brown sugar
2 eggs, lightly beaten
2 cups all-purpose flour
½ tsp. salt

½ tsp. baking powder
2 cups mashed ripe bananas
 (about 3 medium bananas)
¾ cup mini chocolate chips

Cream together butter and brown sugar, add beaten eggs and mix well. Sift flour with salt and baking powder and add to brown sugar mixture, stirring until well blended. Add bananas and beat until mixture is smooth.

(continued)

Fold in chocolate chips, spoon batter into greased mini muffin tins. Bake at 350° for 15 min.

BANANA CHOCOLATE CHIP MUFFINS

Elizabeth Kaye - Age 7
Nathaniel Joseph - Age 9

3 med. bananas, ripe
1/3 c. butter, melted
2/3 c. sugar
1 egg, beaten
1 tsp. vanilla

1³/₄ cup flour
1 tsp. baking powder
1 tsp. baking soda
³/₄ tsp. salt
1/2 c. chocolate chips

Mash bananas and add to melted butter. Mix in sugar and vanilla. Mix in beaten egg. In a separate bowl, mix together flour, baking powder, baking soda and salt. Add flour mixture to banana mixture. Do not over mix. Gently add chocolate chips. Fill lined muffin tins ³/₄ full. Bake at 350 degrees for 15-20 minutes. Remove and cool well. Makes 1 dozen muffins.

BLUEBERRY MUFFINS

Taylor L- Age 13

1 T. soy lecithin granules
1¹/₈ cups fine raw sugar
³/₄ cup banana, mashed
  (approximately 2 large
  bananas)
1/2 cup plain yogurt, nonfate or
  whole
³/₄ T. butter, softened
³/₄ cup milk or plain soymilk,
  low-fate or whole

1¹/₈ cups unbleached white flour
1¹/₂ cups whole-wheat pastry
  flour
2 tsp. baking soda
2 tsp. baking powder
1³/₄ cups blueberries, fresh or
  frozen

Preheat the oven to 375°F. Lightly oil a standard 12-cup muffin tray. Grind the lecithin granules in a coffee grinder or blender to a fine powder. Transfer to a medium bowl. Add the sugar, banana, and yogurt to the bowl and mix well. Cream the butter and stir into the banana mixture. Add the milk and mix well. Sift the dry ingredients (flour, baking soda, baking powder) into a separate bowl and whisk lightly to combine. Quickly but gently mix the dry ingredients into the batter until evenly combined. Gently fold in the blueberries. Scoop the batter into the muffin tray, filling each cup evenly to the top. Bake for 10 minutes, then reduce the heat to 350°F and bake for a further 15-20 minutes, or until golden brown. Cool before serving.

98890-09

BREAD

Ryan - Age 10

1 c. water
3 c. flour
2 T. sugar
¼ c. dry milk

1 pinch salt
4 T. butter, cut up
1½ tsp. yeast

In a bread machine, add all liquids. Put in flour, sugar, dry milk, and salt. Form a little nest shape on top and place yeast in it. Place butter chunks around the edges. Serves 8.

CARAMEL ROLLS

Anna - Age 7
Luke - Age 5
Ashley - Age 3, Jake - Age 2

24 frozen Rhodes dinner rolls
1 box butterscotch pudding
(NOT instant)

½ cup brown sugar
½ cup melted butter

Butter bundt pan and put frozen rolls in. Sprinkle pudding mix on top of frozen rolls. Mix brown sugar in melted butter in separate bowl. Drizzle mixture over the top of the rolls. Let rise 6 - 8 hours. Bake at 350 degrees for 20-30 minutes. Tip upside down and sprinkle with nuts if desired.

CHOC-O-CHIP BANANA BREAD

Sophie Clark - Age 6
Ian Clark - Age 4

½ cup Oil
1 cup Sugar
2 Eggs
3 Medium ripe bananas, mashed
2 cups Flour
½ tsp. Baking Powder

1 tsp. Baking Soda
Dash Salt
3 tblsp Milk
½ tsp. Vanilla
1 tsp. Rum or Rum extract
(6-oz.) oz. Chocolate Chips

Preheat oven to 350°. Beat together the oil and sugar. Add the eggs and bananas, and beat well. Add the sifted dry ingredients, then the milk, vanilla and rum (or rum extract). Mix well. Stir in chocolate chips. Pour into a greased and floured 9 inch loaf pan. Bake for 1¼ hours or until inserted toothpick comes out clean. Cool in pan on wire rack for 5 minutes. Remove from pan and finish cooling. Yield: 1 Loaf.

Variations: Plain, add Craisins. We sometimes make mini muffins or cupcakes (Bake 15 - 25 minutes depending on size of cups). We also use specialty baking tins such as dinosaur, X's and O's, hearts, etc. These also freeze well if you want to make a big batch and freeze it for later use.

CHOCOLATE CHIP PUMPKIN BREAD

Cole Robert - Age 4
Ella Grace - Age 2

1/4 tsp. ground cloves
1 tsp. cinnamon
1/2 tsp. salt
1/2 tsp. baking powder
2 tsp. baking soda
3 cups wheat flour
1 cup canned pumpkin

2 eggs
2/3 cup butter
2/3 cup water
2 cups sugar
1 cup semi-sweet chocolate
chips

Fall favorite, but great anytime as bread or sweet dessert! Preheat oven to 350 degrees. Grease 2 loaf pans (recipe makes two loafs). Mix dry ingredients together in a large bowl (cloves/cinnamon/salt/baking powder/soda/flour/sugar). Mix all wet ingredients in separate bowl (softened butter/eggs/canned pumpkin/water.) Slowly add wet ingredients into dry until smooth. Fold in chocolate chips. Divide evenly into 2 pans and bake for 1 hour. Let fully cool before slicing / removing from pan.

CHOCOLATE PUMPKIN MUFFINS

Bodhi F. Bykowski - Age 1

1 1/2 cups all-purpose flour
1/2 cup sugar
2 tsp. cinnamon
1/2 tsp. salt
1 cup milk
1/2 cup Libby's Solid Pack
Pumpkin (now called 100%
Pure Pumpkin)

1/4 cup margarine or butter
melted
1 egg
1 cup (6 oz. pkg) semi-sweet
chocolate morsels
1/3 cup finely chopped nuts
2 tsp. baking powder

Preheat oven to 400F degrees. Grease 12 (2 1/2") muffin cups. Combine flour, sugar, baking powder, cinnamon and salt in large bowl; make well in center. In small bowl combine milk, pumpkin, butter, and egg; add to well in flour mixture. Add morsels; stir just until moistened. Spoon into prepared muffin cups, filling each 3/4 full. Sprinkle 1 tsp. nuts over each muffin. Bake 18-20 min or until toothpick comes out clean. Cool 5 minutes. Remove from pans. Cool completely on wire racks. Makes 12 muffins. (Or 1 loaf at 350 degrees for 1 hour--do toothpick test.)

98890-09

CINNAMON CRANRAISIN BREAD

Amber Andreen

¾ cup warm water
1 egg, lightly beaten
1 tblsp. margarine
2⅔ cups all-purpose flour
3 tblsp. dry milk powder
2 tblsp. white sugar

2 tsp. ground cinnamon
1 tsp. vanilla extract
1 tsp. salt
1½ tsp. active dry yeast
½ cup sweetened dried
   cranberries

Place warm water, egg, margarine, flour, powdered milk, sugar, cinnamon, vanilla, salt and yeast into the bread machine in the order suggested by the manufacturer. Start the machine. After the first rise, add the cranraisins. Continue baking. Serves 14.

CINNAMON TOAST

Cynthia Marie - Age 12

1 slice Bread
1 tsp. Sugar

1 tsp. Butter or Margarine
1 dash Cinnamon

Place bread in toaster and when done spread butter and sprinkle sugar on toast. Top with sprinkled cinnamon. Cut in 4 pieces. Serve with hot tea or cocoa.

CRAZY CRUST PIZZA DOUGH

Cory James - Age 7

1 cup all-purpose flour
1 tsp. salt
1 tsp. dried oregano

⅛ tsp. black pepper
2 eggs, lightly beaten
⅔ cup milk

Preheat oven to 400 degrees F. Lightly grease a rimmed pizza pan or baking sheet. In a large bowl, stir together flour, salt, oregano and black pepper. Mix in eggs and milk; stir well. Pour batter into prepared pan and tilt until evenly coated. Arrange toppings of choice on top of batter. Bake in preheated oven for 20 to 25 minutes, until crust is set. Remove crust from oven. Drizzle on pizza sauce and sprinkle on cheese. Bake until cheese is melted, about 10 minutes.

DADDY'S SECRET BREAD RECIPE

Gabriel Donna Alesksov - Age 9

1 tsp. salt
4 packets dry yeast
2 eggs
2 sticks margarine
6 lbs. flour
½ tblsp. vegetable oil

1 tsp. sugar
½ cup water
6 or 7 bread pans
Pam to spray the pans
extra large soft cloth
plastic wrap

(continued)

Have all the ingredients at room temperature. To make the yeast mixture add 1 tsp. of sugar in ½ cup of warm water and mix well. Add 4 packets of yeast, dissolve, then cover. Let the mixture stand at room temperature until the yeast rises and crests, 8 - 10 minutes. Place flour in a very large mixing bowl and create an opening in the center approximately 6 by 6 inches. Add the salt in the center and set aside. In a separate bowl melt the margarine then add vegetable oil and approximately 2 cups of warm water - mix well. Pour yeast mixture in the center of the flour and begin to incorporate into the flour. Gradually pour portions of the margarine mixture and blend well until the mixture is fully absorbed into the flour.

Tip: dough should be soft to the touch. Place dough on a floured surface and begin to knead by hand for approximately 15 minutes. when finished the dough should be soft to the touch and should bounce back when pressed. Transfer the dough to a floured bowl; brush the top of the dough with the vegetable oil. Cover loosely with plastic wrap then cover the entire bowl with the soft cloth. Place in warmed oven.

Tip: it is preferred that the oven is warmed by placing a gallon of very hot water in the oven to bring to optimum temperature. The flour will rise to three times its original size - approximately 90 minutes. Transfer the dough to a floured surface and using a pastry scraper and floured hands, gently fold the dough, without punching down. Shape lengthwise and then cut into 6 or 7 equal pieces. Gently shape each piece into a round ball then shape each piece into a loaf shape tucking the creases underneath. Place each loaf in a buttered or sprayed pan and cover with plastic lightly. Let the dough rise for 90 minutes in a warmed oven. When the individual loaves have risen to approximately ⅔ the original size take out of the oven and brush egg mixture on top of each loaf. Position rack in the center of the oven and bake at 375° for 45 minutes. Remove when the crust is browned and the loaf sounds hollow when tapped. When baked, remove from the baking pans, place on a cooling grill and cover with a soft cloth. Makes about 6 - 7 loaves.

FAT FREE BANANA CRUNCH MUFFINS

Jenna C. - Age 13

1 cup flour
½ cup Grape Nuts cereal
½ cup sugar
½ tsp. baking powder
½ tsp. baking soda
¼ tsp. salt

2 medium ripe bananas, mashed
(about 1 cup)
½ cup plain yogurt or sour
cream
¼ cup egg substitute
½ tsp. vanilla extract

Preheat oven to 350°. Spray muffin pan. Mix flour, Grape Nuts, sugar, baking powder, baking soda and salt. Mash bananas, yogurt, egg, vanilla in a separate bowl. Stir in flour mixture until just moist. Spoon into pan. Bake 20 minutes or until golden brown. Makes 24 mini muffins. Muffin: 55 cal., Og. fat, O mg chol., 65 mg. sodium.

98890-09

FUN BREAD

Emily M - Age 13

1 piece of bread   cream cheese
1 cup whole grain cereal

How Funnnnnnnn! The only thing you need for this recipe is creativity. All you need to do is spread the cream cheese on the bread and arrange the cereal into any picture you want.

GHOST TOAST

Brady Douglas - Age 6

1 slice bread   1 T. powdered sugar
2 tsp. butter   4 chocolate chips

Toast the bread in the toaster. Spread with butter. Sprinkle with powdered sugar until bread is completely covered. Cut the slice of bread in half (vertically). This will give you two ghost shaped pieces. Add the chocolate chips for the eyes. Enjoy. This is great for breakfast in October!!!

GREAT GRANDMA'S PUMPKIN BREAD

Andy Gates - Age 12

1 cup vegetable oil   1 tsp. nutmeg
4 eggs   1 tsp. cinnamon
2/3 cup water   2 tsp. baking soda
2 cups canned pumpkin   3 cups sugar
3 1/3 cups flour   Optional: raisins, chocolate,
1 1/2 tsp. salt   cinnamon chips or walnuts

Makes 2 Loaves. Grease 2 9 x 5 inch loaf pans. Mix oil, eggs, water, and pumpkin. Stir in flour, salt, nutmeg, cinnamon, baking soda and sugar. Bake at 350 degrees for 65 minutes, or longer. Test center with clean knife. Cool on wire racks. Recipe can be halved.

GREAT-GRANDMA'S DINNER ROLLS

Sophia Brielle - Age 16 months

2 pkgs. dry yeast   3 eggs, beaten
3 cups warm water   9-10 cups flour
1 cup sugar   6 T. margarine
2 tsp. salt

Dissolve yeast in water. Add sugar, salt, and beaten eggs. Add half the flour; mix well. Add melted margarine, then rest of flour. Dough will be sticky. Form into shape by kneading gently for a few minutes (on a

(continued)

floured surface.) Cover and let rise for about 2 hours in a warm place. Punch down and make into rolls. Let rise 30-45 minutes. Bake 25-30 minutes in 325 degree oven. (This dough will keep in refrigerator over night.)

HIDE & SEEK MUFFINS

Katie Scarlett - Age 11

1½ cup cups Flour
2 level tsp. Baking Powder
½ level tsp. Baking Soda
½ level tsp. Salt
¼ cup cup Sugar
2 Eggs

1 cup cup Milk
½ level tsp. Vanilla
4 level tblsp. Butter, melted
12 med. Strawberries
3 tblsp. Sugar

Preheat oven to 375°. Put paper cups in muffin pan. Crack 2 eggs into bowl. Add 1 cup milk, ½ tsp. vanilla. Melt 4 tablespoons of butter. Whisk. In a separate bowl, mix 1½ cups flour, 2 tsp. baking powder, ½ tsp. baking soda, ½ tsp. salt, ¼ cup sugar. Pour wet into dry mixture. Mix with spoon. Fill the muffin cups halfway. Roll fruit in sugar. Push into center of muffin. Bake 15 min.

HOT HAM BUNS

Kevin Coppin - Age 13

¼ cup soft butter
2 tblsp prepared horseradish
  mustard
2 tsp. poppy seed

2 tblsp finely chopped onions
4 pkgs. hamburger buns split
4 slices boiled ham
4 slices Swiss cheese

Mix butter, mustard, poppy seed and onion. Spread mixture on cut surfaces of buns. Tuck a slice of ham and cheese in each bun. Arrange on baking sheet. Bake at 350 degrees about 20 minutes.

IRISH SODA BREAD

Pauline - Age 4

3½ cups flour
⅓ cup sugar
2 tsp. baking soda
½ tsp. salt
½ tsp. cream of tartar

1½ cups raisins
1⅓ cups buttermilk
1 egg, slightly beaten
¼ vegetable oil

Preheat the oven to 350 degrees. Combine the first five dry ingredients in a large bowl. Stir in raisins. In another bowl, combine buttermilk, egg, and vegetable oil and then add to dry ingredients. Stir dough until moist. Pour into two round pie tins. Bake for 45 minutes or until bread is golden brown on top. Slice and serve plain or with butter. Makes two round loaves.

98890-09

MAGIC MARSHMALLOW CRESCENT PUFFS

Kendall E. - Age 6

¼ c. Sugar
2 T. Flour
1 tsp. Cinnamon
2 cans Pillsbury Crescent
  Dinner Rolls
16 large Marshmallows

¼ c. Butter, melted
½ c. Powdered Sugar
½ tsp. Vanilla
2 tsp. Milk
¼ c. Chopped Nuts, if desired

1. Heat over to 375°F. Spray 16 muffin cups with nonstick cooking spray. In small bowl, combine sugar, flour and cinnamon; mix well. 2. Separate dough into 16 triangles. Dip 1 marshmallow in butter; roll in sugar mixture. Place marshmallow on shortest side of triangle. Roll up starting at shortest side of triangle and rolling to opposite point. Completely cover marshmallow with dough; firmly pinch edges to seal. Dip 1 end in remaining butter; place butter side down in sprayed muffin cup. Repeat with remaining marshmallows. 3. Bake at 375°F for 12 to 15 minutes or until golden brown (be sure to place foil on rack below muffin cups to guard against spills). Remove from oven; cool 1 minute. Remove from muffin cups; place on wire racks set over waxed paper. Be careful not to puncture the puff when removing from the pan or center mixture can run out as the marshmallow has melted. 4. In small bowl, blend powdered sugar, vanilla and enough milk for desired drizzling consistency. Drizzle over warm rolls. Sprinkle with nuts.

MARSHMALLOW CINNAMON ROLLS

Jack Davis - Age 6
Grant Preston - Age 11

1 (8-oz.) pkg. refrigerated
  crescent rolls
8 large marshmallows

½ cup sugar
1 tsp. cinnamon

1. Heat oven to 375° 2. Separate dough into 8 triangles. 3. Mix cinnamon and sugar to make cinnamon sugar and set aside. Place 1 marshmallow right in the middle of each triangle. Sprinkle each marshmallow with some cinnamon sugar. 4. Bring up the sides of the roll to cover the marshmallow. Pinch edges together so none of the marshmallow shows. 5. Cover a cookie sheet with parchment paper. Place the rolls on the parchment paper, making sure none are touching. Sprinkle with more cinnamon sugar. 6. Bake 10 minutes until light brown and puffed up. Makes 8 cinnamon rolls.

MARTIAN MARSHMALLOW PUFFS

Claudia Kathrynee - Age 12

1/4 cup sugar
1 tsp. cinnamon
2 (8-oz.) cans Crescent Dinner
  Rolls

16 lg. marshmallows
1/4 cup margarine, melted

Makes 16 servings. Preheat oven to 375°. Combine sugar and cinnamon. Separate crescent dough into 16 triangles. Dip each marshmallow in melted margarine and roll in cinnamon-sugar mixture. Wrap a triangle of dough around each marshmallow and seal all gaps. Dip again in margarine then place in muffin cups. Bake for 10-15 minutes, or until golden brown.

MINI BLUEBERRY MUFFINS

Kendall Blair - Age 12

6 tsp. unsalted butter, room
  temperature
1/2 tsp. finely grated lemon zest
3/4 cup granulated sugar
2 eggs
1 3/4 cups all-purpose flour
2 tsp. baking powder

3/4 tsp. salt
3/4 cup milk
1 1/2 tblsp. vanilla extract
1 pint fresh blueberries or
  frozen unsweetened
  blueberries, unthawed
6 tblsp. turbino sugar

Preheat oven to 375°. Spray a mini muffin pan with nonstick cooking spray. In the bowl of an electric mixer, beat butter, lemon zest and granulated sugar until light and fluffy (3-4 minutes). Add eggs one at a time. In a bowl stir dry ingredients. Add milk and vanilla to mixer. Add flour mixture until evenly moist. Fold in the blueberries with a rubber spatula only using a few strokes. Spoon batter into mini muffin tins. Sprinkle each muffin with 1/4 tablespoon of turbino sugar. Bake 18-20 minutes until light golden or toothpick comes out clean. Transfer to a wire rack to cool. Makes 24 mini muffins.

MONKEY BREAD

Ellie Mary Colleen - Age 7

4 tube refrigerator biscuits
1 1/3 cups sugar
1 tsp. vanilla

2 tsp. cinnamon
1 stick margarine

Cut each biscuit into 3 pieces - kids can help pull them apart. With a big spoon, mix together 2/3 cup of the sugar and 1 tsp. of cinnamon in a large bowl. Roll each piece of biscuit dough in the mixture. Grease a 12-c bundt pan with a bit of butter. Drop the pieces of dough into the pan. In a small saucepan stir together the remaining sugar, butter, cinnamon and vanilla. Heat on the stove until it reaches a boil. Pour

(continued)

98890-09

over the dough and bake at 350 degrees for 40 minutes. When done, turn the monkey bread onto a plate and serve warm.

MONKEY BREAD

Hanna Claire - Age 9

4 cans small "country style"
  biscuits
2 sticks butter, melted
1 tsp. vanilla
3 T. cinnamon

1 packed cup brown sugar
½ cup sugar
½ cup ground cloves
½ cup ground nutmeg
½ cup pecan pieces

Preheat oven to 350° F. Make topping by combining melted butter, brown sugar, vanilla and ½ tsp. cinnamon. Spray a bundt pan very well with Pam. Place pecans on bottom of pan. Coat biscuits by rolling in mixture of 2+ tablespoons cinnamon, sugar and spices. Place coated biscuits along bottom of bundt pan and cover the gaps as layering. Pour butter mixture over biscuits. Bake at 350° for about 25 minutes. Invert onto a plate before cooling too much.

MONKEY BREAD

Stacy Michele Spangler - Age 16

4 cans refrigerated biscuits
¾ cup sugar
2 T. cinnamon

¾ cup melted butter
2 tsp. cinnamon
¾ cup brown sugar

First, cut biscuits into quarters. Then, combine ¾ cup sugar and 2 T. cinnamon in a large plastic Ziploc bag. Put each quarter of biscuit into the bag and shake to coat bits in cinnamon-sugar. Put the coated pieces into a bundt pan. Combine butters, brown sugar and 2 tsp. cinnamon in an sauce pan Dissolve the sugar, but do not boil. Pour the glaze over biscuit pieces. Bake in preheated oven at 350° for 30 minutes. Wait 5 minutes or so before serving, and enjoy your Monkey Bread!

MONKEY BREAD

Zach David - Age 8

4 cans small "country style"
  biscuits
2 T. cinnamon -- or a little more
  for taste
½ cup sugar
pinch ground cloves

pinch ground nutmeg
2 sticks butter - melted
1 tsp. vanilla
½ - 1 tsp. cinnamon
1 cup packed brown sugar
pecan pieces

Preheat oven to 350° F. Combine over medium heat the ingredients to make the topping (2 sticks butter - melted, 1 tsp. vanilla, ½-1 tsp. cinnamon and 1 cup brown sugar). Spray a Bundt pan with Pam. Place

(continued)

pecans on bottom of pan. Roll biscuits in coating mixture (2 TBS cinnamon -- or a little more for taste, 1/2 cup sugar, pinch of ground cloves and ground nutmeg). Place coated biscuits along bottom of Bundt pan and cover the gaps as layering. Pour topping mixture over biscuits. Bake at 350° F for about 25 minutes. Invert onto a plate before cooling too much.

MONKEY'S BEST BANANA BREAD

Ally Haug - Age 13

2-3 medium ripe bananas, smashed
1/3 cup melted butter
2/3 cup sugar
2 eggs
2 tsp. baking soda
1/4 tsp. salt
1 3/4 cups flour
1/3 cup butter
2 tblsp milk

Pre-heat oven to 350 degrees. Combine 1 cup of flour, sugar, baking soda, and salt in a large mixing bowl. Add mashed banana, butter, and milk. Mix with a wooden spoon until well blended. Add remaining flour and mix until smooth. Pour into a loaf pan and bake for 55-60 minutes. Cool for 10 minutes. Cut and enjoy! (One loaf makes 16 servings)

NANA'S PUMPKIN BREAD

Kamren Christopher - Age 5 1/2
Keaten Lawrence - Age 7

4 Eggs
3 cups Sugar
1-lb. can Pumpkin
2/3 cup Water
1 cup Oil
3 1/3 cups Flour
2 tsp. Baking Soda
1 1/2 tsp. Salt
1 tsp. Cinnamon
1 tsp. Nutmeg

Beat eggs. Add sugar, pumpkin, water and oil to eggs and mix. In another bowl, sift flour, baking soda, salt, cinnamon, and nutmeg. Add dry mixture to egg mixture and stir. Grease 4 large loaf pans and put batter into pans. Bake 350° for 55-60 minutes. Freeze extra loaves or surprise a neighbor with a tasty treat! For a dessert, try adding chocolate chips, YUM!

NO-BAKE CINNAMON

Kailey Smith

2 slices white bread, crusts removed
2 tblsp. butter
2 tblsp. cinnamon sugar
2 tblsp. confectioners' sugar
1/8 tsp. water, or as needed

Roll the bread slices until very flat. Butter the bread and sprinkle with cinnamon sugar. Starting on one side, roll up the bread slice until tight.

(continued)

98890-09

Repeat with the second bread slice. Cut the bread rolls into 1 inch slices. Mix the confectioners' sugar with the water in a small bowl to make a thin frosting. Drizzle frosting over the bread slices, and serve.

OPRAH'S CORN FRITTERS

Oprah Winfrey

⅔ cup yellow cornmeal
⅓ cup self-rising flour
1 cup buttermilk
1 egg, beaten
2 ears of corn, shucked or ½
cup frozen or canned corn

2 tblsp. unsalted butter, melted
milk or water, if needed
(optional)

Microwave the corn on high for 2 or 3 minutes. Slice off the kernels, and set them aside. In a bowl, mix the cornmeal and the flour well, using a wire whisk. This will make your fritters very light. In a separate bowl, whisk together the buttermilk and the egg. Gradually add the wet ingredients to the dry. Don't worry if the batter isn't completely combined; you want to be careful not to over mix it. Fold in the corn and add the butter if desired. If the result is thicker than pancake batter, thin it with a little milk or water. Heat a skillet or a griddle to medium, spray with Pam, and add spoonfuls of batter. Cook the fritters for 2 minutes per side. A great way to tell if they're ready to turn is to look for little bubbles all over the surface. You might have to make a few fritters before they start coming out perfectly. Serve with honey or your favorite syrup. Makes 4 servings.

PISTACHIO BREAD

Issac Noah - Age 7

2 boxes Pistachio Pudding
1 box Yellow Cake
½ cup Oil

1 cup Water
5 Eggs

Mix all ingredients together. Pour into 2 lightly greased and floured 9 x 5 x 3 inch pans. Bake in a 350 degree oven about 55 minutes or until a toothpick comes out clean. Enjoy!

PIZZA ROLLERS

Meghan and Gavin Cahill

2 (10-oz.) packages refrigerated
pizza dough
1 cup pizza sauce

36 slices turkey pepperoni
12 sticks mozzarella cheese

1. Preheat oven to 425 degrees. Coat baking sheet with nonstick cooking spray. 2. Roll out pizza dough on baking sheet to form a 12 x 9-inch

(continued)

rectangle. Cut pizza dough into 6 (4½ x 4-inch) rectangles. Repeat with remaining dough. Spread about one tablespoon of sauce over center third of each rectangle. Top with three slices of pepperoni and a stick of mozzarella cheese. Bring ends of dough together over cheese, pinching to seal. Place seam side down on prepared baking sheet. 3. Bake in center of oven for 10 minutes or until golden brown. Cool slightly. Makes 12 rollers.

POPOVERS

Shivani S - Age 9
Sanjiv N - Age 6

2 tblsp butter
2 eggs
1 cup milk

1 cup flour
¼ tsp. salt

Preheat oven to 375 degrees F, and melt butter. "Paint" the inside of 12 standard muffin cups (no muffin papers needed) with melted butter. In a mixing bowl, break the eggs, add the milk and beat well. Add the flour and salt and whisk until just combined. Pour ¼ cup of batter into each muffin cup until one-half to two-thirds full. Bake for 30 minutes without opening your oven. Remove and enjoy with jam or syrup!

PUMPKIN BREAD

Kyle Thomas - Age 8
Brandon Paul - Age 5

4 eggs
2 c. sugar
2 c. pumpkin
1 c. vegetable oil
⅔ c. water

1 tsp. nutmeg
1 tsp. cinnamon
2 tsp. baking soda
3½ c. flour

Mix all ingredients together in large bowl by beating with an electric mixer. Pour into 2 large or 4 small greased and floured loaf pans. Bake 1 hour at 350 degrees. When cool, remove from pans. Freezes well.

PUMPKIN CHOCOLATE CHIP MUFFINS

Allison Grace - Age 9
Kevin Daniel - Age 7

1⅔ cup flour
1 cup sugar
2¼ tsp. cinnamon
½ tsp. nutmeg
¼ tsp. ground ginger
1 tsp. baking soda

¼ tsp. salt
¼ tsp. baking powder
2 large eggs
1 can pumpkin
½ cup vegetable oil
1 cup chocolate chips

(continued)

98890-09

Heat oven to 350 degrees. Mix flour, sugar, spices, baking soda, salt and baking powder in a large bowl. Break eggs into another bowl. Add pumpkin and oil and whisk until just blended. Stir in chocolate chips. Pour over dry ingredients and fold in until the dry ingredients are just moistened. Scoop batter in muffin cups. Bake 20-25 minutes (or 15 minutes for mini muffins) until puffed and springy in the center. Cool. Store in plastic bags and keep for 1-2 days or freeze them.

PUMPKIN NUT BREAD

Issac Noah - Age 7

4 cups Flour
1 tblsp Pumpkin Pie Spice
2 tsp. Baking Powder
1 tsp. Baking Soda
³/₄ tsp. Salt
1 (15-oz.) can Pure Pumpkin
2 cups Packed Brown Sugar

1 cup Apple Juice
4 Large Eggs
¹/₄ cup Oil
1 tsp. Vanilla
1 cup Chopped Walnuts or
** Pecans**

Combine all dry ingredients and set aside. In a large bowl mix together pumpkin, brown sugar, juice, eggs, oil and vanilla. Mix well. Stir in dry ingredients and ³/₄ cup of the nuts. Spoon into 2 greased and lightly sugared 9 x 5 x 3 loaf pans. Sprinkle with remaining nuts. Bake in 350 degree oven for 60 to 70 minutes or until toothpick inserted in the center comes out clean. Enjoy!

QUICK AND EASY TO MAKE GIANT POPOVERS

Mary Lillie - Age 13

4 large eggs (room temperature)
1¹/₄ cups milk (room
** temperature)**

3 tblsp vegetable oil
1 cup flour
³/₄ tsp. salt

Grease the muffin tin with lots of cooking spray or butter and pre-heat the oven to 425 degrees. With a mixer, blend together the eggs, milk, and oil for 10 seconds on medium speed. Add in the flour and salt and mix for 15 more seconds on medium speed. Put the mixture into the muffin tins about ³/₄ full and bake for about 30 minutes until the popovers have doubled in size and are golden brown. Remove the pan from the oven and dump them onto a work surface or cooling rack, poke them with a wooden skewer or tooth pick to allow steam to escape. Serve immediately with butter or jam. YUM!

(Note: makes 12 Popovers)

SPAGEL

Nolan - Age 14
Gage - Age 12
Tye - Age 8

1 Onion or Plain Bagel　　　**Regular Cream Cheese**
1 slice Spam

Slice bagel in half if it isn't done for you already. Spread both sides with cream cheese. Put the slice of Spam on one side, then cover with the other side of the bagel to form a sandwich. Warm it in a toaster oven set at about 300° for about 5 minutes. Enjoy your Spagel!

STRAWBERRY BREAD

Marissa Nicole - Age 7

2 cup Fresh Strawberries　　**1 tspn Salt**
3¹/₈ cup Flour　　　　　　　**1 tspn Baking Soda**
2 cup Sugar　　　　　　　　**1¹/₄ cup Vegetable oil**
1 tblsp Ground Cinnamon　　**4 Eggs, Beaten**

Preheat oven to 350 degrees. Grease and lightly flour two 9 x 5 inch loaf pans. Slice strawberries and place in a medium sized bowl. Sprinkle lightly with sugar and set aside while preparing bread mixture. Combine flour, sugar, cinnamon, salt and baking soda in a large bowl, mix well. Blend oil and eggs into strawberries. Add strawberry mixture to flour mixture, blending until dry ingredients are moist. Divide batter into pans. Bake for 45 to 50 minutes, or until tester inserted comes out clean. Let cool in pans on wire rack for 10 minutes. Turn loaves out, and cool completely.

SUPER GREAT CINNAMON STICKS

Reed Sincox - Age 13

1 sheet puff pastry, thawed　　**1 tsp. cinnamon**
1 egg　　　　　　　　　　　　**2 tblsp. sugar**

Preheat the oven to 400° F. Lightly butter or spray a baking sheet. Unfold the puff pastry and place it on a large work surface. Beat the egg in a small bowl and brush it over the puff pastry, coating it lightly. Combine the cinnamon and sugar in another small bowl and sprinkle evenly over the puff pastry. Cut the puff pasty into 1-inch-wide strips. Twist each strip several times and place it on the baking Sheet. Bake for 12 minutes, or until lightly brown.

SWEDISH TEA RING

Annabelle Amelia - Age 5
Elizabeth Ella - Age 3
Great Grandma Peifer

1 small pkg. Yeast	1 Egg Beaten
¼ cup Luke Warm Water	Melted Butter
1 cup Scaled Milk	½ cup chopped nuts, raisins or
¾ tsp. Salt	¼ cup blueberries if desired
¼ cup Sugar	sprinkle cinnamon over melted
6 tblsp. Crisco/Shortening	butter if desired
3½ cups Sifted Flour	

Soften yeast in water. Combine scalded milk, salt, sugar and shortening. When lukewarm, add yeast and half the flour and beat well. Let rise until very light, then add egg and remaining flour. Mix well. Let rise. Roll dough into a rectangular sheet on a lightly floured board. Brush with melted butter and sprinkle with nuts or raisins. Roll up like a jelly roll and form into a ring on greased baking sheet. Using a large pair of scissors, cut ring around edge at 2 inch intervals, leaving inner edge intact. Turn each slice to lie flat on pan. Let rise until light and bake in hot oven (400 degrees F) about 30 minutes. Frost while hot with confectioners' sugar frosting. Makes 1 large ring.

WHITE FLATBREAD

Timothy Sebastien - Age 5
Sophia Claire - Age 3

1½ c. flour	1 T. olive oil
¼ tsp. salt	½ c. water

In a food processor, combine the flour and salt. Pulse several times to mix. With the processor running, drizzle in the olive oil, then let the processor run for 10 seconds to blend. With the processor running, drizzle in the water. Continue processing until the dough mostly comes together and forms a ball. Continue processing for another 30 seconds to knead the dough. The dough should be moist but not wet. Transfer the dough to a lightly floured counter and shape into a ball. Divide the dough into six pieces, then use a rolling pin to roll each until very thing and about the size of a salad plate. Do not stack the dough, as they will stick. Heat a grill or large, dry skillet over medium heat. One at a time, place a flatbread in the pan or on the grill. Once the bottom is lightly browned in spots (about one minute) and the bread begins to bubble, use tongs to flip the flatbread. Cook for about another minute. Repeat with the remaining dough. To keep the finished flatbreads warm as you cook, place them on a dinner plate and cover with a pot lid or foil.

WHOLE WHEAT CARROT CRANBERRY MUFFINS
(Dairy Free)

Timothy Sebastien - Age 5
Sophia Claire - Age 3

1 lb. baby carrots, steamed	1¼ tsp. baking soda
1 egg	½ tsp. baking powder
6 T. applesauce	½ tsp. salt
2 T. vegetable oil	½ tsp. nutmeg, grated
1 c. whole-wheat flour	½ tsp. cinnamon
¾ c. white flour	⅛ tsp. allspice
¾ c. sugar	1½ c. dried cranberries

Place carrots, applesauce and oil in a food processor; cover and process until smooth. In a large bowl, combine the flours, sugar, baking soda, salt, and spices. In a small bowl, whisk the puréed carrots mixture and egg; stir into the dry ingredients just until moistened. Fold in cranberries. Fill muffin cups almost full. Makes 12 muffins. Bake at 350 for 20-25 minutes or until a toothpick comes out clean. Cool for 5 minutes before removing from pan to a wire rack. Serve warm.

YUMMY ZUCCHINI BREAD

Griffin Matthew - Age 3

3 cups flour	2¼ cups sugar
1 tsp. salt	3 tsp. vanilla extract
1 tsp. baking soda	2 cups grated zucchini
1 tsp. baking powder	½ cup regular oats
3 tsp. cinnamon	½ cup brown sugar
3 eggs	¼ cup flour
½ cup oil	¼ tsp. cinnamon
½ cup applesauce	¼ cup cold, diced butter

1. Preheat oven to 325°. Grease and flour two 8"x4" loaf pans. 2. Sift flour, salt, baking soda, baking powder, and cinnamon. 3. Beat together eggs, oil, applesauce, vanilla, and sugar. Add the sifted ingredients and beat well. Pour in the grated zucchini, and stir to combine. 4. Pour into prepared loaf pans, and bake 40-60 minutes. 5. While bread is baking, make the streusel topping. Combine oats, brown sugar, flour, cinnamon, and cold diced butter until the mixture forms large crumbs. Top bread with the mixture halfway through baking time. 6. Allow bread to cool in the pan for 20 minutes.

98890-09

ZUCCHINI BREAD

Issac Noah - Age 7

3 Eggs
1 cup Oil
2 cups Sugar
3 cups Flour
2 tsp. Baking Soda
1½ tsp. Cinnamon
1 tsp. Salt

2 tsp. Vanilla
2 cups Shredded Unpeeled
  Zucchini
1 (8-oz.) can Crushed Pineapple
¾ tsp. Nutmeg
¼ tsp. Baking Powder
1 cup Chopped Dates or Nuts

Beat eggs until thick along with oil, sugar and vanilla. Stir in remaining ingredients; mix well. Pour into 2 well greased and lightly floured 9 x 5 x 3 inch loaf pans. Bake about 1 hour in a 350 degree oven or until a toothpick inserted in center comes out clean. Enjoy!

Recipe Favorites

Recipe Favorites

DESSERTS

Helpful Hints

- Keep eggs at room temperature for greater volume when whipping egg whites to make meringue.

- Pie dough can be frozen. Roll dough out between sheets of plastic wrap, stack in a pizza box, and keep the box in the freezer. Defrost in the fridge and use as needed. Use within 2 months.

- Place your pie plate on a cake stand when ready to flute the edges of the pie. The cake stand will make it easier to turn the pie plate, and you won't have to stoop over.

- When making decorative pie edges, use a spoon for a scalloped edge. Use a fork to make crosshatched and herringbone patterns.

- When cutting butter into flour for pastry dough, the process is easier if you cut the butter into small pieces before adding it to the flour.

- Pumpkin and other custard-style pies are done when they jiggle slightly in the middle. Fruit pies are done when the pastry is golden, juices bubble, and fruit is tender.

- Keep the cake plate clean while frosting by sliding 6-inch strips of waxed paper under each side of the cake. Once the cake is frosted and the frosting is set, pull the strips away, leaving a clean plate.

- Create a quick decorating tube to ice your cake with chocolate. Put chocolate in a heat-safe, zipper-lock plastic bag. Immerse it in simmering water until the chocolate is melted. Snip off the tip of one corner, and squeeze the chocolate out of the bag.

- Achieve professionally decorated cakes with a silky, molten look by blow-drying the frosting with a hair dryer until the frosting melts slightly.

- To ensure that you have equal amounts of batter in each pan when making a layered cake, use a kitchen scale to measure the weight.

- Help prevent cracking in your cheesecake during baking by placing a shallow pan of hot water on the bottom oven rack. Do not open the oven door during baking.

- A cheesecake needs several hours to chill and set.

- For a perfectly cut cheesecake, first dip the knife into water, and clean it after each cut. Or hold a length of dental floss taut between your hands and pull the floss down through the cheesecake, making a clean cut across the diameter of the cake.

DESSERTS

"ESPECIALLY DARK" CHOCOLATE CAKE

Sam Bonham

2 cup cups Sugar	1 1 tsp. salt
1-³⁄₄ cup cups all-purpose flour	2 1 pcs. eggs
1³⁄₄ cup Hersheys "special dark" Cocoa	1 1 cup milk
	1½ c. vegetable oil
1 1½ tsp. baking powder	2 1 tblsp boiling water
1 1½ tsp. baking soda	2 1 tsp. vanilla extract

Heat oven to 350°F. Grease and flour two 9-inch round baking pans. Stir together sugar, flour, cocoa, baking powder, baking soda and salt in large bowl. Add eggs, milk, oil and vanilla; beat on medium speed of mixer 2 minutes. Stir in boiling water (batter will be thin). Pour batter into prepared pans. Bake 30 to 35 minutes or until wooden pick inserted in center comes out clean. Cool 10 minutes; remove from pans to wire racks. Cool completely. Frost with "Especially Dark" Chocolate frosting. 10-12 servings.

"Especially Dark" Chocolate frosting.

1 1 stick butter	3 cup c. powdered sugar
²⁄₃ cup c. Hershey's Special Dark Cocoa	¹⁄₃ cup c. milk
	1 1 tsp. vanilla extract

Melt butter. Stir in cocoa. Alternately add powdered sugar and milk, beating to spreading consistency. Add small amount additional milk, if needed. Stir in vanilla. About 2 cups frosting.

5 MINUTE CHOCOLATE MUG CAKE

Judy Pazdan - Age 10

4 tblsp flour	3 tblsp oil
4 tblsp sugar	3 tblsp chocolate chips (optional)
2 tblsp cocoa	
1 egg	splash vanilla extract
3 tblsp milk	1 lg. coffee mug

Add dry ingredients to mug, and mix well. Add the egg and mix thoroughly. Pour in the milk and oil and mix well. Add the chocolate chips (if using) and vanilla extract, and mix again. Put your mug in the microwave and cook for 3 minutes at 1000 watts. The cake will rise over the top of the mug, but don't be alarmed! Allow to cool a little, and tip out onto a plate if desired. EAT! (this can serve 2 if you want to feel slightly more virtuous). And why is this the most dangerous cake recipe in the world? Because now we are all only 5 minutes away from chocolate cake at any time of the day or night!

5 MINUTE CHOCOLATE MUG CAKE

Griffin Pierce - Age 6
Ethan Tracy - Age 9
Tucker George - Age 11

4 T. flour
4 T. sugar
2 T. cocoa
1 egg
3 T. milk

3 T. oil
3 T. chocolate chips (optional)
1 splash vanilla
1 large coffee mug (microsafe)

Add dry ingredients to the mug and mix well. Using a fork, stir the egg in a small bowl before adding it to the mug. Then, add the egg, milk, oil, and vanilla. Mix well. Put your mug in the microwave and cook for 3 minutes at 1000 watts. The cake will rise over the top of the mug, but don't be alarmed! Take it out carefully and let it cool for a few minutes. Tip it out on a plate, add a scoop of ice cream, and enjoy!

A WHOPPER OF A DESSERT

Kelsey Ann - Age 13

3$\frac{1}{3}$ cups malted milk balls
12 oz. frozen whipped topping, thawed

12 frozen ice cream sandwiches
1 cup hot fudge sauce

Place malted milk balls in resealable bag. Tap with rolling pin until coarsely chopped. Reserve $\frac{1}{3}$ cup. Mix remaining crushed malted milk balls and the whipped topping. Arrange ice cream sandwiches in bottom of 13 x 9 x 2 pan. Spread whipped topping mixture over ice cream sandwiches. Sprinkle with reserved malted milk balls. Cover and freeze 2 to 3 hours or until firm. Cut and top with fudge sauce.

ANGEL CUPCAKES

Ashley - Age 12

1 cup milk
6 large eggs whites
1 tsp. vanilla extract
2$\frac{1}{4}$ cups flour
1$\frac{3}{4}$ cups sugar

4 tsp. baking powder
12 tblsp. butter, unsalted, softened, and cut
1 tsp. salt
M&Ms

Makes about 18 cupcakes. Set oven to 350°. Put cup liners into muffin pans. Take a medium bowl and mix the milk, egg whites and vanilla extract together with a fork until blended. At low speed, in an electric mixer, mix the flour sugar, baking powder, and salt together. Add $\frac{1}{2}$ cup of milk mixture to dry ingredients bowl and mix for about 1 minute at medium speed. Add the rest of the milk mixture and mix for about 30 seconds more. Scrape the sides of the bowl and mix for another 20 seconds. Pour batter into muffin cups until about 80% full. Bake cup-

(continued)

cakes for about 20 minutes. Insert a toothpick into center of a cupcake. If it comes out clean they are finished. Let cupcakes cool for 10 minutes. Cool cupcakes for about an hour before frosting. After frosting, add as many M&Ms as desired.

Pastel Frosting

2 sticks unsalted butter	pinch of salt
5 cups sugar	2 tblsp. milk or heavy cream
1 tblsp. vanilla extract	food coloring

Colors with food coloring: Red: 2 drops of red. Orange: 1 drop of yellow and 1 drop of red. Yellow: 2 drops of yellow. Green: 2 drops of green. Blue: 2 drops of blue. Purple: 1 drop of blue and 1 drop of red. Pink: 1 drop of red. Brown: 2 drops of blue, 2 drops of red, 2 drops of yellow, and 2 drops of green. Gray: 1 drop of blue, 1 drop of red, and 1 drop of green. Beat sugar, butter, vanilla extract, heavy cream or milk, and salt in a large bowl. Beat with large spoon for about 8 minutes or until nice and fluffy. Add the food coloring. Blend in the food coloring well with the mixture.

ANGEL FOOD CAKE

Amber Andreen

1 cup cake flour	1½ tsp. vanilla extract
1½ cup white sugar	1½ tsp. cream of tartar
12 egg whites	½ tsp. salt

Preheat oven to 375°. Be sure that your 10 inch tube pan is clean and dry. Any amount of oil residue could deflate the egg whites. Sift together the flour, and ¾ cup of the sugar, set aside. In a large bowl, whip the egg whites along with the vanilla, cream of tartar and salt, to medium stiff peaks. Gradually, add the remaining sugar while continuing to whip to stiff peaks. When the egg white mixture has reached its maximum volume, fold in the sifted ingredients gradually, one third at a time. Do not over mix. Put the batter into the tube pan. Bake for 40-45 minutes, until the cake springs back when touched. Balance the tub pan upside down on the top of a bottle, to prevent decompression while cooling. When cool, run a knife around the edge of the pan and invert onto plate. Serves 14.

ANGEL TOFFEE DESSERT

Heaven Gordon - Age 11

2 (3-oz.) packages cream cheese, softened	5 cup cubed angel food cake
½ cup confectioners' sugar	½ cup chocolate syrup
2 tblsp. milk	½ cup English toffee bits or almond brickle chips, divided
1 (8-oz.) carton frozen whipped topping, thawed	

(continued)

In a mixing bowl, beat cream cheese, sugar and milk until smooth. Fold in the whipped topping. Arrange cake cubes in an ungreased 11-in. x 7-in. x 2 in. dish. Drizzle with chocolate syrup. Set aside tablespoon of toffee bits; sprinkle remaining toffee bits over chocolate. Spread cream cheese mixture over top. Sprinkle with remaining toffee bits. Cover and chill until serving. Store leftovers in the refrigerator.

AUNT JUNE'S ECLAIR CAKE

Kamren Christopher - Age 5½
Keaten Lawrence - Age 7

1 box Graham Crackers
2 small Instant Vanilla Pudding

3½ cups Milk
1 (8-oz.) Cool Whip

Butter a 9 x 13 pan, line with graham crackers. Mix pudding with milk and beat on medium for 2 minutes. Blend in Cool Whip. Pour ½ the mixture over graham crackers. Add another layer of graham crackers, then pudding, ending with graham crackers. Refrigerate at least 2 hours.

AUNT JUNE'S ECLAIR CAKE ICING
(see Aunt June's eclair cake)

Kamren Christopher - Age 5½
Keaten Lawrence - Age 7

2 (1-oz.) pkgs. Pre-melted
  Chocolate
2 tsp. White Karo (Corn Syrup)
2 tsp. Vanilla

3 tblsp Softened Butter
1½ cups Powdered Sugar
3 tblsp Milk

Beat ingredients together. Spread over refrigerated cake. Refrigerate again at least 24 hours.

BANANA "SPLITS"

Samantha Payton - Age 9

8 marshmallows
1 banana
1 pkg. mini M&M's

whipped cream
ice cream

Using a tall glass, add 4 marshmallows, 4 slices of banana, a sprinkle of mini M&M's, a squirt of whipped cream, and a scoop of ice cream. Repeat layers. Top with remaining banana, mini M&M's, and whipped cream. Serve with a long spoon, and enjoy!

98890-09

BANANA DELIGHT

Kallie N. - Age 12

1½ cups Graham Cracker
  Crumbs
¼ cup sugar
6 tblsp. butter, melted
5 large bananas, cut into ¼"
  slices
2 (3.4-oz.) pkgs. banana cream
  flavored instant pudding and
  pie filling

3 cups cold milk
1 (8-oz.) tub frozen non-dairy
  whipped topping, thawed
Garnish (optional):
2 bananas
1 tblsp. lemon juice

Mix together graham cracker crumbs, sugar and melted butter in a bowl. Sprinkle half of crumb mixture in each 10-ounce custard cups or dessert dishes (approximately 2 ½ tablespoons mixture in each dish, enough for 8 cups). Reserve remaining crumb mixture. Place half of banana slices over crumb mixture in dishes. Reserve remaining banana slices. Combine pudding mix and milk in large bowl; beat with a wire whisk for 2 minutes. Spoon half of pudding over bananas in each dish (approximately 2 tablespoons pudding in each dish). Top each with an additional 2 ½ tablespoons crumb mixture and remaining bananas. Cover bananas with whipped topping (a heaping ¼ cup in each dish). Chill at least 15 minutes. Before serving, garnish with sliced bananas dipped in lemon juice, if desired. Makes 8 serving. Prep Time: 25 minutes Chilling Time: 15 minutes

BANANA EGG ROLLS

Alex Ray - Age 8
Robert Anthony - Age 7
Kayli Grace - Age 2

bunch bananas
½ pkg. egg roll wrappers
medium splash sugar
small splash ground cinnamon

small splashes whip cream
1 egg - beaten
1 cup cooking oil

Cut a banana in half, and then cut the half-banana in half, from top to bottom. Roll the 1 slice of the banana in an egg roll wrapper, sealing the wrapper with a touch of the beaten egg. Fry the banana egg roll over medium heat until the egg roll wrapper is a light golden brown; once a light golden brown, remove from the oil, remove excess oil with a paper towel, lightly roll the banana egg roll in the sugar, on a plate. Sprinkle a little cinnamon, top with whip cream and serve!

BANANA PUDDING

Tyshun - Age 10

¾ c. sugar
3 T. all-purpose flour
2 c. milk
3 egg yolks

1 tsp. vanilla
4 T. (½ stick) butter
3 med. bananas, sliced
1 pkg. vanilla wafers

Mix together sugar and flour and slowly add milk. This should be cooked in the top of a double boiler. But you can cook it over low to medium heat, stirring constantly until it thickens. Do not leave unattended. Slightly beat egg yolk and temper with a small amount of the hot custard, stir well. Add vanilla and butter. Add egg mixture to the custard pot and cook. Layer wafers, custard, and bananas. Cook until starts to brown. Serves 8 to 10.

BANANA PUDDING IV

Justin Fernandes

1 (8-oz.) pkg. cream cheese
1 (14-oz.) can sweetened
  condensed milk
1 (5-oz.) pkg. instant vanilla
  pudding mix
3 cups cold milk

1 tsp. vanilla extract
1 (8-oz.) container frozen
  whipped topping, thawed
4 bananas, sliced
½ (12-oz.) pkg. vanilla wafers

In a large bowl, beat cream cheese until fluffy. Beat in condensed milk, pudding mix, cold milk and vanilla until smooth. Fold in ½ of the whipped topping. Line the bottom of a 9 x 13 inch dish with vanilla wafers. Arrange sliced bananas evenly over wafers. Spread with pudding mixture. Top with remaining whipped topping. Chill.

BANANA SPLIT SUNDAE

Jessica Lynn - Age 6
Ryan Robert - Age 4

1 Banana
1 box Neapolitan ice cream
1 bottle Chocolate Syrup (like
  Hershey's)

1 Maraschino Cherry

What a yummy, old fashioned treat. And there is some nutrition, thanks to the banana and cherry! Peel and cut the banana in half, length wise. Set in the bottom of a bowl. Using an ice cream scooper (or a cookie dough scooper for smaller proportions), place a scoop of vanilla, strawberry and chocolate ice cream on top of the bananas. Drizzle on the chocolate syrup and place the cherry on top of the ice cream. Enjoy!

98890-09

BIRTHDAY BASH ICE CREAM CAKE

Patrick Michael - Age 6
Catherine Ashley - Age 4

1 1 pound pkg. Oreos
1 (12-oz.) bag M&Ms
1½ gal. chocolate ice cream
1½ gal. vanilla ice cream

1 bottle Betty Crocker Easy
Flow Decorating Icing
(optional)

Take ice cream out of freezer. Scoop vanilla ice cream into a stand mixer or a large bowl and let sit to soften. Separate the tops from the bottoms of a dozen Oreo cookies. Lay the Oreos (cream side up) on the bottom of a spring-form pan until the entire bottom is covered in a single layer. Scoop out the chocolate ice cream and lay on top of the Oreos. Cover chocolate ice cream with a piece of wax paper. Take the bottom of a heavy cup and pack the ice cream down until it forms a flat layer. Remove and discard the wax paper. Separate the tops from the bottoms of a dozen Oreos. Lay out the Oreos in a single layer (cream side up) until the chocolate ice cream is covered. Mix half the M&Ms into the bowl or mixer with the vanilla ice cream (if using a stand mixer, turn speed on lowest setting). Add additional M&Ms to taste preference. Scoop out the vanilla M&M ice cream and lay on top of the Oreos in the pan. Cover vanilla M&M ice cream with a piece of waxed paper and pack down the ice cream with the bottom of a cup until it forms a flat layer. Remove the wax paper and discard. Cover the entire top of the cake with saran wrap and freeze for 24 hours. After 24 hours, remove side of spring form pan (you may need to let it defrost for a minute or two to loosen clasp of pan). The cake will look festive with the M&Ms. If desired, decorate with Easy Flow Decorating Icing and re-freeze for a few hours to make the icing solid.

BLUEBERRY COBBLER

Mary Beth - Age 13

2 (20-oz.) cans blueberry pie
filling
½ cup softened margarine

1 box white cake mix
1 egg

Spread pie filling in a 9 X 13 baking pan. In a large bowl cream margarine. Add dry cake mix and egg. Blend well. Spoon over pie filling. Bake at 350° for 40 minutes.

BLUEBERRY FRENCH PIE

Caroline Elise - Age 6
Natalie Kate - Age 3

1 cup Crushed graham crackers
1 cup Any type of nuts
1/2 cup melted butter
1 (8-oz.) container cream cheese
1 cup powder sugar
2 boxes dream whip mix

1 tsp. vanilla
1 can blueberry pie filling
1 cup Flour
Small amount of milk for dream
whip

Preheat oven to 400 degrees. For the crust, mix together the flour, graham crackers, nuts and melted butter. Press down into the bottom of an 8 x 8 inch size buttered pan. Bake at 400 degrees for fifteen minutes or until the crust is a little crumbly. For the filling, cream together the cream cheese, powdered sugar and vanilla. Next prepare the dream whip using the instructions on the box. Fold the cream cheese mixture into the dream whip mixture. Spread the cream cheese mixture on top of the cooled crust. Top with blueberry pie filling or whatever flavor you prefer.

BOO BERRY POPSICLES

Marissa Nicole - Age 7

1 1/2 cup Fresh Blueberries
1 cup Ice Cubes

1 cup Milk
4 small Strawberries

Blend blueberries, ice and milk together until no lumps are present. Pour mixture into popsicle forms. Cut strawberries into pieces. Place cut up strawberries into blueberry mixture. Freeze until solid. Remove from popsicle form and enjoy a berry healthy treat!!

BROWN SUGAR ROLL-UP

Kaleigh - Age 10

brown sugar
white or wheat tortilla

butter

Get a tortilla, brown sugar and butter. Place the brown sugar inside the tortilla. Then place the butter on top of that, and fill the inside with brown sugar. Put it in the microwave for one minute and wait until it cools off. Enjoy!

BROWNIE DELIGHT

Heaven Gordan - Age 11

1 package brownie mix
2 packages (one 8 oz., one 3 oz.) cream cheese softened
2 cup confectioner' sugar
1 (16-oz.) frozen whipped topping, thawed, divided

2 cup cold milk
1 package (3.9 oz.) instant chocolate pudding mix
½ cup chopped pecans

Prepare and bake brownies according to package directions. Cool completely on a wire rack. In a large mixing bowl, beat cream cheese and sugar until creamy. Fold in 2 cups whipped topping. Spread over brownies. In a small bowl, whisk milk and dry pudding mix for 2 minutes. Refrigerate for 5 minutes; spread over the cream cheese layer. Spread with remaining whipped topping; sprinkle with pecans. Chill until serving.

BUTTERSCOTCH BARS

Anna - Age 7
Luke - Age 5
Ashley - Age 3, Jake - Age 2

½ cup sugar
½ cup brown sugar
¼ cup butter, softened
2 large egg whites
1 tsp. vanilla

1¼ cup flour
½ tsp. baking powder
¼ tsp. salt
2 cup butterscotch morsels
cooking spray

Preheat oven to 350 degrees. Beat sugars and butter at medium speed. Add egg whites and vanilla. Mix flour, baking powder and salt, stir well with a whisk. Add flour mixture to sugar mixture. Beat at low speed until blended. Spread batter into 8 inch pan coated with cooking spray. Sprinkle evenly with butterscotch chips. Bake at 350 for 28 minutes. Cool in pan on wire rack.

BUTTERSCOTCH BROWNIES

Emma Elizabeth - Age 11
Jacob James - Age 8

¼ cup Butter
1 cup Light Brown Sugar
1 large Egg
¾ cup Flour
1 tsp. Baking Powder

½ tsp. Salt
½ tsp. Vanilla
½ cup Chopped Walnuts (optional)
1 cup White Chocolate Chips

Melt butter over low heat. Remove from heat. Blend in sugar. Cool. Stir in eggs. Blend in flour, baking powder, and salt. Stir in vanilla, nuts, and chips. Pour into a lightly greased 8 X 8 inch pan. Bake for 25 minutes in a 350° preheated oven. DO NOT over bake--bars should be soft and slightly chewy. Cut into bars while still warm.

BUTTERSCOTCH CHIP CAKE
(Best cake in the world!)

Austin Tyler - Age 13
Amy Margaret (Maggie) - Age 8

1 pkg. Butterscotch Instant
  Pudding Mix
2 cups Cold Milk

2 Large Beaten Eggs
1 pkg. Yellow Cake Mix
1 pkg. Butterscotch Chips

Preheat oven to 350 degrees. Grease 9 x 13 inch pan. Make pudding as directed on package in a large mixing bowl; add beaten eggs and cake mix. Blend well and pour into pan. Sprinkle butterscotch chips of top and then bake for 35 minutes. Cool cake and then sprinkle on powdered sugar.

CAMRYN'S CROISSANT DESSERT

Camryn Danielle - Age 9

5 Croissants
2 Medium Sized Chocolate Bars

5 of Your Favorite Fruits
½ cup Milk

Melt the chocolate bars in a bowl in the microwave. Stir in milk until smooth. Slice the croissants in half and fill with pieces of your favorite fruit. I like kiwi! You can cut the fruit filled croissants into bite sized pieces and let people dip them in the chocolate. Or, you can drizzle the chocolate over the croissants and serve them whole. Either way it is delicious!

CANDY SHOP PIZZA

Rachel Sue - Age 5

1 pkg. refrigerated Nestle Toll
  House Chocolate Chip Cookie
  Dough
1 cup Nestle Toll House Semi-
  Sweet Chocolate Morsels

½ cup creamy or chunky
  peanut butter
1 cup coarsely chopped
  assorted candy: Nestle Crunch,
  Butterfinger, Snickers, etc.

Press cookie dough evenly onto bottom of greased 12 -inch pizza pan or 13 X 9-inch baking pan. Bake in preheated 350 degree oven for 14 to 18 minutes or until edge is set and center is still slightly soft. Immediately sprinkle morsels over hot crust; drop peanut butter by spoonfuls onto morsels. Let stand for 5 minutes or until morsels become shiny and soft. Gently spread chocolate and peanut butter evenly over cookie crust. Sprinkle candy in single layer over pizza. Cut into wedges; serve warm or at room temperature. Makes 12 servings.

98890-09

CARAMEL BROWNIES

Erin - Age 10

1 pkg. German chocolate cake
  mix
2 small cans evaporated milk
¾ c. melted butter or margarine

1 T. vanilla extract
1 pkg. light Kraft caramels
1 small pkg. chocolate chips
flour

Preheat oven to 350°. Combine cake mix with ⅓ cup evaporated milk, vanilla, and margarine or butter. Split in half and put half in a 9 x 13 inch glass greased and floured pan. Bake 15 minutes in 350° oven. Melt caramels in double boiler with ⅓ cup of evaporated milk. Pour on cooled cake and spread evenly. Sprinkle chocolate chips on and in small chunks use the rest of cake mix on top. Bake at 350° for 10 to 15 minutes. Watch carefully so caramels don't burn. Serves 25.

CARROT CAKE

Wyatt - Age 13

Carrot Cake

2 cup sugar
1½ cup oil
4 eggs
2¼ cups flour
2 tsp. salt

2 tsp. cinnamon
3 cups grated carrots
1½ cups chopped nuts
2 tsp. baking soda

Combine sugar, oil and eggs; beat 2 minutes at medium speed. Sift dry ingredients; mix with sugar mixture. Add carrots and nuts. Spread in a greased 9 x 13 inch pan. Bake at 300 degrees for one hour.

Icing

(8-oz.) package softened cream
  cheese
¼ cup softened butter

2 tsp. vanilla extract
1-lb. powdered sugar

Mix icing ingredients all together and spread on cooled cake.

CHERRY CHEESE TARTS

Kallie N. - Age 12

1⅛ cups Graham Cracker
  Crumbs
½ cup sugar
2 tblsp. divided butter, softened
2 (8-oz.) pkgs. cream cheese,
  softened

2 eggs
1 tsp. vanilla
1 (21-oz.) can cherry pie filling
cupcake liners

Place cupcake liners into muffin tins. Combine graham cracker crumbs, 2 Tbsp. sugar and butter in a bowl. Cut in butter until it forms small crumbs. Place approximately 1 Tbsp. crumb mixture into each cupcake

(continued)

liner and pat it down. Beat cream cheese and ½ cup sugar until fluffy. Add eggs and vanilla; mix thoroughly. Spoon a layer of cream cheese mixture on top of crusts (fill cups ⅔ full). Bake at 350° for 30 minutes. Cool and spoon cherry pie filling over the top. Refrigerate. Makes about 16. Prep Time: 20 minutes Baking Time: 30 minutes Chilling Time: 1 hour

CHOCOLATE BANANA PARADISE

Reed Sincox - Age 13

3 bananas
1 cup chocolate chips

½ cup toffee chips (optional)

Line a baking pan with parchment or waxed paper. Peel the bananas and cut each one in half crosswise. Insert a skewer or Popsicle stick 2 to 3 inches into one end of each banana half. Place the bananas on the pan and freeze for 30 minutes Place the chocolate chips in a microwave and cook for 2 minutes so they are completely melted. Holding a banana over the bowl, spoon the chocolate over the banana, spreading quickly to cover the entire outside. Sprinkle the banana with the toffee chips and place it on the baking sheet. Repeat with the remaining Bananas. Freeze the bananas for at least 30 minutes. Makes 6 servings.

CHOCOLATE BURFI

Arjun Varma - Age 12

2 cups mawa (can be found in any Indian grocery store)
2 tsp. oil

3 tblsp. cocoa powder
⅓ cups sugar

Crumble mawa into fine granules. Grease tray with oil and keep aside. Cook mawa in a thick-bottomed pan, stirring continuously until it is completely melted and has a thick sauce-like consistency. Do not color. Stir in sugar until it is completely dissolved and mawa is cooked. Remove half of this mixture and pour onto the greased tray. For spreading the mawa evenly on the tray, hold it from two sides and rap it on a hard surface two or three times. Let it cool. Keep the remaining half on a slow flame. Add the cocoa powder and mix well. Pour the cocoa mixture over the earlier mixture. Let it cool completely. Cut into pieces and serve as dessert.

CHOCOLATE CHERRY DROPS

Timothy Sebastien - Age 5
Sophia Claire - Age 3

1½ c. flour
½ c. cocoa
¼ tsp. baking soda
¼ tsp. baking powder
½ c. butter
1 c. sugar

1 egg
½ tsp. vanilla
1 jar maraschino cherries
12 oz. chocolate chips
1 can sweetened condensed
  milk

Combine flour, cocoa, baking soda, baking powder, butter, sugar, egg, and vanilla. Scoop out a small amount and roll into a ball in your hand. Place in mini muffin pan and push into a tart shape. Combine chips and milk and melt together. Add 8 tsp. cherry juice. Place a cherry in each muffin cup, then fill with chocolate sauce. Bake at 350° for 10 minutes.

CHOCOLATE CHIP APPLESAUCE CAKE
(Dairy Free)

Timothy Sebastien - Age 5
Sophia Claire - Age 3

½ c. oil
1½ c. sugar
2 eggs, beaten
2 c. applesauce
2 c. flour
1½ tsp. baking soda
½ tsp. cinnamon

½ tsp. salt
3 T. cocoa powder
2 T. sugar
½ c. chopped nuts (completely
  optional)
1 c. chocolate chips (or carob to
  keep dairy free)

Mix the oil and the 1½ c. sugar. Beat in the eggs. Stir in cinnamon, salt, applesauce, baking soda and cocoa. Add the flour and mix until just moistened. Pour mixture into a greased and floured 13 x 9 inch pan. Sprinkle with 2 T. sugar, nuts (or not), and chocolate pieces. You can lightly stir this in or leave on top. I tend to leave it on top. Bake at 350 degrees for 30 to 40 minutes. If it starts to brown too much on top, cover with foil -- but I've never found the need to do that.

CHOCOLATE CHIP BREAD PUDDING

Allison Horn - Age 9
Nathan Horn

2 large eggs
2¼ cups milk
½ cup sugar
1½ tsp. cinnamon

5 - 6 slices white bread, cubed
  or torn
1½ cups chocolate chips

(continued)

Heat oven to 350°. In a large bowl, mix eggs, milk, sugar and cinnamon. Add bread and stir gently until all of it is completely covered with the egg mixture. Fold in chocolate chips. Pour mixture into lightly greased 8 x 8 inch casserole dish. Bake 45 - 50 minutes or until a knife or toothpick comes out clean and the pudding is lightly browned and puffed up around the edges.

CHOCOLATE CHIP CAKE

Megan Suppes - Age 13

1 pkg. Yellow Cake Mix
1 small box Chocolate Instant
  Pudding
4 Eggs

1 cup Sour Cream
½ cup Oil
1 tsp. Vanilla
1 bag Chocolate Chips

Pre-heat oven to 350 degrees. Mix all ingredients, except chocolate chips, well for about 4 minutes. Fold in chocolate chips. Do not mix with blender. Pour batter into angle food cake pan or bundt pan. Bake for 1 hour. Flip onto plate when done and dust with powdered sugar.

CHOCOLATE CHIP CHEESE BARS

Rachael Dashner
Sheila Lucey, her Mom

(8-oz.) pkg. Cream Cheese
1 Egg
½ c. Sugar

1 tube Chocolate Chip
  Refrigerator Cookies

Heat oven to 350°. In small bowl, beat cream cheese, sugar and egg until smooth. Spread ½ of cookie dough on bottom of ungreased 8x8 pan. Spread cream cheese mixture over the cookie dough. Crumble the remaining cookie dough on top of the mixture. Bake 35-40 minutes. Cool, cut and store in the refrigerator.

CHOCOLATE CHIP FROZEN YOGURT

Akira King - Age 12

½ cup Chocolate Chips
2 cups Vanilla low-fat frozen
  yogurt, softened

Stir chocolate chips into frozen yogurt. Spoon into 4 dessert dishes. 4½ cup servings.

98890-09

CHOCOLATE COVERED STRAWBERRIES

Tatum Elizabeth - Age 5

20 Strawberries
6 ounce semi-sweet chocolate,
** chopped**

Rinse, but do not hull the strawberries. Drain and pat completely dry. Put the chocolate into glass mixing bowl and microwave for one minute. Stir and continue to microwave for 10 seconds at a time until all chocolate is melted and smooth. Dip strawberries into chocolate and place on parchment or wax paper until chocolate is hardened. Enjoy.

CHOCOLATE DIPPED BANANA POPS

Lane - Age 8
Mackenzie - Age 5

1 bunch bananas
1 pkg. semi sweet chocolate
** chips**

1 tblsp. vegetable oil
nut pieces or candy sprinkles
popsicle sticks

At least 4 hours ahead of time, peel bananas, cut them in half, insert a popsicle stick into the cut end and place in a single layer on a tray in the freezer. When you're ready to assemble the pops - In the top of a double boiler, melt one package of semi-sweet chips and one table-spoon of vegetable oil over simmering, not boiling, water. When all the chips are melted and smooth, allow the chocolate mixture to cool for 5 minutes. One at a time, dip each banana into the melted chocolate and sprinkle with your favorite topping. Place back on the tray and back in the freezer for 5 minutes to set the chocolate. YUM!

CHOCOLATE DIPPED STRAWBERRIES

Sara Margaret - Age 6

1 qt. strawberries with caps on
½ cup semi-sweet morsels
1½ tblsp butter

1 tblsp corn syrup
1 tsp. rum flavoring

Wash and pat dry each berry. Set aside. Melt remaining ingredients in the top of a double boiler over hot (not boiling) water. Allow chocolate to cool to 100 degrees before dipping each berry ⅔ into mixture. Rest covered berry stem side down on waxed paper-lined cookie sheet. Chill at least 15 minutes or up to 5 hours in refrigerator before serving. A great confection or garnish.

CHOCOLATE ECLAIR CAKE

Joshua David - Age 7
Jack Robert - Age 3

Butter
1 box graham crackers
2 pkgs. Instant French Vanilla
Pudding

3 cups milk
9 ounce ctn. Cool Whip
1 box Jiffy Chocolate Frosting

This cake tastes best if made the night before as it needs to be refrigerated for about four hours. Butter a 9 x 13 inch pan. Line buttered pan with graham crackers. In a bowl, beat together 2 packages Instant French Vanilla Pudding with 3 cups milk. Add 9 oz. container Cool Whip and mix again. Pour half of this mixture over the graham crackers. Lightly lay another cracker layer over this. Pour remaining mixture on top of crackers. Top with another layer of graham crackers. Frost last layer of graham crackers with your favorite chocolate frosting. Refrigerate over night!

CHOCOLATE MINT HORNS

Amy Podborny - Age 12

2³/₄ oz. Dark chocolate
¹/₃ cup Heavy Cream
1 tblsp Confections' sugar

1 tblsp Crème de menthe
Chocolate coffee beans, to
decorate

Makes 10. Cut ten 3-inch circles of baking parchment. Shape each circle into a cone shape and secure with sticky tape. Melt the chocolate. Using a small pastry brush or clean artists' brush, brush the inside of each cone with melted chocolate. Brush a second layer of chocolate on the inside of the cones and let them chill until set. Carefully peel away the parchment. Place the heavy cream, confectioners' sugar, and crème de menthe in a mixing bowl and whip until just holding its shape. Place in a pastry bag fitted with a star tip and pipe the mixture into the chocolate cones. Decorate the cones with chocolate coffee beans (if using) and then chill until required. Cook's tip: The chocolate cones can be made in advance and kept in the refrigerator for up to 1 week. Do not fill them more than 2 hours before you are going to serve them.

CHOCOLATE PUDDING TORTE

Evan Matthew

1 (3.5 oz.) box instant chocolate
pudding
1 cup whipped cream, divided

1 angel food cake
1 (8-oz.) bag Heath English
Toffee bits, divided

Prepare pudding according to package directions BUT use only 1¹/₃ cups of milk. Chill. In a separate bowl, fold together half of the whipped cream and add about 2 oz. Heath bits. Slice the cake horizontally into

(continued)

3 layers. Combine half of the pudding and half of the whipped cream. Spread the pudding/whip cream mixture between layers of cake. For the frosting, fold the remaining ½ cup of whipped cream into the pudding mixture. Frost the top and sides of the cake. Sprinkle frosted cake with Heath bits. Chill until ready to serve. Makes about 12 servings.

CHOCOLATE STREUSEL BARS

Timothy Sebastien - Age 5
Sophia Claire - Age 3

1¾ c. flour	1 egg
1 c. sugar	1 14 oz. can sweetened
¼ c. cocoa	condensed milk
½ c. butter	2 c. semi-sweet chocolate chips

Heat oven to 350°. Grease 13 x 9 x 2 inch baking pan. In large bowl, stir together flour, sugar and cocoa. Cut in butter until mixture resembles coarse crumbs. Add egg; mix well. Set aside 1½ cups mixture. Press remaining mixture onto bottom of prepared pan. Bake 10 minutes. Meanwhile, melt sweetened condensed milk and 1 cup chocolate chips in a heavy saucepan or double boiler; pour over crust. Add remaining chips to reserved crumb mixture. Sprinkle over top. Bake additional 25 to 30 minutes or until center is almost set. Cool completely in pan on wire rack. Cut into bars. About 36 bars.

CHOCOLATE ZUCCHINI CAKE

William Michael - Age 3

4 eggs	1 tsp. salt
1 cup oil	4 T. cocoa
2 cups sugar	1 tsp. vanilla
2 cups flour	2 cups grated zucchini
2 tsp. baking soda	½ cup nuts
2 tsp. cinnamon	

Beat eggs, oil, and sugar for 2 minutes. Add dry ingredients all at once and mix well until smooth. Stir in vanilla, zucchini, and nuts. Pour into two 9 in. pans or a 9 x 13 inch pan (pans should be greased and floured). Bake at 350 degrees for 40-45 minutes. Frosting: Blend 3 oz. softened cream cheese, 1 stick oleo, 1½ cups confectioners sugar, and 1 tsp. of vanilla. Spread on cooled cake.

COLORFUL CUPCAKES

Candace J. Liu - Age 13

1 box yellow cake mix	sprinkles
vanilla or chocolate frosting	cupcake liners

(continued)

Prepare cake mix as directed on box. Then, add the sprinkles into the mixture. Fill cupcakes liners with batter. Bake as directed on box. Allow to cool completely when done. Spread frosting on each cupcake. You can also place more sprinkles on the top to make it even more colorful! You now have a colorful and pretty cupcake batch!

COOKIE PIZZA

Taylor L- Age 13

1 (16-oz.) pkg. refrigerated sugar cookie dough
2 cups semi-sweet chocolate chips
1 (14-oz.) can sweetened condensed milk
2 cups candy coated milk chocolate candies
2 cups miniature marshmallows
½ cup peanuts

Preheat oven to 375 degrees F. Press cookie dough into 2 ungreased 12- inch pizza pans. Bake 10 minutes or until golden. Remove from oven. In medium sized saucepan, melt chips with the condensed milk. Spread over crusts. Sprinkle with milk chocolate candies, marsh mallows and peanuts. Bake 4 minutes or until marsh mallows are lightly toasted. Cool. Cut into wedges. Enjoy this tasty, sweet, chocolaty, delicious, and crunchy treat!

COOL POLAR BEAR SNACK

Claire Jameson - Age 5
Benjamin Thomas - Age 2

1 cup vanilla ice cream
9 raisins
3 marshmallows
2 tblsp. shredded coconut

Place a scoop of ice cream on a plate. Cut marshmallows in half and use them to make ears, snout and paws. Make eyes, claws, and a nose with raisins. Sprinkle with coconut. Enjoy!

COOL WHIP AND CHIP AHOY COOKIES

Patrick George Grant - Age 16

1 container Cool Whip
saucer of milk for dipping
1 bag Chip Ahoy Cookies

Get a dish like a baking dish. Any size is fine, it just depends on the crowd you want to feed. Fill a saucer with milk. Make a layer of Cool Whip about 1" deep in the baking dish. Then, dip a cookie in the milk for a second to get moist and lay it on top of Cool Whip. Then repeat, whip cream, cookies, whip cream, cookies. Cover and let it sit over night. Just spoon it up and eat. The cookies will just be all soft mixed with whipped cream. This dish goes at every event I take it to. Kids love it too!

98890-09

COOOOCONUT ICE POPS

Ashley - Age 12

3 cups milk
1 cup condensed milk

1 cup coconut
2 tblsp. cinnamon (optional)

Mix the coconut, condensed milk, and regular milk together in a blender. In ice pop containers, sprinkle the cinnamon on the bottom. Plastic cups can also be used instead of ice pop containers. Then, pour mixture into containers or cups. For plastic cups, put aluminum foil or plastic wrap on top of cups. After that, poke a popsicle stick into the cups.

CRAZY PIZZA

Alec David - Age 4.5

graham cracker pie crust
vanilla ice cream
chocolate & caramel sauce

your favorite candies or fruit
whipped cream

Buy graham cracker pie crust at your local grocer. Fill with vanilla ice cream (or your favorite ice cream) - softened or scooped. Top with chocolate sauce and caramel sauce. Sprinkle on a few or all of your favorite sweet treats: M & M's, Crushed Oreo Cookies, Gummy Bears, coconut shavings, chocolate chips. For a healthier flair, add strawberries, blueberries, or peaches instead of candy type treats. Add whipped cream for more fun and a bigger mess!!!

CRAZY WACKY CAKE

Benjamin Daniel - Age 7
Rebekah Marie - Age 4

3 cups flour
2 cups sugar
½ c. cocoa powder
2 tsp. baking soda
1 tsp. salt

2 tsp. white vinegar
2 tsp. vanilla
⅔ c. oil
2 cups water

Preheat oven to 350°. In a 9"x13" pan, sift together the flour, sugar, cocoa, baking soda and salt. Stir to combine. Make 3 holes in the mixture. In one hole place the vinegar, in the next the vanilla, and in the last the oil. Pour the water over all and stir until all the lumps have disappeared and the dry ingredients are completely mixed into the batter. Bake for 35 minutes or until a toothpick inserted in the center of the cake comes out clean.

CREAM CHEESE CHOCOLATE CUPCAKES
(Great Grandma's Best!)

Hannah B. Meyer
Kendra R. Meyer
Maxine Shallenberger

1½ cup Flour
1 tsp. Soda
1 cup Water
½ cup Oil
1 cup Sugar
¼ cup Cocoa
½ tsp. Salt

1 tblsp. Vinegar
1 (8-oz.) Cream Cheese
1 Egg
½ cup Sugar
1 cup Chocolate Chips
Paper cupcake holders

Mix all ingredients from flour to vinegar. Fill paper cups ½ full. In separate bowl, mix cream cheese, egg, and ½ cup sugar. Add chocolate chips. Drop by teaspoon in center of mixture in paper cups. Bake 20 minutes at 375 degrees. (All ovens are different. Check firmness at 15 minutes.)

CREAM PUFF CAKE

Taylor L- Age 13

1 stick butter
1 cup water
1 cup flour
4 eggs
8 oz. Cool Whip

8 oz. cream cheese
¼ cup milk
2 small packages instant vanilla
 pudding
1⅓ cup milk

Heat water and butter until melted. Remove from heat and mix in flour. Beat eggs in one at a time. Spray a 9x13 inch pan with Pam cooking spray. Spread dough in pan evenly. Bake for 25 minutes at 400 degrees. Cool completely. With hand mixer, mix cheese and ¼ cup milk in one bowl until smooth. Mix pudding and 1 and ⅓ cup milk in another bowl. Combine both mixtures and spread over crust. Cover with Cool Whip. Drizzle chocolate syrup over top in fancy design.

CREATIVE BEGINNINGS P-P-P-PIZZA

Sean - Age 5
Meghan - Age 3

12 oz. Chocolate chips

2 oz. white chocolate chips

Line pizza pan with wax paper. Melt chocolate chips and pour into pizza pan. Chill. Melt white chocolate chips and drizzle over pizza. Top with your favorite candy toppers such as mini M&M's, gummies, marshmallows, Reese's pieces, raisins...be creative! When all chocolate has hardened, break into pieces and serve.

98890-09

CREPES
(Great for Breakfast too)

Chloe Elizabeth - Age 9

1 cup all-purpose flour
pinch salt
1 egg, beaten

1-¼ cup milk
1 tsp. butter or oil

In a medium mixing bowl, sift the flour and salt. Make a "well" in the center and add the egg and half the milk. Beat the egg and milk together. Slowly incorporate the flour with the egg/milk mixture. When it is smooth and has no lumps, beat in the rest of the milk. Pour the mixture into a measuring jug, one that has a spout. Heat a non-stick pan over medium heat. Add the butter or oil and swirl it around to cover the whole surface. Pour in enough batter to cover the base of the pan. Swirl it around while tilting the pan so you have a thin, even layer of batter. Cook for 30 seconds or until the bottom is brown. Take a spatula, loosen around the edges, and flip to the other side. Cook the other side until it is golden brown. Repeat, and always add butter or oil to the pan first. Serve the crepes while they are still hot. Try them with sugar or sliced bananas and chocolate sauce. Or go savory and top with melted grated cheese. Fold into quarters or roll them up.

CUPCAKE ICE CREAM CONES

Lucciana Tru - Age 1

1 box your favorite cake mix
24 flat bottomed ice cream
cones

your favorite cake frosting

Preheat oven to 350F. Mix cake mix per directions on box. (If using a white cake mix, divide mix into four separate mixing bowls and use food coloring to make different ice cream "flavors".) Stand ice cream cones in muffin pan or in a 13 x 9 pan and fill about ½ to ¾ full. Bake 15 to 20 minutes or until done. Cool on a wire rack. Let cool completely before frosting then add sprinkles, or whatever you like. Makes 18 to 24 cupcakes

DARN GOOD CHOCOLATE CAKE
(Our Family Favorite for Birthday Cakes)

Travis James - Age 12
Jakob Daniel - Age 10
Trey Vincent - Age 7

1 box (18.25 oz.) plain devil's
food or dark chocolate fudge
cake mix
1 box (3.9 oz.) chocolate instant
pudding mix
4 large Eggs
1 c. Sour cream

½ c. Warm water
½ c. vegetable oil, such as
canola, corn, safflower,
soybean, or sunflower
1½ c. semi-sweet chocolate
chips

1) Preheat oven 350 degrees. Lightly mist a 12 cup Bundt pan with vegetable oil spray, then dust with 1 or 2 Tbs. of cake mix. Set aside. 2) Place the cake mix, pudding mix, eggs, sour cream, warm water, and oil in a large mixing bowl. Blend with an electric mixer on low speed for 1 minute. Scrape sides and continue for 2 to 3 minutes on medium speed until well blended. Fold in chocolate chips. Pour batter into the prepared pan. 3) Place pan in oven on middle rack. Bake 45-50 minutes. Cake will be done when top is pressed with a finger and springs back. Place pan on wire rack to cool for 20 minutes. Run a long sharp knife around the edge of the cake and invert it onto a serving platter. Slice and serve while still warm or wait until completely cool to dust with powdered sugar.

DESSERT DELIGHT SQUARES!!!

Paige McCarthy

1½ cups pecan halved
1¼ cups unsweetened
shredded coconut
5 (1.4 ounces) heath bars
¾ cups (1½ sticks) unsalted
butter
1 cup light brown sugar
½ cup white sugar

2 eggs (lightly beaten)
3 tblsp milk
1 tblsp vanilla extract
1½ cups flour
2 tblsp cornstarch
1 tsp. baking powder
½ tsp. salt

Heat the oven to 350°. Grease the bottom and sides of a light-colored 13 x 9 inch baking pan, then lightly flour it, knocking out the excess. Set the pan aside. On a separate baking sheet, spread the pecan halves and toast them in the oven for 7 minutes. Once they're cool to the touch, set the pan on a solid work surface and use a saucepan to finely crush the pecans. Then transfer them to a medium-size bowl. Toast the coconut in a nonstick skillet over medium heat, stirring with a wooden spoon, until the coconut is light golden in color, about 10 minutes. Transfer the coconut to the bowl with the pecans. Seal the Heath bars in a heavy-duty gallon-size plastic bag, then crush them with a rolling pin. Transfer the bits to the bowl with the pecans and coconut, breaking

(continued)

98890-09

up any larger pieces by hand. Melt the butter, pour it into a large bowl, and let it cool to lukewarm. Using a wire whisk, blend in the sugars until they're smooth. Whisk in the eggs, milk, and vanilla extract. Using a wooden spoon, combine the flour, cornstarch, baking powder, and salt in a medium bowl. Add the dry ingredients to the butter mixture, stirring until they are evenly blended, then stir in the pecans, coconut, and Heath bar bits. Use the back of a large spoon to evenly spread the dough in the prepared baking pan. Bake the bars on the center oven rack until the top is a light, golden brown and the edges are crackly, about 25 minutes. Transfer the pan to a wire rack and cool thoroughly, about 1-1/2 hours, before slicing. Makes 24 bars.

DOUBLE CHOCOLATE COCOA CUPCAKES

Timothy Sebastien - Age 5
Sophia Claire - Age 3

2 c. chocolate chips	1½ c. flour
¾ c. butter, room temperature	½ c. cocoa
1¼ c. sugar	1 tsp. baking soda
2 eggs	½ tsp. salt
1 tsp. vanilla	1 c. milk

Beat butter and sugar until light and fluffy (don't skip this step or short-change it!). Beat in eggs and vanilla until well mixed. Add cocoa, baking soda, and salt. Mix until well combined. Add ⅓ c. milk. Mix again. Add ½ c. flour. Mix until just combined. Add the remaining ⅔ milk and mix well. Add the last 1 c. flour and stir until about halfway mixed in. Add the chocolate chips and stir with a spoon until just mixed in. a) Fill ice cream cones about to the first lip of the cone where it starts to get wide (this makes about 28 cones) or b) fill greased muffin tins with the batter until about ¾ full. Bake at 375 degrees for 20-25 minutes. If you do cones, it will take longer. Be patient; it's worth it. Once cooled, these are GREAT with the strawberry frosting.

DOUBLE DOUBLE BROWNIE FUDGE CAKE

Ashley Nicole - Age 13

½ cup oil	**Frosting Ingredients:**
1 stick butter	1 stick butter
1 cup water	¼ cup cocoa
¼ cup dry cocoa	⅓ cup buttermilk
2 cups sifted flour	1-lb. box powdered sugar
2 cups sugar	½ tsp. salt
½ tsp. salt	1 tsp. vanilla
½ cup buttermilk	½ cup chopped nuts (optional)
1 tsp. baking soda	

Preheat oven to 400 degrees. Combine oil, butter, water, cocoa and bring to a boil. Combine dry ingredients: flour, sugar and salt. Pour

(continued)

above liquid mixture over dry ingredients and mix until smooth. Add buttermilk, soda, eggs, vanilla and blend thoroughly. Bake in 12 x 15 inch buttered pan for 30 minutes. Frosting directions: bring butter, cocoa and milk to boil. Add sugar, vanilla, salt, and nuts (optional) and blend thoroughly. Put icing on cake while cake is warm. Umm, umm, good!!!!! ENJOY!!!!

EASY AS PIE

Elise Marie - Age 13

4 eggs
1 stick margarine or butter
½ cup flour

1 cup flaked coconut
2 cup milk
¾ cup sugar

Blend together eggs, butter, flour, coconut, milk, and sugar in a blender. Then pour the mixture into a 10-inch pie pan and bake for an hour at 350°. After baking, let the pie cool. Bon Appetite!

EASY EGG FREE BROWNIES
(Lowfat Brownies)

Brooke Caroline - Age 6
Gibson "Gibby" Louis - Age 4

1 box Brownie Mix

1 cup diet coke

Add 1 cup of diet coke with any brand of boxed Brownie Mix. Stir brownie mix and diet coke until well blended. Spread into 13 x 9 greased pan. Bake at 350 for about 26-28 minutes. My son has an egg allergy, so this is a family favorite, plus they are yummy and easy!!

EGG NESTS

Madison Michelle - Age 6

2 cups mini marshmallows
¼ cup butter

4 cups chow mein noodles
egg shaped candy's

Butter a 12 cup muffin tin. Combine marshmallows and butter over medium heat in a saucepan. Stir until the butter and marshmallows have melted. Stir in the chow mein noodles, coat well. Butter fingers and press the mixture into the bottom and sides of the prepared muffin tin. Refrigerate until firm. Remove from tin and fill with Robin's Eggs or Jelly Beans. Makes a great Easter or Spring treat for the kids. Yields 12 nests.

98890-09

FABULOUS CAKE

McCall Farrington - Age 13

1 box yellow cake mix
1 box instant vanilla pudding
 mix
2 cups sour cream
2 eggs

¼ cup vegetable oil
orange flavoring
1 cup white chocolate chips
⅛ cup confectioners sugar for
 dusting

Preheat oven to 350°. Grease 9" bundt pan. Mix all ingredients except chocolate chips and confectioners sugar together until blended. Add in white chocolate chips. Bake for 1 hour or until done. Cool cake for 10 minutes on a wire rack. Turn cake out and dust with sugar.

FAIRY PRINCESS MARSHMALLOW POPS

Jessica Noelani - Age 8

Assorted candies and sprinkles
Food coloring (optional)
1 pound Vanilla candy coating
 or vanilla almond bark

12 Craft sticks, colored or plain
12 Large marshmallows, colored
 or white

Place assorted candies or sprinkles in several small bowls. Melt 6 squares of vanilla coating according to package directions. Mix in food coloring, if desired. Insert a craft stick into the bottom of each marshmallow. Holding the stick, dip each marshmallow into the melted coating and then dip coated marshmallow into assorted candies. Place marshmallow pops on a baking sheet and put in freezer for 5 minutes to harden the coating quickly. Keep marshmallow pops in the freezer until ready to eat. When ready to serve, tie a little ribbon around the stick for decoration, if desired.

FANCY SCHMANCY CUPCAKES
(these cupcakes are photographed in this book)

Taylor - Age 13
Sarah

1 recipe Vanilla Cupcakes (see
 additional recipe)
2 cans Vanilla Frosting
Decorating Sugar, assorted
 colors

Mini Nonpareils, assorted colors
M&Ms Mini Candies

Place a generous dollop, about 2 tablespoons, of frosting on each cup cake. Using a knife or a small offset spatula, spread the frosting over the cupcake and smooth to make as round as possible. Coat each cupcake, either by sprinkling or gently dipping, with a chosen color of decorating sugar. Once completely coated you can reshape the frosting by pressing lightly with your hands to remove any rough edges. Fill a

(continued)

small pastry bag or plastic freezer bag with the remaining frosting. If using a piping bag and tip, use the smallest round tip available. If using a freezer bag, cut off about 1/16" of the corner to make a very small hole. On top of the decorating sugar pipe any desired design. Sprinkle over mini nonpareils and using a toothpick push any stray sprinkles to completely coat the design. Continue in this manner, color by color, until you achieve your desired design. Use M&Ms Minis and other candies as desired.

FLORENCE'S SOUR CREAM COFFEE CAKE

S. Ferrari

½ lb. margarine	¼ tsp. salt
1 cup sugar	8 oz. sour cream
2 eggs	**Filling:**
1 tsp. vanilla	1 tsp. cinnamon
2 cups flour	¼ cup sugar
1 tsp. baking soda	**Optional: unsalted crushed**
1 tsp. baking powder	**walnuts or pecans**

Cream together margarine and 1 cup sugar, set aside. In another bowl, mix together eggs, vanilla, four, baking soda, baking powder, salt and sour cream. Add margarine and sugar mixture to batter. Mix with electric mixer on medium until batter is smooth. Fill half of greased and floured tube pan or bundt pan with batter. Sprinkle filling (reserve enough for top of cake). Add remaining batter and sprinkle with remaining sugar/cinnamon mixture. Bake at 350° for 30-40 minutes.

FLUFF

Annabel Marie - Age 7
Abigail Leigh - Age 4
Atley Catherine - Age 2

1 (12-oz.) tub Cool Whip	1 (14-oz.) can sweetened
1 (16-20 oz.) can cherry pie	condensed milk
filling	
1 (20-oz.) can crushed pineapple	
(drained)	

Gently FOLD all ingredients in a large bowl until mixed well. Serve cold.

FOUR LAYER DESSERT

Cael Matthew - Age 7

1 cup flour
½ cup pecans
1 stick butter
8 oz. cream cheese
1 cup powdered sugar

1 carton Cool Whip
2-3 oz. packages of vanilla or
  chocolate pudding
3 cups milk
nuts

Combine flour, pecans and butter for the first layer. Press into a 9 x 13 inch pan. Bake at 350 for 20 minutes. Cool. For second layer, combine cream cheese, powdered sugar and 1 cup of Cool Whip. Blend and spread onto crust. Combine both pudding mixes and milk. Spread on top for third layer. Top with remaining Cool Whip and nuts.

FRIED APPLES

Ian Pitcher

1 cup Milk
½ cup Sugar
½ tspn Baking soda

Flour
4 Apples

Peel apples and cut into small pieces. Mix all ingredients into bowl. Use a table spoon to put the apples pieces with the mixture on a pan with hot oil. Flip to the other side and cook. Fry both sides till brown.

FROSTED BANANA BARS

Timothy Sebastien - Age 5
Sophia Claire - Age 3

Bars

½ c. butter
2 c. sugar
3 eggs
4 med. ripe bananas

1 tsp. vanilla
1 tsp. baking soda
2 c. flour
pinch salt

In mixing bowl, cream butter and sugar. Beat in eggs, bananas, and vanilla. Combine the flour, baking soda, and salt; add to creamed mixture and mix well. Pour into a greased 15 x 10 x 1 inch baking pan. Bake at 350° for 25 minutes or until bars test done. Cool.

Frosting

¾ c. butter, softened
1½ 8 oz. pkgs. cream cheese,
  softened

6 c. confectioners sugar
3 tsp. vanilla

Cream butter and cream cheese in a mixing bowl. Gradually add confectioners' sugar and vanilla; beat well. Spread over bars.

FROSTED CHEWS

Mrs. Retzlaff's Fifth Grade Class

1 cup sugar
1 cup white corn syrup
1 cup peanut butter
6 cups Special K cereal
Frosting:

1 (6 oz.) cup of semi-sweet
chocolate chips
1 (6 oz.) cup of butterscotch
chips or peanut butter/
chocolate chips

Place sugar and corn syrup in medium size saucepan. Stir constantly on medium heat until mixture comes to a boil. Remove from heat. Add peanut butter, stir to mix well. Press into a greased 9 x 9 inch pan. Add cereal, mix well. Melt chocolate chips and butterscotch chips on very low heat. Spread over cooled bars. Cut into squares when frosting has hardened.

FROSTED PUMPKIN BARS & CREAMY ICING

Allison Lynn - Age 11
Mallory Jean - Age 8
Ryan - Age 4

2 cups sugar
2 cups flour
1 (15-oz.) can pumpkin
1 cup canola oil
4 eggs
2 tsp. baking powder
1 tsp. baking soda

1 tsp. cinnamon
1 (8-oz.) pkg. cream cheese,
softened
6 tblsp. butter, softened
4 cup powdered sugar
1 tsp. vanilla

Combine all ingredients. Pour into ungreased 15½ X 10½ inch jelly roll pan. Bake at 350° for 25-35 minutes or until toothpick inserted comes out clean. These have a cake texture. Cool. Frost with: Creamy Icing. Cream together cream cheese and butter. Beat in vanilla and powdered sugar. Refrigerate frosted bars.

FROSTY MINT ICE CREAM PIE'S

Danny Roewer - Age 13

1 pkg. Devil's Food or Dark
Chocolate Cake Mix
1 can Chocolate Fudge Frosting

¾ cup Water
6 cups Mint Chocolate Chip Ice
Cream, slightly softened

Heat oven to 350°F. Generously grease bottom sides and rim of two 9-inch pie pans. In a large bowl, combine cake mix, ¾ cup of the frosting, and water. Blend at a low speed until moistened; beat 2 minutes at high speed. Spread half of batter (2½ cups) in bottom of each greased pan. Do not spread up sides of pan. Bake at 350°F for 20 to 27 minutes. DO NOT OVERBAKE. Cakes will collapse to form shells. Cool completely. Spoon ice cream evenly into each shell. In small saucepan over

(continued)

low heat, heat remaining frosting until just melted, stirring occasionally. Drop the frosting by teaspoons over ice cream; lightly swirl with tip of knife. Freeze until firm. Let stand at room temperature 10 to 15 minutes before serving. Recipe should make about 12 servings.

FROZEN GRAPES

Jacob Russell - Age 3

1 lb. Red or Green Seedless Grapes   **Water**

Pull grapes off of stem and wash them. Dry grapes and place them in a freezer container overnight or until grapes are frozen. Take out a bunch for a snack on a hot day. Enjoy!

Tip: Cut in half for little ones.

FROZEN STRAWBERRY YOGURT PIE

Mary Beth - Age 13

2 (8-oz.) containers strawberry yogurt
3½ cups Cool Whip

2 cups sliced or chopped strawberries, sweetened
1 graham cracker pie crust

FOLD: yogurt into Cool Whip, blend well, fold in strawberries SPOON: into crust FREEZE: until firm (4 hours or overnight) Let stand at room temperature 10 minutes before serving. Store leftover pie in freezer.

FRUIT COBBLER

Freida - Age 6
Beata - Age 5

1⅓ cup all-purpose flour
2 tblsp. sugar (plus 1 tblsp. for sprinkling on dough before baking)
¾ tsp. baking powder
¼ tsp. baking soda
½ tsp. fine sea salt
5 tblsp. cold unsalted butter, cut into small pieces
½ cup sour cream

¼ cup heavy cream (plus 2 tblsp. for brushing dough before baking)
Filling Ingredients:
6 cups peeled & pitted, or cored fruits (apples, peaches, pears, any berry, etc.)
½ cup sugar
4 tblsp. cornstarch
zest and juice of one lemon

Preheat oven to 375°. Topping: In a large bowl, whisk together the flour, sugar, baking powder, soda and salt. Add butter and toss together with dry ingredients. Using a pastry cutter or two knives, cut the butter into the dry ingredients until the mixture resembles coarse bread crumbs. In a small bowl, combine sour cream, and heavy cream and

(continued)

whisk together. Add to flour and butter mixture. Mix with a wooden spoon, rubber spatula or fork only until the dough comes together and can be rolled or patted. Gently knead the dough in the bowl 5-10 times if needed, turning and pressing any loose pieces into the dough. Gently roll small pieces of the dough into balls, flatten each one slightly, and place it on the fruit. Lightly brush each "biscuit" with a bit of cream and then sprinkle with sugar. Filling: In a small bowl, combine the fruit, sugar, cornstarch, zest and juice. Transfer to a buttered 2 quart baking dish (about 2" deep) and top with "biscuit" topping. Place baking dish on a parchment paper lined baking sheet and bake for 40-45 minutes, until the filling is bubbly and the top is golden. Let stand for about 15 minutes before serving. Serve warm or at room temperature.

FRUIT DIP

Rachael Dashner
Sheila Lucey, her Mom

(8-oz.) pkg. Cream Cheese   **1 tsp. Lemon Juice**
(12-oz.) jar Marshmallow Creme

Blend all ingredients with mixer until combined. Serve with strawberries, bananas, apples, kiwi or whatever fruit you like. Enjoy!

FRUIT DIP

Griffin - Age 10

1 c. vanilla yogurt   **⅛ tsp. cinnamon**
½ c. peanut butter   **½ c. Cool Whip**

Put all ingredients in the blender. Put top on the blender. Blend on high until well mixed. Then pour it in a dessert bowl. Then serve with any fruit you like and you got some fruit dip. (Especially good with apples.) Serves 4 - 8 people.

FRUIT PIZZA

Cade Ivan - Age 2

1 pkg. Sugar Cookie Dough   **1 can mandarin oranges**
1 kiwi   **1 tub cream cheese**
1 ctn. strawberry

Make sugar cookies by following the directions on the package. When the cookies have cooled, spread softened cream cheese on top of each cookie. Then put slices of fruit on top and serve! Yummy and healthy dessert.

FRUIT PUDDING

Reed Sincox - Age 13

1 pkg. frozen raspberries in
  syrup, thawed
4 eggs
½ cup milk

½ cup heavy cream
¼ cup flour
¼ cup plus 1 tblsp. sugar
½ tsp. vanilla extract

Preheat the oven to 375°. Lightly butter a 9-inch pie plate or a 1-quart shallow baking dish. Spread the raspberries and their syrup evenly over the bottom of the pie plate. Make the batter: In a blender or food processor, combine the eggs milk, cream, flour, ¼ cup of the sugar and the vanilla, and blend well. Pour the batter over the fruit. Sprinkle with the remaining 1 tablespoon sugar. Bake for 20 to 25 minutes, or until the pudding is set and golden around the edges.

FUDGE

Stephen - Age 10

4 c. sugar
1 c. milk
1 tsp. vanilla
1 c. butter
13 oz. Hershey's Milk Chocolate
12 oz. Hershey's Semi-Sweet
  Chocolate

2 oz. Hershey's Unsweetened
  Chocolate
25 Large marshmallows
1 c. nuts (optional)

Boil sugar, milk, vanilla, and butter for 2 minutes, stirring constantly. Turn off heat and add marshmallows, stirring until melted. Add each chocolate, one at a time, stirring until melted. You may need to turn the heat on low for a short time to finish melting the chocolate. Add nuts. Quickly pour the mixture into a greased 9" x 15" dish. Refrigerate until set. Cut into ½" squares with a warm knife. Serve at room temperature. Keep unused portions refrigerated. The fudge freezes well, but cover it with wax paper inside an airtight container.

FUDGE CAKE BROWNIES

Campbell - Age 4

6 tblsp Unsweetened Cocoa
1 cup Sugar
½ cup Butter, Melted
2 Large Eggs
½ cup Self Rising Flour

1 tblsp Vanilla Extract
½ cup Chopped Pecans,
  Toasted (optional)
Powdered Sugar

Combine cocoa and sugar. Add melted butter, eggs, flour, vanilla and pecans stirring just until combined. Pour mixture into a lightly greased 8-inch square pan. Bake at 350° for 25 to 30 minutes. Cool. Cut into

(continued)

2-inch squares and dust with powdered sugar before serving. Have Fun and Enjoy!

FUDGE COATED FRUITS

Ashley - Age 12

1 banana
3 strawberries
7 grapes
(can use other desired fruits)

½ cup mini chocolate chips
2 tblsp. unsalted butter
toothpicks

Fill a pot half way full of water and put over medium heat. Put a smaller stove top bowl over the boiling water. Add the butter to the smaller bowl and spread it out. Afterwards, add the chocolate chips and stir until smooth. Add a little bit of milk at a time when and if necessary to make chocolate smoother. When chocolate is all smooth, stick a toothpick into the fruits and dip the fruits into the chocolate carefully. When done put in the freezer for about an hour or two to harden.

FUN FRUIT KEBOBS

Lara H.

1 apple
1 banana
⅓ cup red seedless grapes
⅓ cup green seedless grapes

⅔ cup pineapple chunks
1 cup yogurt of your choice
¼ cup dried coconut, shredded

1. Prepare the fruit by washing the fruit and cutting them into small squares and chunks as desired. 2. Spread coconut onto a large plate. 3. slide pieces of fruit onto a skewer and design your kebobs by putting as much or as little of whatever fruit you want until the stick is almost covered from end to end. 4. hold your kebob at the ends and roll it in the yogurt so the fruit gets covered. Then roll it in the coconut. 5. Repeat these steps with the remaining fruits.

GEORGE AND MIA'S FAVORITE ICE CREAM PIE!

Mia T. Carroll - Age 5
George James Carroll - Age 7

1½ cups Cold milk
1 box Instant pudding (4 serving size)
3 cups Whipped topping, thawed

1 Packaged chocolate or graham cracker crust

Pour milk into a large bowl. Add pudding mix. Beat with a wire whisk until well blended. Let stand 5 minutes until slightly thickened. Fold whipped topping into pudding mixture. Spoon the filling into crust. Cover

(continued)

98890-09

pie and freeze until firm, about 6 hours, or overnight. When you take this pie out of the freezer, it will look and taste just like ice cream!! Enjoy!!

GIANA'S TAFFY APPLE DIP

Giana Marie - Age 4

2 (8-oz.) pkgs. cream cheese
1½ cup light brown sugar
1 (8-oz.) pkg. Heath Bits Toffee Chips (found in the baking aisle)
1 (16-oz.) container T. Marzetti Old Fashioned Caramel Apple Dip (found in the produce dept.)

3-5 green and red apples, sliced
1¾ cup chopped peanuts

Mix cream cheese, brown sugar, and Heath Bits and spread on the bottom of a glass pie plate. Spread caramel apple dip over cream cheese. Sprinkle chopped peanuts over caramel dip. Place sliced apples around the pie plate, alternating colors. You can place extra apples in a bowl and serve them on the side. Keep dip refrigerated until ready to serve. Enjoy!!!

GIANT GINGERBREAD MAN

Colin Harrison - Age 5
Bradley Wayne - Age 5
Ella Oakes - Age 2

1 box gingerbread mix
1 can pam

1 box raisins
⅓ cup water

Preheat oven to 375°. Pour the gingerbread mix into a bowl. Pour the water in the bowl and stir with a big spoon. Stir and Stir. Stir HARD. Stir until all the gingerbread mix is wet. Now, you have gingerbread dough! Put the dough in the refrigerator for 15 minutes. While you wait, prepare the cookie sheet by spraying with pam. Remove the dough from the refrigerator. Create the gingerbread man: For the head, take some dough in your hands and make a gingerbread ball. Make it the way you make a snowball. Put the gingerbread ball on the cookie sheet and press it down. Make it flat and round. For the body, take a bigger handful of dough and make a bigger gingerbread ball. Press it flat and round. For the legs, roll some dough in the hands, like your making a thin stick. Stick it on the body. Press it flat and make another leg the same way. For the arms, use just a little dough for each arm. Make the arms the same way you made the legs, but smaller. If you have some dough left, make some gingerbread cookies. Put them on the cookie sheet with the gingerbread man. Before you put the giant gingerbread man into the oven, give him a face and some buttons using the raisins. Into the hot oven goes the giant gingerbread man! He will be baked in

(continued)

15 to 20 minutes. Look to see if he is golden brown. Take him out when he looks done.

GOODIE BALLS (UNBAKED)

Erin - Age 8

3 oz. cream cheese, softened
3 T. peanut butter
2 T. honey
2 T. dry milk powder
¼ cup sunflower seeds

2 T. chopped nuts
½ cup unsweetened shredded
  coconut
Optional: wheat germ or
  coconut

Mix all ingredients together. Shape into small balls. May be rolled in wheat germ or coconut. Refrigerate. Vary the amounts in the recipe according to your family's tastes. ("Whole Food for the Whole Family" La Leche League International Cookbook, 1981.)

GOOEY BARS

Serena Grace - Age 2

1 box yellow cake mix
1 cube margarine
3 egg

1 (8-oz.) pkg. cream cheese
1 box powdered sugar
crushed nuts (optional)

Serves 24. Preheat oven to 350°. Mix the cake mix, margarine and 1 egg together. Pour this mixture into an ungreased 9 x 13 inch pan. In another bowl, mix 2 eggs, cream cheese, and sugar together. Pour this mixture on top of the cake mixture in the pan. Sprinkle nuts on top. Bake for 30-35 minutes.

GRAHAM AND PEANUT BUTTER BON BON

Kallie N. - Age 12

1 cup Graham Cracker Crumbs
1¼ cups crunchy peanut butter
½ cup powdered sugar

1½ cups crisped rice cereal
12 oz. almond bark (white or
  dark chocolate)

Set almond bark aside; mix remaining ingredients together in a bowl. Refrigerate for 1 hour. Melt almond bark. Form crumb mixture into balls and dip in melted almond bark, place on waxed paper. Allow the almond bark to cool and set up. Makes 44 to 48 Bon Bons. Prep Time: 25 minutes

GRAHAM CRACKER BROWNIES

Mary Beth - Age 13

2 cups graham cracker crumbs
1 cup chocolate chips

1 can Eagle Brand Milk

(continued)

98890-09

Combine the graham cracker crumbs, chocolate chips and milk together. Bake in a 9 X 9 inch greased pan. Bake for 20-25 minutes at 350°.

GRANDMA'S FUDGE FROSTING

Kaitlin Lee

2 squares Bakers Semi Sweet Chocolate
1/4 cup Butter or Margarine

1/4 cup Milk
1 cup Sugar

Mix all ingredients in a sauce pan over medium heat until just melted. Once everything is melted stop stirring and let bubble across the entire top of mixture (Make sure you don't stir during this step). Then, take off heat and stir briskly until thick (about 5 minutes).

TIP: Smooth over your dessert right away as this frosting is more like fudge than frosting and is hard to spread once it's cool. Is great over brownies or drizzled over angle food cake, but the absolute best part for us is licking the spoon!

GRANDMA'S PEACH KUCHEN

Timothy Sebastien - Age 5
Sophia Claire - Age 3

1½ c. flour
1/4 tsp. baking powder
2 tsp. cinnamon
3/4 c. sugar
1 egg

1 c. milk
1 stick butter
1 29 oz. can sliced peaches (or 3-4 fresh)

Preheat oven to 375°. Mix cinnamon and all but 1 t. sugar, and set aside. Cut together butter, flour, and 1 t. sugar. Pat into pie pan. Drain and rinse the peaches (or cut fresh peaches into slices - skin optional). Layer artfully over flour mixture, and bake 30 minutes. Mix egg and milk. Pour into pan, and bake another 30 minutes. Let stand 15 minutes before serving.

HAILEY AND VAN'S NO SMOKE SMORES!

Van - Age 6
Hailey - Age 8

2-3 pkgs. graham crackers
1-2 jars marshmallow fluff

1 pkg. milk chocolate chips

Break graham crackers in half. Spread generous layer of fluff between crackers (sandwich style). Melt chocolate chips in microwave. Holding one end of sandwich, dip remaining end in melted chocolate. Cool on wax lined baking sheet and refrigerate until ready to serve. Remove from fridge 10 mins. before serving. Easy dessert for kids to make!

HANNA'S HELLO JELLO CAKE

Hanna Marie - Age 4

1 box White Cake Mix
1 (3-oz.) box Jello Gelatin Mix
  (your choice of flavor)

1 (8-oz.) pkg. Cool Whip
Topping

Prepare cake mix as per instructions on box. Pour batter into a 13 x 9 inch cake pan and bake according to directions. Mix gelatin with 1 cup of boiling water, stirring until completely dissolved. Poke random holes in cake with a tooth pick. Pour gelatin mixture over the top of the cake and let set for 15 minutes before frosting. Frost with Cool Whip topping. Cut strawberries and fresh blueberries can be placed on top as well. We like to form the stars and stripes with fresh fruit on our cake for the holidays.

HOLIDAY ICE CREAM CAKE

Anthony Michael - Age 7

1 (5-oz.) pkg. Oreo cookies
1 stick butter
½ gal. peppermint ice cream

chocolate fudge topping
Cool Whip

Crush 1 pkg. of Oreo cookies and mix with 1 stick of melted butter. Press into a 9 x 13 inch pan and freeze for 1 hour. Place softened peppermint ice cream (or any other flavor) on top of crust. Freeze for 1 hour. Top with fudge topping and spread evenly. Freeze for 30 minutes or overnight. Spread Cool Whip on top of fudge and serve.

HOME MADE ICE CREAM SANDWICHES!!!

Camryn Schmidt

2-⅓ cup all-purpose flour
1 tsp. baking powder
½ tsp. salt
1 cup butter
⅔ cup packed brown sugar
½ cup sugar
1 tblsp. vegetable oil

1 tblsp. light corn syrup
1 egg
2 tsp. vanilla extract
1 (10-oz.) pkg. chocolate chips
  or chunks, regular or mini
  sized m&m's
5 cups vanilla ice cream

To make the cookies, preheat the oven to 350 degrees and lightly butter several large baking sheets. In a large bowl, stir together the flour, baking powder, and salt. In a separate bowl, stir the butter, sugars, oil, and corn syrup until combined. Add the egg and vanilla extract until blended, and then the flour mixture. Stir in the chocolate chips and nuts, if desired. Using a ¼ cup measurer, drop the dough onto the prepared baking sheets, leaving about 3 inches between the cookies. (For smaller cookies, use 2 tablespoons of dough). Bake for 15 to 18 minutes or until the cookies are browned lightly. Remove the sheets to wire racks

(continued)

98890-09

and cool for about 5 minutes. Using a metal spatula, transfer the cookies to racks and cool completely. Repeat until all the dough is used. To assemble sandwiches, let the ice cream soften in the refrigerator for about 30 minutes. Spread 1/2 cup of ice cream on the bottom of one cookie. Place a second cookie, bottom side down, on top of the ice cream. Repeat until all the cookies are used, wrapping each sandwich individually in plastic wrap or aluminum foil. Freeze for about two hours or until firm. If the sandwich cookies have become too hard, let them stand at room temperature before serving. Makes 8 large or 16 small ice cream sandwiches!!!

HOMEMADE FRUIT SKWASH

Braelyn Grace - Age 6
Blake Emmitt - Age 4

7 lg. strawberries
20 blueberries
1 lg. banana

2 (6-oz.) fruit yogurt
1 tsp. ground cinnamon

Cut all fruits into bite sized pieces and put them into a bowl. Add the 2 containers of yogurt and the cinnamon to the bowl and stir. Whala......you have just made a healthy fruit desert for two!

ICE CREAM PARFAIT

Ford - Age 5

3 dollops ice cream flavor of
   choice
3 dollops bottled chocolate
   sauce

3 dollops whipped cream
1 maraschino cherry with a
   stem

Put one dollop of ice cream in the bottom of a parfait glass (tall glass). Add one dollop of chocolate sauce. Add one dollop of whipped cream (squirty kind is the best). Repeat above two more times. Add maraschino cherry on top. This is best eaten with a parfait spoon which is long enough to reach the bottom of the glass.

ICE CREAM SALAD

Emily M - Age 13

1 ice cream cone
1 cup yogurt

1/2 cup chopped fruits

We all scream for ice cream. No, we all scream for fruits. You just need to put the 1 cup of yogurt into the ice cream cone and then put the chopped fruits on top. So then you have your mini ice cream salad. What did you really think? Its ice cream!

ICE CREAM SANDWICH

Kelsy Elizabeth - Age 11

2 Large cookies per sandwich
1 scoop of ice cream of choice

1 can of whipped cream
chocolate sprinkles

Take one cookie and turn over so the backside is face up. Place scoop of ice cream on top of this cookie. Add the second cookie on top of the ice cream with the right side up. Add the whipped cream and decorate with the sprinkles.

ICE CREAM SNACK

Michael Vitale - Age 5
Matthew Vitale - Age 3

2 Large Graham Crackers
2 cups Vanilla Ice Cream (or
  your choice)

3 shakes Colorful Sprinkles

Lay 1st graham cracker on plate, add ice cream on top of cracker. Add sprinkles. Place 2nd graham cracker on top to make a sandwich. Enjoy.

ICE CREAM SODA CUPCAKES

Maria & Sarah

1 box of Funfetti Cake Mix
Package of ice cream cones
  (with flat bottom)
1 can of white frosting
Twizzlers or Pixie Sticks (will be
  used as "straw")

red gumballs or any red candy
  (used as "cherry")
multi-colored sprinkles

Follow cake mix directions. Put ice cream cones in a cupcake tin. Fill cones with cake batter ⅔ - ¾ full, not to the top of the cone. Follow baking directions on cake box. Let cool when done. Frost cupcake - make it look swirly like an ice cream soda. Cut a Twizzler in half and poke it through to look like a straw or use a Pixie Stick. Place red gumball on top as the "cherry" or any red candy. Top with sprinkles.

ICE CREAM SUNDAE

Sara Margaret - Age 6

ice cream (any flavor)
whip cream
cherries

hot fudge
cherry

Take out a bowl and scoop two scoops of ice cream into it. Pour hot fudge onto the ice cream. Spray some whip cream on top, then place a cherry on the top to finish it off.

JELLO JIGGLERS

Lauren Caffe - Age 9

4 cups Pure white grape juice, cranberry juice cocktail or other clear juice

4 envelopes unflavored gelatin

Sprinkle the gelatin over 1 cup of the juice. Allow to stand for a few minutes. Heat remaining 3 cups of juice to a boil and pour over the gelatin mixture. Stir until dissolved. Pour into 9 x 9 inch pan, chill until firm (3 hrs). Cut into shapes.

KATE'S FAVORITE COFFEE CAKE

Katie Mae

Batter

2 sticks butter
1 c. sugar
2 eggs
2 c. flour
1 tsp. baking powder

1 tsp. baking soda
½ tsp. salt
1 c. sour cream
1 tsp. vanilla

Cream butter and sugar together until light and fluffy. Add eggs. Sift flour with baking powder, baking soda, and salt in a large bowl. Add dry ingredients to creamed mixture, alternating with sour cream until well mixed. Stir in vanilla. Turn half of the batter into a greased 9 X 13 inch baking dish. Sprinkle with half of the brown sugar mixture. Cover with the rest of the batter and top with remaining brown sugar mixture. Bake at 350° for approximately 35 minutes or until toothpick comes out clean. Freezes well.

Filling & Topping

⅓ c. brown sugar, firmly packed
¼ c. white sugar

1 tsp. cinnamon
1 c. chopped walnuts

Mix together brown sugar, white sugar, cinnamon and walnuts in a medium sized bowl.

KEY LIME PARFAIT

Timothy Sebastien - Age 5
Sophia Claire - Age 3

1½ lbs. graham cracker crumbs
1 T. powdered sugar
1 T. cinnamon
½ lb. butter

4½ oz. cream cheese
7 oz. sweetened condensed milk
2½ oz. key lime juice

Heat oven to 300°. Melt butter and mix well with sugar, cinnamon, and crumbs. Layer on sheet pan, and bake for 15 minutes. Cool and break into pieces. With an electric mixer, beat the cream cheese on low speed

(continued)

until smooth. Slowly add the condensed milk and continue, scraping down the sides. Mix for two minutes on low speed after all the condensed milk has been added. Slowly add the key lime juice and scrape the sides well. Layer in a glass with graham pieces. Chill and garnish with lime zest. Serves 10.

KEY LIME PIE

Issac Noah - Age 7

1 box Sugar free lime flavor
  gelatin
¼ cup Boiling water
2 (8-oz.) ctn. Key Lime Pie
  flavored light yogurt

1 (8-oz.) ctn. Frozen fat free
  whipped topping, thawed
1 9" Graham cracker pie crust

In a large heat resistant bowl, dissolve gelatin in boiling water. With a wire whisk, stir in yogurt and whipped topping. Transfer mixture to prepared crust. Refrigerate overnight or at least 2 hours. Enjoy!

KISSES IN A WINDOW
(Chocolate Pretzel Treats)

Gavin Smith - Age 5
Annabelle Smith - Age 7
Gavin and Jennifer Smith

1 bag Square Pretzels
1 bag Large Chocolate Chips,
  either milk or dark chocolate,
  like Hershey's Kisses

1 bag Candy-coated chocolate
  pieces like M&M's

Heat oven to 250 degrees F. Place pretzels on a cookie sheet. Unwrap large chocolate chips and place one on each pretzel. Place cookie sheet in oven and heat until the chocolate starts to melt, about 5-10 minutes. Remove cookie sheet from oven and press candy-coated chocolates into each pretzel so that the pointed top of the chocolate chip flattens out. Let cool and harden.

KOLACHIES

Jack S - Age 13

1 lb. butter
1 pint vanilla ice cream

4 cups flour
powdered sugar

Soften butter and ice cream in a bowl. Gradually add flour. Dough will be quite moist. Take 1 spoonful of mixture and place on ungreased cookie sheet. Fill centers with solo can filling. Bake 20-25 minutes in 350 degrees oven. Sprinkle with powdered sugar while hot.

98890-09

KRAZY KAKE

Eileen Mary - Age 12

2 tsp. baking soda
1 tsp. salt
2 cups sugar
3 cups flour
½ cup cocoa

2 tsp. vinegar
1 tsp. vanilla
¾ cup oil
2 cups water

Preheat oven to 350 degrees. Mix DRY ingredients together in 8 x 8 baking pan. Smooth out the dry ingredients. Using a spoon or cup bottom make three large holes in dry mix. In 1 hole pour vanilla, next vinegar, then oil and last pour water over entire mix. Stir with a fork until thoroughly mixed. Bake at 350 degrees for 35-40 minutes. Cool and top with powdered sugar or frosting.

LAZY DAISY CAKE

Joey Jankowicz
Elise Jankowicz

3 cups Flour
1 tsp. Baking Soda
2 cups Sugar
1 tsp. Salt
1 cup Cocoa

⅔ cup Oil
1 tblsp Vinegar
1½ cups Cold Water
1 tsp. Vanilla

Preheat oven to 350°. Mix all ingredients in an ungreased 9 x 13 inch pan. Bake for 40 min.

LEMON BARS

Issac Noah - Age 7

1½ cup Flour
⅔ cup confectioner's sugar
¾ cup butter, softened
3 Eggs, lightly beaten

1½ cups Sugar
3 tblsp Flour
¼ cup Lemon juice
Additional confectioner's sugar

Combine flour, confectioner's sugar and butter, pat into a greased 13 x 9 inch baking pan. Bake at 350 degrees for 20 minutes. Meanwhile, in a bowl whisk eggs, sugar, flour and lemon juice until frothy. Pour over hot crust. Bake and additional 20 to 25 minutes in the 350 degree oven or until light golden brown, Cool on a wire rack. Dust with confectioners sugar. Enjoy!

LEMON BARS

Isaiah - Age 10

⅓ c. Margarine or Butter
1 c. Sugar
1 c. All Purpose Flour
2 Eggs
2 T. All Purpose Flour

2 tsp. Finely Shredded Lemon
  Peel
3 T. Lemon Juice
¼ tsp. Baking Powder
Powdered Sugar (optional)

Beat margarine with an electric mixer on medium to high speed for 30 seconds. Add ¼ cup of the sugar. Beat until combined. Beat in the 1 cup of flour until crumbly. Press into the bottom of an ungreased 8 x 8 x 2 inch baking pan. Bake in a 350° oven for 15 to 18 minutes or until just golden. Meanwhile, combine eggs, the remaining sugar, 2 tablespoons flour, lemon peel, juice, and baking powder. Beat for 2 minutes or until thoroughly combined. Pour over hot baked layer. Bake in a 350° oven about 20 minutes more or until lightly browned around the edges and the center is set. Cool on a wire rack. If desired, sift powdered sugar over top. Cut into bars. Makes 20 servings.

LEMON SQUARES

Mary Beth - Age 13

1 box Angel Food Cake Mix   1 can Lemon Pie Filling

Mix the cake mix and pie filling together and bake in a 9 X 13 greased and floured pan at 350° for 20-30 minutes. Sprinkle with powdered sugar when cool.

LUSCIOUS LEMONADE PIE

Kelsey Ann - Age 13

1 Graham Cracker Pie Crust
1 qt. vanilla ice cream, softened
1 (12-oz.) can frozen pink
  lemonade concentrate, thawed

4 oz. frozen whipped topping,
  thawed
few drops red food coloring

Bake and cool Graham Cracker Crust. Mix all other ingredients in a bowl. Mound the mixture in the crust. Cover and freeze about 4 hours or until firm. Let pie stand at room temperature a few minutes before cutting.

98890-09

MACKENZIE'S PUMPKIN BARS

Mackenzie Virginia - Age 7

4 eggs
1 c. oil
2 c. flour
1²/₃ c. sugar
16 oz. pumpkin

2 tsp. baking powder
1 tsp. salt
2 tsp. cinnamon
1 tsp. baking soda

Preheat oven to 350 degrees. Beat 4 eggs with 1 cup oil until fluffy. Add: flour, sugar, pumpkin, baking powder, salt, cinnamon, and baking soda. Pour into a jelly roll pan. Bake 25-30 minutes. Frost with cream cheese frosting when cool.

MAEVE'S MARVELOUS MALTED MILK SHAKES

Maeve Eileen Murphy - Age 1

6 heaping cups Vanilla Ice-
cream
2½ tblsp Malted-Milk Powder

1½ cups Milk
2 tblsp. Chocolate syrup
few shakes rainbow sprinkles

Add ice-cream, powder, milk and syrup to blender and blend until desired consistency....add sprinkles before serving and serve with a spoon and a straw.....enjoy!

MARBLED RING CAKE

Morgan McGrew - Age 15

4 oz. (115g) plain chocolate
12 oz. (350g) plain flour
1 tsp. Baking powder
1 lb. (450g) butter, at room
temperature

1 lb. 10 oz. (740g) caster sugar
1 tblsp Vanilla essence
10 Eggs, at room temperature
Icing sugar, for dusting

Serves 16. Preheat a 350°F gas oven. Line a 10X4" (25X10cm) ring mould with greaseproof paper and grease the paper. Dust with flour. Melt the chocolate in the top of a double boiler, or in a heatproof bowl set over a pan of hot water. Stir occasionally. Set aside. In a bowl, sift together the flour and baking powder. In another bowl, cream the butter, sugar and vanilla with an electric mixer until light and fluffy. Add the eggs, 2 at a time, then gradually incorporate the flour mixture on low speed. Spoon half of the mixture into pan. Stir the chocolate into the remaining mixture, then spoon into the tin. With a metal spatula, swirl the mixtures for a marbled effect. Bake until a skewer inserted in the center comes out clean, about 1 hour 45 minutes. Cover with foil halfway through baking. Let stand 15 minute.

MEET AND EAT THE EARTH'S TREATS

Mrs. Dato's Second Grade Class
Countryside School

12 popsicle sticks
12 red or orange gum drops
1 batch Rice Krispie treats
 (slightly chilled)

15 Oreo cookies, crushed

Form a Rice Krispie ball around a gumdrop. Roll in crushed Oreo cookies. Push in a popsicle stick. Place on cookie sheet and chill. Oreo layer = Earth's crust, Rice Krispie layer = Earth's mantle, Gum Drop = Earth's core

MICROWAVE S'MORES

Faith Aurora - Age 9
Sarah Denise - Age 11
Benjamin Daniel - Age 7

2 graham crackers
2 lg. marshmallows

2 pcs. chocolate bar, milk or
 dark

Place 1 graham cracker on microwave-safe plate. Put chocolate bars on crackers and marshmallows on top. Microwave on high for 15-20 seconds. Marshmallows will puff up and might fall onto plate. If this happens carefully place them back on the chocolate on the graham crackers; cover with the remaining graham cracker. Cool slightly before eating. Serves 1.

MIKEY'S MONKEY BREAD

Michael Prinner - Age 3

1⅓ cup cups Sugar
4 tube refrigerator biscuits
2 tsp. Cinnamon

1 tsp. Vanilla
1 stick butter

Tear each biscuit into 3 pieces (4 for larger biscuits). Mix ⅔ cut of sugar and 1 teaspoon of cinnamon into bowl and biscuit pieces in mixture. Grease 12 cup bundt pan with a bit of butter. Drop covered biscuit pieces into bundt pan. Place bunt pan on foil lined cookie sheet. In small sauce pan stir together remaining sugar, butter, cinnamon & vanilla. Bring to a boil Pour over biscuits and bake at 350° for 40 minutes. When done, turn onto plate sprinkle with powdered sugar and serve warm.

98890-09

MINTY CHOCOLATE SUNDAE

Annie Catherine - Age 7

2 scoops Mint Frozen Yogurt
4 drops Chocolate Sauce
4 Mint Oreos

2 Mini Brownies
Whipped Cream
½ cup Chocolate Chips

First, get a bowl and put in 2 scoops of mint frozen yogurt. Then, crush up the mint oreos. Take the mini brownies and crush them. Mix in a half cup of chocolate chips. Top with whipped cream and chocolate sauce.

MOCHA MILK SHAKE

Danielle Cassidy - Age 13

3½ cups vanilla low-fat ice
  cream
¾ cup cold coffee

¼ cup fat-free hot fudge
  topping
1½ cups ice

Combine vanilla ice cream, cold coffee, hot fudge topping, and ice in container of an electric blender; cover and process until smooth. 4 servings.

MUD PIE CAKE

Payton Steven - Age 7

1½ cups all-purpose flour
1 cup sugar
¼ cup unsweetened cocoa
  powder
1 tsp. baking soda

½ tsp. salt
⅓ cup cooking oil
1 tblsp. vinegar
1 tsp. vanilla
1 cup water

Place flour, sugar, cocoa powder, soda, and salt in a plastic bag. Mix well and then put the flour mixture into an ungreased 8 x 8 x 2 in baking pan. Use a fork to make a hole in the middle of the flour mixture. Combine oil, vinegar, and vanilla and pour the mixture into the hole. Add the water to the hole. Stir together all ingredients with a fork. Bake in 350-degree oven for 40 to 45 minutes. Let cool and then top a piece of cake with a scoop of vanilla ice cream, chocolate syrup, and a maraschino cherry.

NANA SQUARES

Griffin - Age 4
Lexi - Age 2
Leighton - Age 1

13 Graham Crackers
(16-oz.) Chocolate Chips

1 can Sweetened Condensed
  Milk

(continued)

Mix crumbled graham crackers, chocolate chips and condensed milk together. Press into a well greased 13 x 9 inch pan. Bake for 20 minutes at 375 or once edges look browned.

NO BAKE PEANUT BUTTER BALLS

Eileen Mary - Age 12

½ cup peanut butter
½ cup honey
1 cup crushed corn flakes
  cereal

2 tblsp powdered milk

Set corn flakes aside. Mix all other ingredients well and roll into balls. Then roll again in cornflakes until covered. Refrigerate leftovers. This is a yummy snack that is great with milk!

NUTCRACKER SWEETS

Erin - Age 8

½ cup butter
brown sugar
graham crackers

pecans or walnuts (omitted
  because Erin didn't like nuts,
  except peanuts.)

Get graham cracker. Split in half on dots. Preheat oven to 325 degrees. Cover cookie sheet with foil. Put graham crackers on sheet. Put butter on them. Put brown sugar on them. (Add pecans or walnuts if desired.) Put in the oven for five minutes. Take out and enjoy! (This was a traditional treat for the kids to take when skiing with their aunt.)

OLIVIA'S MARSHMALLOW SURPRISE!

Olivia Patricia - Age 6
Freddie James - Age 4

1 bag Small Marshmallows
1 bottle Chocolate Syrup with
  Squirt Top

1 bottle Caramel Sauce with
  Squirt Top
1 bottle Sprinkles

Line small marshmallows in 8 x 8 inch pan. Pour chocolate syrup and caramel sauce over the top. Put sprinkles on top. Enjoy!

OREO BALLS

Caitlin Therese - Age 6

1 1-lb. pkg. Oreos
1 (8-oz.) pkg. Cream Cheese

1 1-lb. pkg. Almond Bark

Crush oreos and mix with softened cream cheese. Form into bite-sized balls and refrigerate until cold. Melt almond bark, dip balls to cover, and place on lined cookie sheet. Refrigerate, enjoy!

98890-09

OREO COOKIE CAKE

Alessandra Elizabeth - Age 6

1 (20-oz.) pkg. chocolate
  sandwich cookies
½ cup butter
1 (16-oz.) container frozen
  whipped topping, thawed

2 pkgs. cream cheese
1 cup confectioners' sugar
2 cups milk
1 (3.4-oz.) pkg. instant vanilla
  pudding mix

Crush cookies into bite size pieces. Reserve 1 cup for top. Melt butter and mix with rest of cookies. Press into 9 x 13 pan. Put in freezer for 5 minutes. Blend ½ of the whipped topping, all of the cream cheese and confectioners' sugar. Spread over crust and place cake back in freezer. Prepare instant pudding with the milk according to package directions then spread over top of cake. Spread the remaining whipped topping on top of the pudding then sprinkle with the remaining cookies. Keep cake refrigerated.

OREO STUFF

Kyle Thomas - Age 8
Brandon Paul - Age 5

1 (15-oz.) pkg. Oreo cookies,
  crushed
⅓ cup butter, melted

½ gal. ice cream, any flavor
1 (20-oz.) bottle chocolate syrup
1 (9-oz.) pkg. Cool Whip

Put the Oreo cookies in a zip lock bag and crush them with mallet or rolling pin. Mix crushed cookies together with melted butter. Press into the bottom of a 9"x13" pan. Spread ice cream over crust. Pour chocolate sauce over ice cream. If ice cream melts a bit, freeze dessert until solid before spreading Cool Whip over the top of the chocolate syrup. Freeze overnight.

OREO SURPRISE DESSERT

Jake Patrick - Age 3
Jonathan Ryan - Age 1

2 pkgs. Instant Vanilla Pudding
  Mix
3 cups Milk
1 (8-oz.) container Cream
  Cheese

1 cup Powdered Sugar
1 container Cool Whip
1 bag Oreo cookies

Mix together pudding and milk and set aside. Mix together cream cheese and powdered sugar. Combine both of the above plus a carton of Cool Whip. Layer crushed Oreo's in the bottom of a dish; then pudding mixture, and top with more Oreo's. For special holidays, add lots of sprinkles to the top. Chill in the refrigerator for one hour. Enjoy!

OREO TRUFFLES

Samantha Lewandowski - Age 14
Matthew Lewandowski - Age 9

1 (18-oz.) pkg. Oreo Cookies
1 (6-oz.) pkg. White Chocolate
  Bark (Almond Bark)

1 (8-oz.) pkg. Cream Cheese
  (softened)

Using a food processor, crush Oreos. Add cream cheese to Oreo mixture. Roll into small bite size balls and place on a cookie sheet. Refrigerate until firm. Meanwhile melt white chocolate. Dip Oreo ball in melted white chocolate and allow to dry on wax paper, in the refrigerator.

PEANUT BUTTER CRISPY BARS

Annabel Marie - Age 7
Abigail Leigh - Age 4
Atley Catherine - Age 2

4 c. Cheerios
2 c. crispy rice cereal
2 c. M&M's
2 c. dry roasted peanuts

1½ c. creamy peanut butter
1 c. light corn syrup
1 c. sugar
1 tsp. vanilla extract

In a large bowl, combine first four ingredients and set aside. In a saucepan, bring corn syrup and sugar to a boil. Cook and stir until sugar is dissolved. Remove from heat; stir in peanut butter and vanilla. Pour over cereal mixture and toss to coat evenly. Spread into greased 9-in. x 13-in. or larger baking pan. Cool. Cut into bars.

PEANUT BUTTER CUP SQUARES

Brandan Michael - Age 17
Allie Marie - Age 10
Avery Madison - Age 7

2 sticks Salted Butter
1 cup Creamy Peanut Butter
2 cups Graham Cracker Crumbs
2½ cups Powdered Sugar
1 (10-oz.) bag Milk Chocolate
  Chips

1 (10-oz.) bag Semi-Sweet
  Chocolate Chips
1 tblsp Vegetable Oil

In a big saucepan, melt butter then mix in peanut butter. Turn off heat and mix in graham cracker crumbs and powder sugar. Mix well and spread into a cookie sheet; pat mixture into pan. Topping: put both bags of chocolate chips in microwave safe bowl and add 1 tblsp oil. Stir; then melt in microwave for one minute. Mix again and melt one more minute. Mix; then pour over top of peanut butter in cookie sheet. Put into fridge until chocolate on top is set. Take out and soften for approximately 30 minutes then cut into squares.

PEANUT BUTTER OATMEAL TREATS

Bennett John - Age 4
Annabelle Kady - Age 2

1¼ cups flour
½ tsp. salt
1 tsp. baking soda
1 cup butter
¾ cup sugar
¾ cup light brown sugar (firmly
  packed)

2 eggs
1 tsp. vanilla
1 (16-oz.) jar peanut butter
2 cups oats
1 cup mini-chocolate chips

In a small bowl mix together flour, baking soda and salt. Set aside. In a large bowl, cream butter, peanut butter and both sugars. Beat in eggs and vanilla. Stir in flour mixture, oats and chocolate chips. Do NOT over beat. Place mixture in rectangular pan, pressing down slightly to fill the pan. Bake at 350 degrees for 15 to 17 minutes. (Side note: this gets crumbly when over baked, and tastes much better a bit under bake.)

PEANUT BUTTER PIZZA

Madie Rose - Age 7

1 Flour Tortilla
Peanut Butter

1 Banana
Raisins

Take 1 flour tortilla. Spread peanut butter all over the tortilla. Slice 1 banana into thin circles and put them in different spots on top of the peanut butter. Then sprinkle raisins all over. Cut into triangles and eat !!

PEANUT BUTTER TRUFFLES

Samantha Lewandowski - Age 14
Matthew Lewandowski - Age 9

½ level cup Peanut Butter
3 level tblsp Butter (softened)

1 level cup Sifted Powder Sugar
1 (8-oz.) pkg. Chocolate Bark

Mix peanut butter & butter, gradually add powdered sugar. Shape into 1 inch balls. Refrigerate until firm. Meanwhile melt chocolate. Dip balls in melted chocolate and allow to dry on wax paper, in the refrigerator.

PENGUIN CUPCAKES

Mrs. Bellagamba Kindergarten Class
Countryside School

vanilla cupcakes
vanilla frosting
mint chocolate cookies (cut in
  half, 3 halves per cupcake)

Dried apricots or orange candy
  slices (cut into triangles for
  beak & feet)
brown M&M's for eyes

(continued)

Bake cupcakes and frost. To make the Penguin, place one half of mint cookie (flat side down) horizontally on top of cupcake (this is the head). Take two other halves of mint cookie and place them vertically below the center of the head. Slightly spread the bottom of the cookies apart from each other to allow space for the penguin feet. For the face, add two small M&Ms on top of a dot of frosting. Add a triangle piece of orange candy for the beak. Add two more triangle pieces for the feet between the two halved cookies.

PEPPERMINT PARADISE

Delaney Michelle - Age 10

⅔ cup milk
2 tblsp peppermint syrup

14 oz. peppermint ice cream
sprigs of fresh mint (optional)

Pour the milk and the 2 tbsp. of the peppermint syrup into a blender and blend gently until combined. Add the peppermint ice cream and blend until smooth. Pour the mixture into two tall glasses and decorate with the sprigs of fresh mint. Add colorful straws and serve to your wonderful guests.

PHILADELPHIA SOUR CREAM-TOPPED CHEESECAKE
(New York Style)

Moriah Jamison

1½ cups Honey Maid graham
  Cracker Crumbs
¼ cup (½ stick) butter, melted
1¼ cup sugar, divided
4 pkg. (8 oz. each) Philadelphia
  Cream Cheese, softened

2 tsp. vanilla, divided
1 container (16 oz.)
  Breakstone's of Knudsen Sour
  Cream, divided
4 eggs
2 cups strawberries, sliced

Heat oven to 325°. Line a 13 x 9 inch pan with foil, with ends extending over sides of pan. Mix crumbs, butter and 2 tblsp. sugar; press into bottom of pan. Beat cream cheese, 1 cup of remaining sugar and 1 tsp. vanilla in a large bowl with mixer until well blended. Add 1 cup sour cream; mix well. Add eggs, at a time, beating on low speed after each just until blended. Our over crust. Bake 40 minutes or until center is almost set. Mix remaining sour cream, sugar and vanilla; carefully spread over cheesecake. Bake 10 minutes. Cool completely. Refrigerate 4 hours. Use foil handles to lift cheesecake from pan just before serving; top with berries.

KRAFT Kitchen Tips: Great news! You'll save 80 calories, 9 g of fat and 7 g of saturated fat per serving by preparing with margarine, Philadelphia ⅓ Less Fat Cream Cheese and Breakstone's Reduced Fat or Knudsen Light Sour Cream. Substitute 1½ cup crushed Oreo Cookies for the graham.

98890-09

PIPES & BOULDERS

Carson Bruce - Age 5

1 bag large marshmallows
1 bag large pretzel rods

1 bag melting chocolate chips
Nonpareils for decoration

This is so easy, but delicious and beautiful on any table! Pour chocolate chips into a microwavable bowl. Microwave for 30 seconds and then stir. Repeat 2-3 more times until completely melted. Spread out a large piece of wax paper on the counter. Pour your jar of nonpareils into a shallow bowl. Dip only the bottom surface of the marshmallow in the chocolate and wipe of the excess on the side of the bowl. Gently dip the chocolate end of the marshmallow into the nonpareils. You should only be able to see the nonpareils and no chocolate if done correctly. Place chocolate side up on wax paper to dry. These look amazing in a glass bowl and you can change the colors of the nonpareils for the holiday. (note: we have tried other types of sprinkles and they don't look as nice). Dip the pretzels in the chocolate half way. Over a separate dish, shake nonpareils or your favorite sprinkles on the pretzel. Dry on wax paper. These look great standing up in a cylinder shape dish or vase.

PISTACHIO PUDDING CAKE

Jimmy Gill

1 box yellow cake mix
1 (3.5 oz.) box instant pistachio
  pudding

8 oz. sour cream
4 eggs
1½ cup vegetable oil

Mix all ingredients together. Bake at 350° for 50 minutes.

PISTACHIO PUDDING GREEN CAKE

John (Jack) Benton
Andrew Benton

1 pkg. Pistachio Flavor Instant
  Pudding
1 pkg. Yellow Cake Mix
½ tsp. Almond Extract
4 Eggs

1¼ cups water
¼ cup oil
Several drops green food
  coloring, optional
confectioner's sugar, optional

Combine all ingredients. Pour into greased and floured 13 x 9 inch pan or bundt pan. Bake at 350 degrees for 45-50 minutes. It is very moist and light. Enjoy!

PRETZEL JELLO

Stephanie Louise - Age 16

2 cups pretzels, crushed
1½ stick butter, melted
2 tsp. sugar
8 oz. cream cheese
1 cup sugar

9 oz. Cool Whip
6 oz. strawberry Jello
2 cups boiling water
1 can (20 oz.) frozen
  strawberries

Dissolve Jello in 2 cups of boiling water. Add frozen strawberries to Jello, stir well, let it stand until it's consistency of egg whites. In a separate bowl, combine pretzels, butter, and 2 tsp. sugar. Press mixture into a 9 x 13 inch pan and bake at 375° for 10 minutes. Whip cream cheese, 1 cup sugar, Cool Whip and spread on cooled pretzel crust. Pour Jello mixture over whip cream, cover with plastic wrap and refrigerate overnight.

PUMPKIN PATCH BARS WITH CREAM CHEESE ICING

Braelyn Grace - Age 6
Blake Emmitt - Age 4

1½ cups all-purpose flour
1½ tsp. baking powder
2 tblsp cinnamon
¼ tsp. salt
¼ tsp. nutmeg
1¼ cups canned pumpkin
1¼ cups sugar

¾ cup vegetable oil
3 large eggs
1 (8-oz.) cream cheese
3 tblsp unsalted butter
1 tsp. vanilla extract
3 cups confectioners sugar

Pumpkin Bars- Preheat oven to 350 degrees. Prep a 13 x 9 inch glass baking pan by spraying with vegetable oil cooking spray. Using a mixer...on medium... beat together the pumpkin, sugar, vegetable oil and eggs until well incorporated. Add the cinnamon, salt and nutmeg followed by the baking powder and all-purpose flour. Make sure to scrape down your bowl to make sure that all of the ingredients are being blended well. Pour the batter into the 13 x 9 pan and bake for 25 to 30 minutes. Test with a toothpick or cake tester in the center to make sure that the cake is done.....it will come out clean if it is. Remove from the oven and allow to cool completely. Icing-Using a mixer......cream the butter and cream cheese until well blended......make sure to scrape down the bowl to make sure everything is being blended in. Add the vanilla and slowly add the confectioners sugar until fully incorporated. When the cake is completely cool.......spread the icing on the pumpkin bars. Yummy!!!! Refrigerate bars.

98890-09

PUMPKIN PIE

Issac Noah - Age 7

¾ cup Sugar
1 tsp. Ground Cinnamon
½ tsp. Salt
1 tsp. Pumpkin pie spice
2 Eggs

1 (15-oz.) can Pure Pumpkin
1 (12-oz.) can Evaporated Milk
1 Unbaked (9-inch) deep dish
  pie shell

Mix sugar, cinnamon, salt, pumpkin pie spice in a small bowl. In a large bowl beat the eggs. Stir in the pumpkin and evaporated milk. Add sugar and spice mixture. Pour into the pie shell. Bake in a preheated 425 degree oven for 15 minutes. Reduce oven temperature to 350 degrees and bake 40 to 50 minutes or until a knife inserted in the center comes out clean. Cool for 2 hours on a rack then refrigerate. Enjoy!

PUMPKIN PUFFS

Ella Albright - Age 11

1 tblsp Sugar
1 tblsp Brown Sugar
1 tsp. Beaten Egg
1 tsp. Oil
2 tsp. Butter Milk
1 tblsp Pumpkin
1¼ cup Flour sifted

1 tsp. Soda
⅛ tsp. Salt
¼ tsp. Allspice
¼ tsp. Cinnamon
¼ tsp. Cloves
½ tblsp. Raisins
½ tblsp. Nuts chopped

Preheat oven to 375°. Combine white and brown sugar, beaten egg, oil, butter milk and pumpkin in a bowl. Stir thoroughly. In a separate bowl, combine flour (sifted), soda, salt, allspice, cinnamon and cloves. Combine 2 Tablespoons of flour mixture, raisins and nuts. Stir just to moisten flour. Bake in 2 small lines muffin tins 15-18 mins.

PUPPY TO THE CHOW!!!

Becca McCarthy

½ cup peanut butter
¼ cup butter
1 cup chocolate chips
½ tsp. vanilla

9 cups Chex cereal or Corn
  Chex cereal
1-½ cups powdered sugar

1. Combine peanut butter, butter and chocolate chips in a microwave safe bowl. 2. Microwave for one minute then stir to blend all ingredients thoroughly. Add ½ tsp. vanilla. Stir well. 3. Place the 9 cups of Crispix cereal in a very large bowl. 4. Pour the peanut butter-chocolate mixture over the cereal and toss evenly, making sure all the cereal gets a good covering. 5. Coat with powdered sugar, sprinkling evenly over the cereal and tossing as you sprinkle to cover each piece well.

RAINBOW ICE CREAM SANDWICHES

Kendall Blair - Age 12

1 box chocolate cake mix
½ cup vegetable oil
2 eggs

2 tblsp. water
M&M's
ice cream

Preheat oven to 350°. In a large bowl, combine the oil, eggs, and water, then blend ingredients into cake mix until smooth. Drop generous teaspoons of the dough two inches apart on a cookie sheet. Bake for 8-10 minutes while the cookies are still soft press the M&M's into the top of each one, let them cool completely. Put ice cream between two cookies. Makes 18 to 24.

RASPBERRY CHOCOLATE CHIP CHEESECAKE

Andrew - Age 10

1 (8-oz.) pkg. Philadelphia cream cheese, softened
½ c. sugar
½ tsp. vanilla
2 eggs

½ c. mini semi-sweet chocolate chips
1 (6-oz.) Oreo pie crust
3 T. red raspberry preserves

Mix cream cheese, sugar and vanilla at medium speed with electric mixer until well blended. Add eggs; mix until blended. Stir in ½ cup of the chocolate chips. Pour into Oreo crust. Dot top of cheesecake with preserves. Cut through batter with knife several times for marble effect. Bake at 350° for 40 minutes or until center is almost set. Cool. Refrigerate 3 hours or overnight. Serves 8.

RASPBERRY CREAM

Anna Marie - Age 11

1 Large container French vanilla yogurt

1 pkg. frozen raspberries (don't thaw)

Take a half of container of yogurt and add to a mixing bowl. Add the package of frozen raspberries to the yogurt. Just mix until combined, trying not to mash the raspberries. Add to serving dishes and add a garnish.

RASPBERRY-LAYERED WHITE CHOCOLATE BROWNIES

Ella Albright - Age 11

1 package Brownie Mix
½ cup Water
½ cup Oil

1 Egg
¾ cups Raspberry Preserves or jam

(continued)

98890-09

Heat over to 350°. Grease 13 x 9-inch pan. In large bowl, combine brownie mix, water, oil and egg; beat 50 strokes by hand. Spread in greased pan. Bake at 350° for 33-35 minutes or until set. DO NOT OVERBAKE. Cool brownies 10 minutes; spread with preserves. Cool completely.

White Chocolate Buttercream

1 (6-oz.) White Baking Bar (or 3 cubes almond bark or 1 cup vanilla milk chips)

¾ cup Butter or Margarine, softened
¼ cup Powdered Sugar

In small saucepan over low heat, melt white baking bar, stirring constantly. Remove from heat; cool 30 minutes. In small bowl, beat butter and powdered sugar until fluffy. Gradually beat in cooled baking bar until smooth and fluffy. Carefully spread over preserves. Store in refrigerator. Allow to stand at room temperature 5-10 minutes before serving. Makes 36 bars.

RICE KRISPIE EASTER EGGS
(as seen on the Today Show)

Maggie Thompson - Age 3
Quinn Thompson - Age 2

6 c. Rice Krispies
1 bag large marshmallows
1 bag chocolate discs (any color)

1 bunch colored sprinkles

Have an adult melt all the marshmallows in a pan on the stove over low heat. When marshmallows are melted, add the Rice Krispies. Mix up well. Spray little hands with cooking spray. Scoop out ¼ c. of mixture on to little hands to mold into an Easter egg shape then set on wax paper. Have an adult heat chocolate discs in a mug in the microwave according to package directions. With an adult's supervision, dip one end of the egg into the chocolate then sprinkle it and set back on wax paper. Repeat for all eggs. When your first egg looks like the chocolate has 'set', dip the other end and repeat the process for all eggs. Soak all clothing/aprons worn by cooks in Oxi-Clean for one week, then wash.

RICE PUDDING DU JOUR

Gertrude Mary - Age 15

1 packet instant white rice
1 dash cinnamon
1 dash nutmeg

1 handful of raisins
¼ cup sugar
⅓ cup milk

Cook rice as packet states. When done, add sugar, milk, raisins, nutmeg and cinnamon. Spoon into bowl and enjoy on a cold winter's day!!

ROCKY ROAD BARS

Kallie N. - Age 12

1³/₄ cups Graham Cracker
  Crumbs
¹/₄ cup sugar
¹/₂ cup butter, melted
1¹/₂ cups semi-sweet chocolate
  morsels, divided

¹/₂ cup almonds, chopped,
  divided
1¹/₂ cups mini marshmallows

Combine Graham Cracker Crumbs, sugar and melted butter in a bowl. Press mixture onto the bottom of a greased 9 x 13 inch-baking pan. Sprinkle with 1 cup chocolate morsels. Bake at 350° (325° glass dish) for 15 minutes. Remove from oven and spread melted chocolate evenly across crumb layer. Sprinkle with half of the almonds and the marshmallows. Top with remaining 1 cup chocolate morsels and remaining 1 cup almonds. Continue baking 10 minutes or until marshmallows are lightly browned. Cool. Cut into bars. Makes 12 3x3 pieces. Prep Time: 10 minutes. Baking Time: 25 minutes

ROCKY ROAD BROWNIES

Carson Bruce - Age 5

1 box Plain Brownie Mix
1 cup mini marshmallows
¹/₂ cup chopped nuts of your
  choice

1 tsp. mint extract
1 tsp. vanilla extract
vanilla ice cream

Prepare box of brownie mix as indicated on box. Add the marshmallows, nuts, mint and vanilla extract. Mix. Bake as indicated on box. Serve with vanilla ice cream.

S' MORES PIE

Bennett John - Age 4
Annabelle Kady - Age 2

2 cups golden grahams
2 cups mini marshmallows

1 (12-oz.) bag chocolate chips

Fill an enamel or a foil pie pan with golden grahams, marshmallows and chocolate. Place on a grill while the fire is cooling down, but still hot. Cover for a couple of minutes, until the marshmallows melt. Cool before serving.

98890-09

S' MORES SANDWICH
(The PB&J of Desserts!)

Brodie Thomas - Age 4
Kassie Anne - Age 18 months

2 Slices of Bread
1 tblsp Smooth Peanut Butter
1 tblsp Chocolate Hazelnut
  Spread (Nutella)

1 tblsp Marshmallow Fluff

Toast your bread. Spread Peanut Butter on one slice and Chocolate Hazelnut Spread on the other slice. Spread Marshmallow Fluff on top of the peanut butter slice. Put the two slices together and cut as desired! If you have a panini press or sandwich iron, you do not have to toast the bread. This is a messy, gooey, tasty treat that any kid can help create!

S'MORES ON A STICK

Johnny Sanfilippo - Age 6

1 (14 oz.) can Eagle Sweetened
  Condensed Milk, divided
1½ cups milk chocolate mini
  chips, divided
1 cup mini marshmallows
11 whole graham crackers,
  halved crosswise

Toppings: chopped peanuts,
  mini candy-coated chocolate
  pieces, sprinkles
11 wooded craft sticks

Microwave half can of sweetened condensed milk in microwavable safe bowl on high (100% power) for 1½ minutes. Stir in 1 cup chips until smooth; stir in marshmallows. Spread chocolate mixture evenly by heaping tablespoons onto 11 graham cracker halves. Top with remaining graham cracker halves; place on wax paper. Microwave remaining half can of sweetened condensed milk for 1½ minutes, stir remaining ½ cup chips, stirring until smooth. Drizzle mixture over cookies and sprinkle with desired toppings. Let stand for 2 hours; insert wooden craft stick into center of each cookie.

SHREK CAKE

Jane Stewart - Age 7

1 box yellow cake mix
5 eggs
2 pkgs. pistachio instant
  pudding

½ cup milk
½ cup water
½ cup vegetable oil

Mix ingredients with electric mixer for two minutes. Pour into a greased bundt pan and bake at 375° for 45-55 minutes or until toothpick comes out clean. Sprinkle confectioners' sugar on cooled cake. Enjoy!

SIMPLICIOUS FLAN

Xavier Mendoza - Age 13

1 cup sugar (to make the
  Caramel)
1 can evaporated milk

1 can condensed milk
5 eggs
1 tblsp vanilla extract

Preheat oven to 350 degrees. Heat sugar in a pan until caramelized. Pour quickly into a round, 9 inch, oven proof pan. Spread covering only bottom of pan. Set Aside. Add all of Flan ingredients into an electric mixture. Mix on medium for about 20 seconds, or you can use a whisk. Using a strainer pour the mixture into the caramelized Pan (straining makes a smoother Flan). Put the whole pan with the Flan mixture into another rectangular pan, filling the rectangular pan with 1 inch of water. Creating a "bath" for your Flan. Place all in the oven for 1 hour. Let cool 2 hours before Flipping over onto a plate. Cool in refrigerator for 1 hour before serving. Enjoy!

SMORE

Zachary Trussell

1 graham cracker
1 marshmallow

1 chocolate bar

With help from an adult, prepare a camp fire. Find a roasting stick for your marshmallow. Hold the stick over the flame until golden brown. Place the chocolate bar on half of the graham cracker. Top with the golden marshmallow and the other half of the graham cracker.

SMORE

Tom Kuliavas

1 Graham Cracker
1 Marshmallow

1 Chocolate Bar

Place chocolate bar on half of graham cracker, followed by the marshmallow. Place the second half of the graham cracker on top. Place the smore in the microwave for 30 seconds. Now, you have a Smore!

SOUR CREAM POUND CAKE

Amanda - Age 10
Westchester Intermediate School

1 lb. butter (room temp.)
3 c. sugar
6 eggs
3 c. flour

$1/2$ tsp. salt
$1/4$ tsp. baking soda
1 c. sour cream
1 tsp. vanilla

(continued)

98890-09

Preheat oven to 350°. Using a mixer, cream butter and sugar, mix well. Add one egg at a time, beating well after each egg. Mix dry ingredients together and add alternating with sour cream to the first mixture, beating until smooth. Blend in vanilla; pour batter into well greased tube, bread, or bundt pan. Bake at 350° for 1 hour and 20 minutes. Watch closely at end of cooking time.

SPOON DELIGHT

Aidan Francis - Age 6

1 heaping tblsp creamy peanut butter

1 bag semi-sweet chocolate chips

Take a dinner tablespoon (not measuring spoon) and scoop a large spoonful of peanut butter. Open up the chocolate chip bag. Take the spoonful of peanut butter and dip it into the chocolate chips. Pull out and start eating.

STRAWBERRY CAKE

Timothy Sebastien - Age 5
Sophia Claire - Age 3

1 box white cake mix
½ 6 oz. box strawberry Jell-O
4 eggs
⅔ c. oil

2 c. strawberries
⅓ c. milk
1½ tsp. lemon juice

Mix the cake mix and Jell-O in a bowl. Add the eggs and oil to a measuring cup and whisk until well blended. Pour the wet ingredients on top of the dry and then mix. Hull the strawberries, and place them and the milk into a blender. Purée. Pour the puréed strawberries into a sieve to remove the seeds. Use a spatula to push the purée through the sieve until you have essentially only seeds remaining. Stir it all together, and add the lemon juice. Stir. Pour it into a prepared 13 x 9 inch pan, and bake at 325° for 30 minutes or until a toothpick inserted into the middle comes out clean.

STRAWBERRY CREAM POUND CAKE

Xavier Mendoza - Age 13

1 Pound Cake
1 tub Whip Cream

1 pkg. Fresh Strawberries

Cut pound cake into ½ inch slices. Lay half of your slices on a plate. Spread whip cream on the slices (as much as you would like). Cut strawberries into halves. Place on top of whip cream. Lay rest of sliced pound cake On top. Spread whip cream on top and more strawberries. Enjoy!

STRAWBERRY FROSTING

Serena - Age 7

Bread
Colored Frosting

Strawberries
Cracker Crumbs

Make a shape with bread using a cooking cutter or knife (with a grown up). Put it in the toaster or grill pan so you could harden it a little bit. Put the colored frosting on the bread. Next, make tiny lines on the bread with a knife. Put strawberries on it. Next, put cracker crumbs on it.

STRAWBERRY FROSTING

Timothy Sebastien - Age 5
Sophia Claire - Age 3

¼ **c. butter**
⅓ **c. milk, heated**
½ **pkg. strawberry Jell-O**

3 c. powdered sugar
1 tsp. vanilla

Cream the butter. Heat the milk until simmering, then add the Jell-O and stir until the Jell-O is dissolved. Let the milk cool to room temperature. Add the milk to the butter and beat to combine. Add the vanilla and powdered sugar (slowly) and mix until well combined. If you're adding strawberry purée instead of Jell-O, add it at with the milk (not heated). Strawberry purée will be more healthful. Purée about ½ c. hulled strawberries, and then strain them. You'll also want to increase the powdered sugar.

STRAWBERRY POPSICLES

Krista Brummet

4 cups Rinsed off ripe
strawberries
⅓ **cup Kool-Aid Tropical Punch**
mix

Flavored Soft Drink Mix
6 Small paper cups
6 Small wooden popsicle sticks

Remove stems from strawberries. Measure ⅓ cup of Kool-Aid mix and level it with the straight part of a knife. Place the strawberries and Kool-Aid mix in a blender and blend on low speed for 1½ to 2 minutes, until smooth. Pour the blend equally into the 6 paper cups. Freeze for 1 hour, then put 1 wooden stick in per paper cup and then freeze for 3 more hours until hardened. After it is frozen, completely peel off the cup over a sink and let it sit at room temperature to soften a little bit before serving. Enjoy!

98890-09

SUGAR AND SPICE TWISTS

Meghan and Gavin Cahill

1 tblsp. sugar
¼ tsp. ground cinnamon

1 pkg. 6 count of refrigerated breadsticks

1. Preheat oven to 350 degrees. Spray baking sheet with non stick cooking spray; set aside. 2. Combine sugar and cinnamon in shallow dish or plate; set aside. 3. Divide breadstick dough into 6 pieces. Roll each piece into 12-inch rope. Roll in sugar-cinnamon mixture. Twist into pretzel shape. Place on prepared baking sheet. Bake 15 to 18 minutes or until slightly browned. Remove from baking sheet. Cool 5 minutes. Serve warm. Makes 6 servings.

Hint: use colored sugar sprinkles in place of the sugar in this recipe for a fun "twist" of color.

SUPER FUDGE BROWNIES

Ashley Nicole - Age 13

½ cup butter or margarine
2 squares unsweetened
chocolate
1 cup sugar

2 eggs
1 tsp. vanilla
¾ cup flour
½ cup walnuts (optional)

Number of servings, 16. Grease an 8 x 8 x 2 inch baking pan. Melt butter and chocolate in a saucepan. Remove from heat; stir in sugar. Add eggs and vanilla; just until blended (don't over beat or brownies will rise too high, then fall). Stir in flour and nuts. Spread batter in pan. Bake in a 350 degree oven for 30 minutes. Cool and then cut into bars.

SWEET AND SALTY SURPRISES

Meagan Reigh - Age 12

12 Pretzels
12 Rolos (or chocolate caramel candy)

12 Pecans or Marshmallows

Preheat oven to 200 degrees. Place Pretzels on tray and then place Rolos on Pretzels. Put Pan in oven for 2 minutes or until the candy begins to melt. Pull out of oven. Put pecans or marshmallows on the top and push down. Makes a dozen. Enjoy!

SWEET SWEET FUDGE

Jaime M - Age 12

⅔ cup margarine
3 cups sugar
⅔ cup evaporated milk
1 (12-oz.) pkg. semi-sweet
  chocolate chips

(7-oz.) marshmallow creme
1 tsp. vanilla

Lightly grease 9 x 13 inch pan. In a heavy 3 quart pan, combine margarine, sugar, and evaporated milk. Bring mixture to a full boil on medium heat, stirring constantly. Continue boiling over medium heat for 5 minutes or until thermometer reaches 234 degrees, stirring constantly to prevent scorching. Remove from heat and add chocolate chips until melted; and marshmallow creme and vanilla and mix well. Spread into prepared pan and cool at room temperature; cut into squares and serve.

TASTY TREATS

Daniella Dolores - Age 12

2 cups mini marshmallows
3 cups Cocoa Krispies

1½ tblsp. butter or margarine

Melt margarine or butter in medium saucepan over low heat. Add marshmallows and stir until completely melted. Remove from heat. Place medium saucepan on cooling rack. Add COCOA KRISPIES cereal. Stir until well coated. Using wax paper, press mixture evenly into 9 x 9 inch pan sprayed with cooking spray. Cut into 2 inch squares when cool.

TEDDY HAS GONE BANANAS!

Anne - Age 12

Nabisco Teddy Grahams -
  chocolate

banana pudding

In a tall glass, layer the Teddy Grahams with banana pudding. Repeat layers until the top of the glass. Very easy and quick and great tasting. If you are watching the sugar...you can use sugar free pudding. Teddy Grahams are a good source of Calcium and made with 5 grams whole grain per serving (24 pieces).

THE BEST BROWNIES

Jack S - Age 13

½ cup vegetable oil
1 cup sugar
1 tsp. vanilla extract
2 eggs
½ cup unsifted flour

⅓ cup Hershey's cocoa
¼ tsp. baking powder
¼ tsp. salt
½ cup chopped nuts (optional)

(continued)

98890-09

Blend oil, sugar, and vanilla in bowl. Add eggs, beat well. In a separate bowl, combine flour, cocoa, baking powder, and salt. Gradually add eggs to mixture until blended well. Stir in nuts. Spread in greased square pan. Bake 20-25 minutes at 350 degrees.

THE BEST CHOCOLATE CAKE EVER
(made by Daddy)

Kamren Christopher - Age 5½
Keaten Lawrence - Age 7

Devil's food cake mix
package of instant chocolate
**   pudding**

4 eggs
½ cup Crisco oil
1¼ cups water

Preheat oven to 350°. Grease and flour 10 inch bundt pan. Combine ingredients into large bowl. Beat at medium speed for 2 minutes. Bake for 50-60 minutes. Cool in pan for 25 minutes. Place on cooling rack until completely cool.

THE BEST SOUR CREAM APPLE PIE

John - Age 4
Janie - Age 2

¾ cup sugar
¼ tsp. nutmeg
⅛ tsp. salt
1 egg
1 unbaked pie shell
1 tsp. pure vanilla extract
2 tblsp flour
1 cup sour cream
3 cups Granny Smith apples,
**   peeled and thinly sliced**

⅓ cup sugar/light brown sugar
**   (mix together)**
¼ cup butter (cut into small
**   squares)**
⅓ cup flour
1 tsp. cinnamon
⅛ tsp. ground cloves (optional)

In a bowl, combine sugar, flour and salt. Stir in sour cream, egg, vanilla and nutmeg - mix until smooth. Add apples and pour mixture into unbaked pie shell. Bake at 400 degrees for 15 minutes. Reduce oven to 350 degrees and bake 30 minutes longer. Prepare topping: Combine sugar, flour, butter and spice(s). Sprinkle on top of baked pie. Return to oven and bake 15 minutes or until light brown. Enjoy!

THE BEST VANILLA FROSTING EVER

Mary Lillie - Age 13

1½ sticks butter (room
**   temperature)**
3¼ cups powdered sugar

¼ cup milk
2 tsp. vanilla extract
1 dash salt

(continued)

With an electric mixer, beat together the ingredients for about three minutes, or until smooth. You can dye the frosting whichever color you choose and use it to frost a cake or cupcakes, it tastes just as good plain too!

THE BOMB BROWNIES

Millie Claire - Age 13

1 box Brownie Mix
1 King Size bag M & M's

1 can Chocolate Frosting
1 cup Marshmallow Fluff

Bake brownie mix according to directions on the box. Let brownies cool and frost the brownies with the can of chocolate frosting. Spread marshmallow fluff on top. Finally, sprinkle bag of M&M's on top for an amazing brownie!

THE CAKE DOCTOR'S ALMOND CREAM CHEESE POUND CAKE

Sophie Clark - Age 6
Ian Clark - Age 4

vegetable oil spray for misting the pan
flour for dusting the pan
1 (18.5 oz.) pkg. butter recipe golden cake mix
1 (8-oz.) package cream cheese, at room temperature

4 large eggs
1/2 cup water
1/2 cup vegetable oil, such as canola, corn, safflower, soybean, or sunflower
1 tsp. pure vanilla extract
1 tsp. pure almond extract

Place a rack in the center of the oven and preheat the oven to 350°. Lightly mist a 10-inch tube pan with vegetable oil spray, then dust with flour. Shake out the excess flour. Set the pan aside. Place the cake mix, cream cheese, eggs, water, sugar, oil, vanilla, and almond extracts in a large mixing bowl. Blend with an electric mixer on low speed for 1 minute. Stop the machine and scrape down the sides of the bowl with a rubber spatula. Increase the mixer speed to medium and beat 2 minutes more, scraping the sides down again if needed. The batter should look well blended. Pour the batter into the prepared pan, smoothing it out with the rubber spatula. Place the pan in the oven. Bake the cake until it is golden brown and springs back when lightly pressed with your finger, 35 - 40 minutes. Remove the pan from the oven and place it on a wire rack to cool for 20 minutes. Run a long, sharp knife around the edge of the cake, invert it onto a rack, then invert it onto a serving platter so that it is right side up. Slice the cake while it is still a little warm. *Store this cake, covered in plastic wrap or under a glass dome, at room temperature for up to 1 week. Or freeze it, wrapped in aluminum foil, for up to 6 months. Thaw the cake overnight on the counter before serving.

98890-09

THE CAKE DOCTOR'S FRESH ORANGE CAKE

Sophie Clark - Age 6
Ian Clark - Age 4

vegetable oil spray for misting
  the pan
flour for dusting the pan
1 (18.5 oz.) pkg. yellow cake mix
  with pudding
1 cup fresh orange juice (From
  about 5 medium oranges) or
  from the carton
½ cup vegetable oil, such as
  canola, corn, safflower,
  soybean, or sunflower

¼ cup granulated sugar
1 tsp. pure vanilla extract
4 large eggs
Glaze:
1 cup confectioners' sugar,
  sifted
3 tblsp. fresh orange juice (from
  about 1 medium orange) or
  from carton
1 tsp. fresh grated orange zest
  (from about 1 medium orange)

Place a rack in the center of the oven and preheat the oven to 350°. Lightly mist a 12-cup Bundt pan with vegetable oil spray, then dust with flour. Shake out the excess flour. Set the pan aside. Place the cake mix, orange juice, oil, sugar, vanilla, and eggs in a large mixing bowl. Blend with an electric mixer on low speed for 1 minute. Stop the machine and scrape down the sides of the bowl with a rubber spatula. Increase the mixer speed to medium and beat for 2 minutes more, scraping the sides down again if needed. The batter should look thick and well blended. Pour the batter into the prepared pan and place it in the oven. Bake the cake until it is golden brown and just starts to pull away from the sides of the pan, 45 - 47 minutes. Remove the pan from the oven and place it on a wire rack to cool for 20 minutes. Run a long, sharp knife around the edge of the cake and invert it onto a rack to cool completely, 30 minutes more. Meanwhile, prepare the glaze. Combine the confectioners' sugar, fresh orange juice, and orange zest in a small bowl and stir with a wooden spoon until smooth. Place the cake on a serving platter and pour the glaze over the top, letting it drizzle down the sides and into the center. Let the glaze set for a few minutes before slicing. *Store this cake under a glass cake dome or covered in plastic wrap at room temperature for up to 1 week. Or freeze it, wrapped in aluminum foil, for up to 6 months. Thaw the cake overnight on the counter before serving.

THE GREATEST CHOCOLATE COVERED BANANAS

John W. - Age 13

2 Bananas (ripe, but firm)
6 oz. milk chocolate (chopped
  or chocolate chips)

2 tblsp vegetable oil
Sprinkles (optional)
4 Popsicle sticks

First, line a baking sheet with nonstick foil or parchment paper. Cut the bananas in half and insert a Popsicle stick into each half. Place them on the baking sheet and freeze for 15 minutes. Meanwhile, melt the chocolate with the oil in a measuring cup or small bowl in the microwave

(continued)

(check it every 30 seconds). Roll each banana half in the milk chocolate, then put the sprinkles on if using. Freeze until the chocolate sets, approximately 30 minutes.

THE "BEST" BROWNIES

Elise Marie - Age 13

1 stick butter
1 cup sugar
4 eggs
1 can Hershey's syrup
1 cup flour
1 - 1½ cup walnuts

Frosting ingredients as follows:
1½ cup sugar
6 T. butter
6 T. milk
½ cup chocolate chips

Mix the butter, sugar, eggs, syrup, flour, and walnuts together. Beat this very well. Pour the mixture into a greased 11 x 15-inch pan. Bake this for 25-30 minutes at 350°. Frosting: Boil sugar, butter, and milk for 30 seconds. Then add chocolate chips and beat. Pour over baked brownies and refrigerate.

TROPICAL BEACH DESSERT

Claire Jameson - Age 5
Benjamin Thomas - Age 2

1 packet blue Jello gelatin
1 packet gummy dolphins
10 graham crackers

6 clear plastic cups
6 tropical drink umbrellas

Prepare 1 package of blue gelatin Jello. Pour Jello into 6 clear, plastic cups. Add a couple of gummy dolphins into each cup. Refrigerate until Jello is ready. Take 10 graham crackers and place into a ziploc bag. Smash up the graham crackers until they look like sand. Sprinkle "sand" on top of the Jello cups but leave half of the cup blue so that it looks like half sand and half water. Add drink umbrellas to each cup and enjoy! This is a great recipe for summer birthday parties too!

TURTLE BARS

Kallie N. - Age 12

1½ cups Graham Cracker
  Crumbs
½ cup butter, melted
1 (12-oz.) pkg. semi-sweet
  chocolate morsels

pecans, chopped (optional)
1 (12.25-oz.) jar caramel topping

Combine Graham Cracker Crumbs and melted butter in a bowl. Press mixture onto the bottom of a 9 x 13 inch baking pan. Sprinkle with chocolate morsels and pecans. Top with caramel topping. Bake at 350°

(continued)

98890-09

(325° glass dish) for 15 minutes or until morsels melt. Cool in pan on a wire rack. Refrigerate 30 minutes; cut into squares. Makes 12 3x3 pieces. Prep Time: 10 minutes Baking Time: 15 minutes Chilling Time: 30 minutes

ULTIMATE BROWNIE RECIPE

Shpat Alili

8 1 oz. Squares of unsweetened chocolate
1 cup Butter
5 Eggs
3 cups Sugar

1 tblsp Vanilla
1 tspn Salt
2½ cups Chopped pecans or walnuts, toasted

Preheat oven to 375 degrees F. Grease a 9 X13 inch pan. Melt chocolate and butter in a saucepan over low heat; set aside. In a mixer, beat eggs, sugar and vanilla at high speed for 10 minutes. Blend in chocolate mixture, flour and salt until just mixed. Stir in the nuts. Pour into prepared pan. Bake for 35-40 minutes. (Don't over bake) Cool and frost if desired (but not necessary). This is one of the best brownie recipes ever!

VANILLA CUPCAKES

Taylor - Age 13
Sarah

2½ cups All-purpose Flour
2 tsp. Baking Powder
½ tsp. Baking Soda
½ tsp. Salt
½ cup Milk

½ cup Vegetable Oil
1 tsp. Vanilla Extract
1 stick Unsalted Butter, softened
1 cup Sugar
3 Large Eggs

Preheat oven to 350°. Line two 12 cup muffin pans with paper liners. Combine the flour, baking powder, baking soda and salt in a medium bowl. In small bowl, whisk together the milk, oil, and vanilla extract. Using an electric mixer on medium speed, cream the butter and sugar together, about 3 minutes. Add the eggs, one at a time, to the butter and sugar mixture, beating well after each addition. Reduce the speed and alternately add the flour mix and the milk mix, beginning and ending with the flour mixture and beating until just combined. Fill the lined cupcake tins with the batter and bake until a toothpick inserted in the center comes out clean, 15 to 20 minutes. Cool completely on a wire rack.

VANILLA CUPCAKES WITH STRAWBERRY FROSTING

Elizabeth Marie - Age 5

Cupcakes

3½ cups all-purpose flour
2 cups sugar
2 tsp. baking powder
½ tsp. salt

⅔ cup plus 1 T. vegetable oil
2 T. cider vinegar
2½ tsp. vanilla extract
2 cups water

Preheat oven to 350°. Line two muffin tins with cupcake liners. Combine flour, sugar, baking powder, and salt in a large bowl and set aside. In another bowl, combine oil, vinegar, vanilla and water and add to dry ingredients. Whisk together until well blended. Fill cupcake cups about two thirds full. Bake 33-35 minutes or until the cake springs back when lightly touched. Cool completely before frosting.

Frosting

4 T. strawberry jam
¼ cup butter or butter
 substitute, softened

2½ cups powdered sugar

In a microwave-safe container, microwave the jam for 20-30 seconds until melted. Combine all ingredients. Using a mixer, beat ingredients until well blended. Spread on cooled cupcakes. Makes 24 cupcakes.

VANILLA FLAN

Adreanna Buster - Age 18

¾ cup granulated sugar
1 (12-oz.) can Nestle Carnation
 Evaporated Milk
1 (14-oz.) can Nestle Carnation
 Sweetened Condensed Milk

3 Large eggs
1 tblsp. vanilla extract

Preheat oven to 325°F. Heat sugar in small, heavy-duty saucepan over medium-low heat, stirring constantly, for 3 to 4 minutes or until dissolved and caramel colored. Quickly pour onto bottom of deep-dish 9 inch pie plate; swirl around bottom and side to coat. Combine evaporated milk, sweetened condensed milk, eggs and vanilla extract in medium bowl. Pour into prepared pie plate. Place pie plate in large roasting pan; fill roasting pan with warm water to about 1-inch depth. Bake for 45 to 50 minutes or until knife inserted near center comes out clean. Remove flan from water. Cool on wire rack. Refrigerate for 4 hours or overnight. To serve: Run small spatula around edge of pie plate. Invert serving plate over pie plate. Turn over; shake gently to release. Caramelized sugar forms sauce. Makes 8 servings.

98890-09

VERY BERRY RICE KRISPIES

Samantha
Sydney
Brendan

4 tblsp. Butter
1 bag Large Marshmallows
3 cups Rice Krispies

3 cups Captain Crunch - Crunch
Berry Cereal

Melt the butter in a pan and add marshmallows until melted. Add Rice Krispies and Crunch Berry Cereal and mix until well blended. Pour into a 9 x 12 inch pan and let cool. Enjoy! The kids (and Moms) love them too!!!!

WALNUT BROWNIES

Sachi Bhobe

1 cup Butter
4 1 oz. Squares unsweetened
  chocolate
2 cups White sugar
3 Eggs

1 tspn Vanilla extract
1 cup All-purpose flour
1½ cups Chopped walnuts
1 cup Semisweet chocolate
  chips

Melt butter and 4 squares unsweetened chocolate in a medium size saucepan over moderate heat. Remove from heat. Preheat oven to 350 degrees F (175 degrees C). Beat in sugar gradually with a wooden spoon until thoroughly combined. Add eggs, one at a time, beating well after each addition; stir in vanilla. Stir in flour until thoroughly combined. Stir 1 cup of the walnuts. Spread into greased 13 x 9 x 2 inch pan. Combine remaining ½ cup walnuts with chocolate chips; sprinkle over top of brownie mixture, pressing down lightly. Bake in a preheated oven for 35 minutes or until top springs back when lightly pressed with fingertip. Cool completely in pan on wire rack. Cut into bars or squares.

WATERMELON GRANITA

Timothy Sebastien - Age 5
Sophia Claire - Age 3

4 c. watermelon, cut into pieces
¼ c. sugar

1 lemon, juiced

Freeze a 13 x 9 pan to ensure it is cold before you begin. Purée the watermelon in a food processor. Once smooth, add the sugar and lemon juice and pulse to combined. Pour into the frozen pan, then place into the freezer. After an hour, use a fork to rake the mixture to break up the ice crystals. Return to the freezer. Rake every half hour and continue freezing until it is completely ice crystals fluffed by the fork. Place in an airtight container and keep frozen. If the mixture melts, simply repeat the freezing process. Rake again before serving.

WILL AND CHARLIE'S CAKE

William John - Age 4
Charles Thomas - Age 2
(with Grandmother Karma Crowell)

1 box plain Angel food cake mix
1 (20-oz.) can crushed pineapple
 with the syrup
1 tsp. vanilla
toasted coconut (optional)
toasted slivered almonds
 (optional)

Cream Cheese Icing Ingredients:
(8-oz.) cream cheese
(4-oz.) butter
1 lb. confectioners sugar
1 tsp. vanilla

Mix the cake mix, pineapple and vanilla together in a bowl. Pour into an ungreased 9 x 13 inch cake pan. Bake for 30-40 minutes in a 350° oven. To make the icing, beat the cream cheese, butter, sugar and vanilla together. After the cake has cooled, you may ice the cake with the frosting. Top with toasted coconut or toasted slivered almonds, if desired.

WORM DIRT

Aidan Francis - Age 6

1 cup ready-made chocolate
 pudding
1/4 cup crushed, chocolate wafer
 cookies

2 gummy worms

Scoop out chocolate pudding into a serving dish. Make sure dish is not too large. Add the gummy worms and mix just until the worms are incorporated. Sprinkle the crushed cookies on top for the dirt. Enjoy!

YUMMY CHOCOLATE COVERED STRAWBERRIES

Elizabeth Jonah - Age 7

16 oz. milk chocolate chips
2 tblsp. shortening

1 lb. fresh strawberries with
 leaves

Insert toothpicks into the tops of the strawberries. In a double boiler, melt the chocolate and shortening, stirring occasionally until smooth. Holding them by the toothpicks, dip the strawberries into the chocolate mixture. Turn the strawberries upside down and insert the toothpick into Styrofoam for the chocolate to cool.

98890-09

YUMMY PUDDING GRAVEYARD (MUD PIE)

Brianna Logan
Taylor Nicole - Age 15
Kaleigh Mackenzie - Age 13

2 (4-oz.) pkgs. jell-o chocolate instant pudding
3½ cup Milk 2 % is best or whole milk
1 (12-oz.) ctn. Cool Whip whipped topping thawed

1 (16-oz.) pkg. chocolate wafer cookies (by ice cream toppings in grocery store)
1 pkg. Milano cookies
1 bag pumpkin candy corn
1 tube black decorators icing

Prepare pudding as directed using 3½ cups milk. Stir in 3 cups of whipped topping and ½ of the cookie crumbs. Layer in 9 X 13 pan and cover top with remaining crushed cookie crumbs. Decorate using dollops of whipped topping as ghosts. Write "RIP" or "Boo" on Milano cookies and stick into pudding to look like gravestones. Decorate with pumpkin candies. Refrigerate after making. Could also be used in Spring time decorated with Gummy worms sticking out of "mud" pudding and real flowers. We've made individual serving in cute plastic cups and put into mini- flower pots for the perfect spring birthday party treat.

YUMMY S'MORES

Nicholas Butera - Age 11
Joshua Butera - Age 8

2 graham crackers
6 Hershey's milk chocolate squares

2 marshmallows
1 stick

Put marshmallows on a stick; heat them over an open flame until gooey and burnt (have an adult help you!!). Put the chocolate squares on a graham cracker; put the melted marshmallow on the chocolate; put the other graham cracker on top of the marshmallow and voila!! Makes 1 YUMMY S' MORE.

YUMMY TOFFEE BARS

Olivia Patricia - Age 6
Freddie James - Age 4

1 box Graham Crackers
2 sticks Butter

½ cup Dark Brown Sugar
1 cup Chocolate Chips

Preheat Oven to 350°. Line a 9 x 13 inch pan with Graham Crackers. Melt the butter in a pan. Add the sugar. Boil for 2 minutes. Pour over crackers. Bake 10 Minutes. Let cool a few minutes, add chips, let melt a minute, spread. Cool, break apart, and Enjoy!

Recipe Favorites

98890-09

cookies & candy

Helpful Hints

- Unbaked cookie dough can be covered and refrigerated for up to 24 hours or frozen in an airtight container for up to 9 months.

- Bake one cookie sheet at a time using the middle oven rack.

- Decorate cookies with chocolate by placing cookies on a rack over waxed paper. Dip the tines of a fork into melted chocolate, and wave the fork gently back and forth to make wavy line decorations.

- Some cookies need indentations on top to fill with jam or chocolate. Use the rounded end of a honey dipper.

- Dip cookie cutters in flour or powdered sugar and shake off excess before cutting. For chocolate dough, dip cutters in baking cocoa.

- Tin coffee cans make excellent freezer containers for cookies.

- If you only have one cookie sheet on hand, line it with parchment paper. While one batch is baking, load a second sheet of parchment paper to have another batch ready to bake. Cleaning is also easier.

- When a recipe calls for packed brown sugar, fill the correct size measuring cup with sugar, and then use one cup size smaller to pack the brown sugar into its cup.

- Cut-up dried fruit often sticks to the blade of your knife. To prevent this problem, coat the blade of your knife with a thin film of vegetable spray before cutting.

- Instead of folding nuts into brownie batter, sprinkle on top of batter before baking. This keeps nuts crunchy instead of soggy.

- Only use glass or shiny metal pans. Dark or nonstick pans will cause brownies to become soggy and low in volume.

- When making bars, line pan with aluminum foil and prepare as directed. The bars can be lifted out, and cleanup is easy.

- Cutting bars is easier if you score the bars right as the pan leaves the oven. When the bars cool, cut along the scored lines.

- Use a double boiler for melting chocolate to prevent it from scorching. A slow cooker on the lowest setting also works well for melting chocolate, especially when coating a large amount of candy.

- Parchment paper provides an excellent nonstick surface for candy. Waxed paper should not be used for high-temperature candy.

COOKIES & CANDY

AMERICAN FLAG COOKIE

Charlie James - Age 7

1 tube prepackaged sugar
  cookie dough
1 pint blueberries

1 pint strawberries - sliced
Cool Whip

Spread out sugar cookie on greased pan. Bake according to directions. Let cool. Cover with Cool Whip. Place 50 blueberries in upper left corner. Spread out strawberries in horizontal lines like stripes for the flag.

ANDES PEPPERMINT CRUNCH DARK CHOCOLATE COOKIES

Sam Bonham

2 sticks butter, softened
2 cups sugar
2 eggs
2 tsp. vanilla extract
¾ c. Hershey's "Special Dark"
  Cocoa

1 tsp. baking soda
½ tsp. salt
(10-oz.) pkg. Andes Peppermint
  Crunch baking chips

Heat oven to 350°F. Beat butter and sugar in a large bowl until creamy. Add eggs and vanilla; beat until light and fluffy. Stir together flour, cocoa, baking soda and salt; gradually blend into butter mixture. Stir in crunch. Drop by rounded teaspoons onto ungreased cookie sheets. Bake 8 to 9 minutes. (DO NOT OVERBAKE; COOKIES WILL BE SOFT. they WILL PUFF WHILE BAKING AND FLATTEN UPON COOLING.) Cool slightly. Remove from cookie sheets to wire racks; cool completely. makes about 4½ dozen cookies.

AUNT ALMA'S OATMEAL COOKIES
(Grant's favorite!)

Grant Woodward - Age 12

1 cup Lard (½ lb)
1¼ cup Sugar
2 Eggs beaten lightly
½ tsp. Salt
1 tsp. Baking Soda dissolved in
  2 T. Molasses
2 cups Flour sifted

½ tsp. Nutmeg
½ tsp. Cinnamon
¼ tsp. ground Cloves
2 cups rolled Oatmeal (not
  instant)
½ cup Nuts, chopped
½ cup Raisins

Sift flour with nutmeg, cinnamon and ground cloves. Set aside. Melt lard in 3 or 4 quart saucepan. Let cool. In another bowl, add sugar, beaten eggs and molasses with baking soda. Mix in flour mixture. Mix

(continued)

in oatmeal, nuts and raisins. Cover and refrigerate a couple of hours or overnite. Preheat oven to 400°. Form cookies into 1" balls on ungreased cookie sheet. (12 balls per sheet). Bake 10 minutes (5 minutes on lower rack and 5 minutes on middle rack). Remove cookies to cool on rack.

BELLY BUTTON COOKIES

Allison Lynn - Age 11
Mallory Jean - Age 8
Ryan - Age 4

Jewel Brand Pretzel Rings   **M&M Candies**
Hershey's Hugs Kisses

Line cookie sheet with parchment paper. Place pretzel rings flat on sheet. Place one unwrapped Hershey Kiss in center of each pretzel ring. Heat in 200 degree oven, about 4-5 minutes, until candy softens. Remove from oven and press one M&M candy into center of each pretzel, flattening out the tips on the melted Hershey Kiss candy. Place in freezer for a few moment to allow them to set back up. Remove from sheet and store in tightly closed container. Kids have fun making these for all holidays using the different colored M&M candies.

BRIONNA'S CHOCOLATE CHIP COOKIES

Susan B. Johnson
Brionna Rae Lalis

¾ cup white sugar   **2½ cups flour**
¾ cup brown sugar   **½ cup oatmeal**
1 cup butter   **(12-oz.) chocolate chips**
2 med. eggs   **(preferably dark chocolate) 18**
1 tsp. vanilla extract   **oz. for real chocolate lovers**
1 tsp. salt

These some how turn out better if you can mix the ingredients by hand. Mix the sugars and butter until creamy. Add the eggs and vanilla and mix till fully blended. Add salt and baking soda and slowly add flour, mixing portions in at a time. Add oatmeal and chocolate chips. Spoon onto cookie sheet with about 1 inch between cookies. Bake at 350 degrees for 12-13 minutes. Let them cool a bit before you eat them (so they don't fall apart), but you must try one while still warm! Brionna has been making these cookies since she was a child. We have shipped them all over the country as she competed with her 2 uncles for 'the best chocolate chip cookie'. She now lives in Athens, Greece and still makes the cookies when she can get chips brought to her from the States.

BUCKEYES

A Rule

3 lbs. confectioners sugar
2 lbs. creamy peanut butter
1 lb. margarine (softened)

12 oz. bag chocolate chips
(2-oz.) paraffin wax

Mix confectioners sugar, peanut butter, and margarine together. A pie crust cutter works well for this job. Form into balls, approximately the size of a walnut and let cool at least 1 hour. Melt chocolate chips and wax. Keep stirring to prevent burning. Dip balls into chocolate not quite submerged. Store in a cool area.

BUTTERFLY COOKIES

Mackenzie - Age 10

2¼ c. all-purpose flour
¼ tsp. salt
1 c. sugar
¾ c. (1½ sticks) butter,
  softened

1 egg
1 tsp. vanilla
1 tsp. almond extract

Combine flour and salt in medium bowl; set aside. Beat sugar and butter in large bowl with an electric mixer at medium speed until fluffy. Beat in egg, vanilla, and almond extract. Gradually add flour mixture. Beat at low speed until well blended. Divide dough in half. Cover; refrigerate 30 minutes or until firm. Preheat oven to 350°. Grease cookie sheets. Roll half of dough on lightly floured surface to ¼ inch thickness. Cut out cookies using cookie cutters. Repeat with remaining dough. Bake 12 to 15 minutes or until edges are lightly browned. Remove to wire racks; cool completely. Makes about 20 cookies.

CADE'S CHOCOLATE CHIP COOKIES

Cade Edward - Age 6

¾ cup sugar
¾ cup packed brown sugar
1 cup butter, softened
2 large eggs, beaten
1 tsp. vanilla extract
2¼ cups all-purpose flour

1 tsp. baking soda
¾ tsp. salt
2 cups semi-sweet chocolate
  chips
1 cup chopped pecans, if
  desired

Preheat oven to 375 degrees. Mix sugar, brown sugar, butter, vanilla and eggs in a large bowl by hand. Stir in flour, baking soda, and salt. The dough will be very stiff. Stir in chocolate chips and pecans if desired. Drop dough by rounded tablespoonfuls 2 inches apart onto ungreased cookie sheet. Bake 8 to 10 minutes or until light brown. The centers will be soft. Let cool completely then remove from cookie sheet.

CHOCOLATE BALLS
(A Healthy Snack or Dessert)

Baylee Danielle - Age 4
Callie Mari - Age 2

1½ cups Walnuts
1 dash Salt
12 Pitted Dates
2 T. Water

⅓ cup Nestle Cocoa Powder or
   Raw Cacao
½ tsp. Vanilla

In a food processor, chop the walnuts and salt using the S blade then pour into a bowl and set aside. Using the processor and the S blade again, blend the dates and water until smooth. You may need to add more water 1 tsp. at a time. Add the remaining ingredients including the chopped nuts and process until mixed well. Form into balls and you're done!

TIPS: We like these room temperature but they store best in the refrigerator. You can roll them in chopped nuts or cocoa powder or roll them around a cashew. But our favorite way is to press your thumb into the ball to create a well. Add a raspberry or raspberry sauce (just blend some raspberries and pour into the well).

CHOCOLATE BALLS

Claire Elizabeth - Age 9

4 whole graham crackers
⅓ cup sugar

¼ cup chocolate syrup
¼ tsp. flour

Crush the graham crackers into crumbs. Mix all ingredients together. Shape the mixture into small balls and place on wax paper-lined pan. If the mixture is too thin, add more crushed graham crackers. Put the balls into the freezer for an hour. When you remove them from the freezer, sprinkle with powdered sugar. Share them with your friends.

CHOCOLATE CHOCOLATE-CHIP BROWNIES

Elizabeth Kaye - Age 7
Nathaniel Joseph - Age 9

½ c. unsalted butter (1 stick)
2 (1-oz.) squares unsweetened
   chocolate
1 c. sugar
½ c. flour
½ c. chopped pecans or
   walnuts

½ tsp. baking powder
1 tsp. vanilla extract
2 eggs, slightly beaten
1 c. semi-sweet chocolate chips

Preheat oven to 350 degrees. Butter an 8-inch square pan. Melt butter and unsweetened chocolate. In a mixing bowl combine butter/chocolate with sugar, flour, nuts, baking powder, and vanilla. Stir well. Add eggs

(continued)

98890-09

and mix thoroughly. Add chocolate chips. Pour batter into pan and bake for 30-40 minutes.

CHOCOLATE COVERED STRAWBERRIES

Jennifer Sue - Age 12

strawberries   **chocolate**

Melt the chocolate of your choice. Dip strawberries in the melted chocolate. Refrigerate.

CHOCOLATE CRINKLE COOKIES

Mary Lillie - Age 13

½ cup powdered sugar
1⅔ cup flour
½ cup unsweetened cocoa powder
1½ tsp. baking powder
¼ tsp. salt

1 stick butter (room temperature)
1¼ cups sugar
2 large eggs
½ tsp. vanilla extract

Preheat the oven to 350 degrees and grease two baking sheets with baking spray or butter. Using a wooden spoon, stir together the flour, cocoa, baking powder, and salt. In another bowl, with an electric mixer, on medium speed for about three minutes, beat together the butter and sugar, add the eggs and keep beating until they blend in. Slowly add the flour mix into the butter mixture and mix on low just until blended. Put the powdered sugar into a bowl and take golf ball sized chunks of rounded dough and roll in the powdered sugar. Put the dough onto a baking sheet 2 ½ inches apart from each other. Bake the cookies for 15 minutes.

CHOCOLATE RICE KRISPIE DROP COOKIES

Georgina Olivia - Age 9

Rice Krispies   **Baking chocolate**

Break the chocolate in to squares, melt the chocolate, add Rice Krispies. Line a baking sheet with parchment paper, put the mix on the paper in individual portions. Then refrigerate until the chocolate is set. Then eat!

CHOCOLATE RINGS

Eric Puccini

1 bag Pretzel Rings   **1 bag M&M's**
1 bag Hershey Kisses

(continued)

Preheat Oven to 350 degrees. Put pretzels on a cookie sheet. Put the Hershey Kisses on the pretzels Put it in the oven for two minutes. Take them out of the oven and immediately put the M&M's on top of the Hershey Kisses. Let cool & enjoy!

CHOCOLATE SURPRISE

Whitney Keana - Age 8

⅔ cups powder sugar
1 tsp. cinnamon
2 tblsp chocolate milk powder
⅔ cups water

1 tspn dark brown sugar
2 cups milk
vanilla ice cream

Add all ingredients to a mixing bowl EXCEPT the ice cream. Mix until smooth. Scoop vanilla ice cream into a serving bowl. Drizzle the chocolate syrup over the ice cream and enjoy.

CHOCOLATE WAFER COOKIES

Kendall Blair - Age 12

2 cups flour
¾ cups cocoa powder
1 tsp. baking soda
½ tsp. salt

1¼ cups butter
2 cups sugar
2 large eggs
2 tsp. vanilla

Mix butter, sugar, and eggs until smooth, add vanilla, gradually add any remaining ingredients. Chill 1 hour. Roll into 1 inch balls, roll balls in granulated sugar, and bake on parchment paper at 350° for 9 minutes. When done, let cool for 5 minutes.

COCONUT COOKIES

Issac Noah - Age 7

2 pkgs. Shredded coconut (fine)
1 can Sweetened Condensed
   Milk

1 Extra Large Egg

Mix all the ingredients together. Line cookie sheet with parchment paper. Use a small cookie scoop and place on paper. Bake in 350 degree oven until the tops are lightly brown (about 8 minutes). Enjoy!

98890-09

COOKIE CUTTER COOKIES

Jenna C. - Age 13

½ cup margarine or butter,
  softened
1 cup sugar
1 large egg
1 tblsp. lemon juice (optional)

1 tsp. vanilla
2 cups flour
½ tsp. baking soda
½ tsp. salt

Cream butter and sugar until fluffy. Beat in egg, lemon, and vanilla. In a separate bowl, combine flour, baking soda, and salt. Gradually add into butter mixture until well blended. Separate and tint with food color if desired. Divide dough in half. Flatten into 1 inch thick disk - wrap in plastic wrap. Refrigerate until firm, 2 hours or longer. When ready roll out dough ⅛ inch thick. Cut with a 3 inch cookie cutter. Place 1 inch apart on pan. Bake 8-10 minutes and 350°.

COOKIE MONSTER'S COOKIE RECIPE

Gabrielle Marie - Age 9

¾ cup butter/margarine
1 cup sugar
2 eggs
1 tsp. vanilla

2½ cups flour
1 tsp. baking powder
1 tsp. salt

Mix all ingredients together. Chill overnight or at least one hour. Roll dough and cut out desired cookie shapes. Decorate with sugar sprinkles. Bake at 350 degrees for 7 minutes or until golden.

COOKIES ON A STICK

Mrs. Fitzpatrick's Kdgn. Class
Countryside School

1 cup soft butter
⅔ cup sugar
2 eggs

2 tsp. vanilla
3 cups flour
½ tsp. salt

Cream butter until fluffy, beat in sugar, eggs and vanilla. Blend in flour and salt. Chill. Roll chilled dough ⅛ inch thick. Cut out 2 sizes of hearts. Place large heart on a cookie sheet. Press stick into dough. Put smaller heart on top of large heart and stick. Bake 350° on ungreased cookie sheet for 10 minutes. Cool. Decorate with frosting, etc.

COOKIES WHILE YOU SLEEP

Ryan Matthew - Age 6
Clayton Anthony - Age 11

3 extra large egg whites
⅞ cup sugar

1 cup miniature chocolate chips

(continued)

1. Preheat the oven to 375 degrees. 2. Beat the egg whites in the bowl of an electric mixer until they just begin to thicken. Add a pinch of salt and gradually add the sugar. Beat for several minutes until the mixture should look like Marshmallow Fluff. 3. Line 2 rimmed baking sheets with parchment paper. Gently fold the chocolate chips into the meringue mixture and drop by the tablespoonful onto the baking sheets. Place in the oven on the middle rack and turn the oven off immediately. Leave the door closed until morning. Sweet dreams. Makes about 28.

COOL KALEIDOSCOPE

Caprece - Age 10

1 c. sugar
1/2 c. butter
1 large egg
2 T. milk
2 tsp. baking powder
2-1/4 c. flour

1/2 tsp. vanilla
1/4 tsp. salt
red, yellow, and blue food
  coloring
1/3 c. each blue, yellow, pink and
  clear sugars

In a large bowl, using an electric mixer set on medium, beat sugar and butter until fluffy, about 2 minutes. Add egg, milk and vanilla; beat until combined. In a medium bowl, combine flour, baking powder and salt. Gradually add flour mixture to butter mixture, beat until a soft dough forms. Turn dough onto a lightly floured surface. Cut dough into 4 equal sections. Using red food coloring, tint one section light pink. Then using yellow food coloring, tint another section pale yellow. Using blue coloring tint another section light blue; leave remaining piece plain. Roll each piece into a 12 inch rope. Cut ropes in half. Stack the cut ropes, alternating colors, to form a log. Twist the stacked pieces together to blend colors. Gently roll and stretch dough to form a 10-inch log. Wrap the dough in wax paper and refrigerate until firm, about 1 hour. Preheat over to 375°. Grease 2 baking sheets. Pour colored sugars into strips on a plate. Slice the logs into 1/4 inch thick slices. Roll slices across sugars. Arrange on baking sheets two inches apart. Bake until lightly golden, 8 - 10 minutes. Place baking sheet on wire racks, cool for 10 minutes. Transfer cookies to racks; cool completely. THE COOKIE WIZARD SAYS.....When slicing the chilled cookie dough, give the log a 1/4 turn every few slices in order to keep the cookie round. Makes about 4 dozen.

CRISPY CANDY SUSHI SNACKS

Rachel Sue - Age 5

1/4 cup butter
4 cups mini marshmallows
6 cups crisped rice cereal

20 gummy worms
1-2 boxes fruit leather

Grease a 12 x 17 inch baking sheet. Melt butter in a 2 qt. saucepan over medium heat. Add the marshmallows and stir mixture. Remove

(continued)

98890-09

the mixture from the heat and stir in the rice cereal until it's evenly coated. Turn the baking sheet so that the shorter ends are at the top and bottom. Then press the marshmallow mixture onto the sheet, distributing it evenly. Starting at one side an inch up from the lower edge, place gummy worms atop the mixture end to end in a horizontal line. Gently roll the lower edge of the marshmallow mixture over the gummy worms. Then stop and cut the log away from the rest of the mixture. Use the same method to form 4 more logs. Slice each log into 1-inch thick "sushi" rolls and wrap them individually with a strip of fruit leather. Makes 4 to 5 dozen.

CRUNCHY FUDGE COOKIES

Jay Torres - Age 15

1 box Betty Crocker fudge brownie mix
2 cups Fiber One original bran cereal
2 tblsp. Miniature semi-sweet chocolate chips
1/8 tsp. Ground cinnamon
1/3 cup Water
1 tblsp. Canola oil
2 tsp. Vanilla
1 Egg

Start to finish: 50 minutes. Makes about 3 1/2 Dozen Cookies. Heat oven to 350°F. Spray cookie sheets with cooking spray. In large bowl, mix all ingredients with spoon. Onto cookie sheets, drop dough by rounded tablespoonfuls 2 inches apart. Bake 10 to 12 minutes or until set. Cool 2 minutes; remove from cookie sheets to cooling rack. Cool completely. Store in tightly covered container. Freeze up to 2 months if desired.

EASY BREEZY ICE CREAM COOKIES

Madison Elizabeth - Age 7

1 cup milk
1 pkg. favorite pudding
2 cups Cool Whip
36 large cookies

Make the pudding mix with milk. Add in the Cool Whip and blend well. Spread the filling on the flat side of the cookie and set another cookie on top. Press lightly and smooth the edges. Freeze for at least 3 hours. Store in a covered container.

EASY CHOCOLATE CHIP COOKIES

Justin Michael - Age 7

1 (18-oz.) pkg. yellow cake mix
1/2 cup butter, softened
1 tsp. vanilla extract
2 cups semi-sweet chocolate chips

Preheat oven to 350 degrees F. Pour the cake mix into a large bowl. Stir in the butter, eggs and vanilla with an electric mixer until well

(continued)

blended. Stir in the chocolate chips. Drop by rounded spoonfuls onto cookie sheets. Bake for 11 to 15 minutes in the preheated oven, until the edges are golden. Cool on baking sheets for a few minutes before removing to cool on wire racks.

EASY OREO TRUFFLES
(Oreo Balls)

Clair Bonham
Sam Bonham

1 (16-oz.) pkg. OREO chocolate sandwich cookies
1 (8-oz.) pkg. PHILADELPHIA Cream Cheese, softened

2 (8-oz.) pkgs. Baking Chocolate, melted

Crush 9 of the cookies to fine crumbs in a food processor: reserve for later use. (Cookies can also be finely crushed in a resalable plastic bag using a rolling pin.) Crush remaining 36 cookies to fine crumbs; place in a medium bowl. Add cream cheese; mix until well blended. Roll cookie mixture into 42 balls, about 1-inch diameter. Dip balls in chocolate; place on wax paper-covered baking sheet. (Any leftover chocolate can be stored at room temperature for another use.) Sprinkle with reserved cookie crumbs. Refrigerate until firm, about 1 hour. Store leftover truffles, covered, in a refrigerator.

ENORMOUS CHOCOLATE COOKIES

Reed Sincox - Age 13

1 pkg. semi-sweet chocolate chips
2 tblsp. milk
1 cup plus 2 tblsp. flour
2 tblsp. unsweetened cocoa powder

$\frac{1}{2}$ tsp. baking soda
$\frac{1}{2}$ tsp. salt
1 stick butter, softened to room temperature
$\frac{2}{3}$ cup packed brown sugar
1 egg

Preheat the oven to 375°. In a small saucepan, combine $\frac{1}{3}$ cup of chocolate chips and the milk and let it sit over very low heat until the chocolate is melted, 5 to 10 minutes. Stir the chocolate mixture until smooth and blended. Remove the pan from the heat and set aside. In a medium bowl, stir together the flour, cocoa baking soda and salt. In another medium bowl, cream the butter with the sugar until well blended. Beat in the egg until well blended, then blend in the chocolate mixture. Beat in the dry ingredients just until combined, then stir in the remaining chocolate chips. Drop $\frac{1}{4}$-cup portions of dough on an ungreased baking sheet leaving about 3 inches between them. Gently flatten the dough to form 2 $\frac{1}{2}$-inch rounds. Bake the cookies for 10 to 12 minutes, or until the bottoms are lightly browned. Let the cookies cool on rake. Makes 12 servings.

FANTASTIC FUDGE

Hannah - Age 7

12 oz. package semi-sweet chocolate chips
6 oz. package butterscotch chips or peanut butter chips

1 can Eagle sweetened condensed milk
½ stick butter

Line cookie sheet with wax paper. Combine all ingredients in a microwave safe bowl. Microwave until melted, stirring frequently. Pour fudge onto waxed paper. Refrigerate overnight and cut into pieces.

FROSTED BANANA COOKIES

Taressa Anne

Cookie Ingredients

¾ c. shortening (Crisco)
¾ c. sugar
1 egg
½ tsp. vanilla extract

2 ripe bananas, mashed
¼ tsp. salt
1 tsp. baking soda
2 c. sifted all-purpose flour

Preheat oven to 350°F. Cream shortening, add sugar and blend. Add egg, vanilla and mashed bananas. Sift together flour, salt and baking soda. Add banana mixture to flour mixture and blend thoroughly. Place by teaspoonfuls onto greased baking sheet. Bake for 8 Minutes (cookies will brown on edges only). Frost cookies while still warm.

Frosting

6 T. light brown sugar
4 T. butter
4 T. evaporated milk

1 box powdered sugar
¾ tsp. vanilla

Bring brown sugar, butter and milk to boil. Remove from heat and add enough powdered sugar to make runny, but spreadable. Add vanilla. Keep pan over warm water to keep frosting soft. Frost and enjoy!

FRUIT JUICE GUMMIES

John W. - Age 13

1 cup fruit juice (pure juice, not a fruit flavored drink) or nectar

1¼ ounce pkg. gelatin

The fruit juice (pure juice, not a fruit flavored drink) or nectar, such as Goya, Mott's, or Kern's, should be chilled or at room temperature. Lightly coat 16 tartlet molds or mini-muffin tins with oil (or however many you want). Place ¼ cup of the juice in a medium bowl and sprinkle in the gelatin. Let sit for 1 minute. Meanwhile, in a small pan, bring the remaining juice to a boil. Add it to the gelatin mixture, stirring until the gelatin is dissolved. Spoon the mixture into the molds. Chill in the refrigerator until set, 2 hours. Pop the tartlets out. Serve them cold or

(continued)

at room temperature within 2 hours, or store them in an airtight container in the refrigerator for up to 3 days.

FUDGEY COCOA NO-BAKE TREATS

Kendall E. - Age 6

3 c. Quick-rolled oats
2/3 c. creamy peanut butter
2 c. sugar
2 tsp. vanilla extract

1/2 c. butter (or margarine)
1/2 c. milk
1/3 c. cocoa
1/2 c. chopped peanuts (optional)

Line cookie sheet with wax paper or foil. Measure oats, peanut butter and optional peanuts. Set aside. Combine sugar, butter, milk and cocoa in medium saucepan. Cook over medium heat, stirring constantly, until mixture comes to a rolling boil. Remove from heat. Stir in peanut butter and vanilla. Add oats and optional peanuts; stir quickly, mixing well. Immediately drop mixture by heaping teaspoons onto wax paper. Cool. Store in cool dry place. Makes about 4 dozen.

Note: You can use a combination of quick oats and old fashioned oats (half of each). It will make the cookies a bit heartier.

GLAZED APPLE COOKIES

Uncle Jeff

4 1/2 cups flour
2 tsp. baking soda
1 tsp. ground cloves
1 tsp. nutmeg
2 tsp. cinnamon
1 tsp. salt
1 cup shortening
2 2/3 cups brown sugar
2 eggs
1 cup apple cider (or milk)

2 cups apples, unpeeled & finely
  chopped
1 cup walnuts, broken (optional)
1 cup raisins
3 tblsp butter, softened
3 3/4 cups powdered sugar
1/4 tsp. salt
6 1/2 tblsp apple cider (or milk)
1 tsp. vanilla

Preheat the oven to 375 °F. Sift together the flour, baking soda, cloves, nutmeg, cinnamon, and salt. Set this mixture aside. Using a mixer, combine the shortening and brown sugar. Add eggs, apple cider, and apples. Then add in the sifted ingredients and mix well. Add the walnuts and raisins to the mixture. Using a spoon, place onto a cookie sheet. Bake at 375°F for 10-12 minutes. Mix the butter, powdered sugar, salt (1/4 tsp.), apple cider (6 1/2 tbsp.), and vanilla. Glaze the cookies with this while they are still hot. Makes 7 dozen cookies.

98890-09

GRANDMA'S SUGAR COOKIES

Kelli Kermath
Marcia Alexander
Alexander Kermath

1½ cups 10X Sugar
1 Large Egg
1 cup Butter, room temperature
1 tsp. Vanilla

2½ cups Flour
1 tsp. Baking Soda
1 tsp. Cream of Tartar

Cream sugar and butter, then add egg and vanilla. Mix dry ingredients in a separate bowl. Stir dry ingredients into cream mixture and mix medium speed with a hand mixer. Chill for 2-3 hours. Pre-heat oven to 375°. Roll dough out on flour surface and cut with cookie cutters or glass. Sprinkle with or ice after baking. Bake 7-8 minutes. Makes approximately 2 dozen cookies

GRANT'S GREAT FUDGE

Grant Channing - Age 4

2 tblsp Butter or Margarine
⅔ cup Evaporated Milk
1½ cup Granulated Sugar
¼ tsp. Salt

2 cup Miniature Marshmallows
2 cup Milk Chocolate Morsels
1 tsp. Vanilla Extract

Combine butter, evaporated milk, sugar, and salt in a medium sized saucepan. Bring to a boil over medium heat. Stir often for 5 minutes. Remove from heat. Stir marshmallows, chocolate morsels, and vanilla for 1 minute or until all marshmallows are melted. Pour into foil lined 8 inch square baking pan. Chill until firm in refrigerator. Cut into ½ inch squares.

GREAT-GRANDMA NANCY'S CRESCENT COOKIES

Mary Rose - Age 10

½ lb. butter (2 sticks) unsalted
5 tblsp sugar
1 T. water
2 tsp. vanilla extract

2 cups Flour-sifted
½ tsp. salt
1 cup pecans or walnuts-
   optional

Cream butter and sugar in mixing bowl then add water and vanilla. Sift flour and salt in separate bowl, blend together with butter mixture, then add nuts and mix well. Using portions about the size of a walnut, shape into crescent shapes and place on cookie sheet. Bake at 325 degrees for 20 minutes or until lightly browned. Immediately roll into powdered sugar or sift on top. Can also dip one side of cookie into dipping chocolate.

HAPPY FACES

Anna Marie - Age 11

1 pkg. refrigerated sugar cookie
  dough
1 pkg. semi-sweet chocolate
  baking chips

red or pink colored sugar
licorice sliced thin for smiles

Follow cookie dough package directions. Before baking the cookies, add two chocolate chips for the eyes to the cookies. Bake according to directions. When the cookies come out of the oven, sprinkle the colored sugar on for cheeks. Take one small thin piece of licorice and add it for its mouth. Push in a little. Let the cookies cool and enjoy with your friends.

HOLLY WREATH COOKIES

Timothy Sebastien - Age 5
Sophia Claire - Age 3

1 stick butter
30 large marshmallows
7-10 drops green food coloring

2 tsp. vanilla
4 c. corn flake cereal
Red M&Ms

Put the butter and marshmallows into a pan and heat on medium low, stirring occasionally until they're all melted and combined. Remove them from the heat and add the vanilla. Add the green food coloring. You'll want to make it a bit darker than you think, as it will look much lighter once it's thinned out amongst the corn flakes. Add in the corn flakes and very, very gently stir them together. If you do it like you're folding in eggs, you'll break fewer flakes which is the goal. Very quickly, you'll want to use a spoon to scoop out the mixture to make small "wreaths" and place them on waxed paper (or in my case, a silpat). Again, working quickly, place the M&Ms (or traditionally red hots, just not in my family) on top of the wreaths to make the holly berries. If you let the mixture cool before putting in the M&Ms, they won't stick. If you're doing it, you'll want to make sure the M on the M&Ms are facing down. If you're letting small children do this, trust me when I say that explaining this concept just doesn't work.

HOLLY WREATHS

Issac Noah - Age 7

30 Large Marshmallows
½ cup Butter
1½ tsp. Green Food Coloring

3 cup Corn Flakes
Red Cinnamon Candies

Melt Butter and marshmallow and green food coloring in a microwave for 2 to 2½ minutes. (Use a very large microwavable bowl) Stir together

(continued)

98890-09

and add the corn flakes. Wet hands and shape into wreaths and place on wax paper. Place several red cinnamon candies on each. Enjoy!

ISSAC'S CREAMY FUDGE

Issac Noah - Age 7

4 cups Sugar
1 cup Milk
½ lb. Butter (no substitute)
25 Big Marshmallows

1 (12-oz.) bag Semi Sweet Chips
2 oz. Unsweetened Chocolate
13 oz. Hershey Bars (broken up)
1 cup Chopped nuts

Add sugar, milk and butter to a large saucepan (5 qt. Dutch oven works well). Heat over medium heat until the sugar is dissolved. Add 25 big marshmallows. Cook until the marshmallows are melted. Remove from heat. Stir in chocolate. Stir until all chocolate is mixed in well. Add the nuts if desired. Pour into a cookie sheet sprayed with Pam and lined with wax paper. Refrigerate. Cut into squares while still soft. Enjoy!

JACKIE'S ENGLISH TOFFEE

Jackie Kapcheck

3 T. water
1 cup sugar
½ lb. salted butter sticks

1 cups milk chocolate chips
1 cup chopped toasted pecans
   or walnuts (optional)

Place the butter, sugar, and water in a large heavy-bottomed skillet over medium heat and cook until the mixture comes to a low boil. Lower the heat to medium and cook, stirring constantly, until the mixture turns a cinnamon color with streaks of brown and reaches the hard-crack stage (when you drop a bit into cold water, it will form a brittle mass), about 12 minutes, or reaches about 300 degrees on a candy thermometer. Immediately pour the candy into a shallow 8 x 12 metal, baking pan and let sit until just warm, about 5 minutes. Sprinkle with the chocolate, and, when the chocolate has melted, smooth down with a knife. Just before it has hardened, add the nuts or sprinkles, if using. Refrigerate until cold and then break into pieces.

Notes: Store in the refrigerator or at room temperature in an airtight container up to 1 month. This recipe takes practice to reach perfection. Don't be discouraged on the 1st try - it really becomes simpler with each batch.

K BARS
(Grandma's Best)

Hannah B. Meyer
Kendra R. Meyer
Doby Meyer

1 cup Sugar
1 cup White syrup
1½ cups Creamy peanut butter

6 cups Special K cereal
1½ cups Chocolate chips

Heat sugar and syrup until sugar is dissolved and brought to a boil. Remove from heat and add peanut butter and stir and until peanut butter melts. Add cereal. Stir until coated. Put in a buttered 9 x 13 pan. Top with a generous amount of chocolate chips. Once chips melt, spread chocolate evenly over treat. (Can substitute cereal with Rice Krispies.)

LEMON BARS

Megan Suppes - Age 13

2 cups sifted flour
½ cup powdered sugar
1 cup butter
4 eggs, beaten

2 cups granulated sugar
⅓ cup lemon juice
¼ cup sifted flour
½ tsp. baking powder

Preheat Oven to 350 degrees. Sift together 2 cups flour and powdered sugar. Cut in butter until mixture clings together. Press mixture into 13 x 9 x 12 inch baking pan and bake for 20 minutes or lightly browned. Beat together the eggs, granulated sugar and lemon juice until syrupy. In a separate bowl, stir together ¼ cup sifted flour and baking powder. Stir into egg mixture. Pour mixture over baked crust. Bake at 350 for 20-25 minutes. Sprinkle with additional powdered sugar. Cool and Cut into squares.

M&M PRETZELS

Kyle Hendzel

bag of pretzels
melted chocolate

M&M's
sugar

Melt chocolate in a microwavable bowl. Dip bottom of pretzel in chocolate. You can add sugar if desired. For the final touch, place an M&M on each hole of pretzel. Now, you have M&M Pretzels.

98890-09

MICROWAVE FUDGE

Alexander Bennett - Age 5

½ cup Butter
2 cups Sugar
½ cup Unsweetened Cocoa
  Powder
⅛ tsp. Salt
½ cup Milk

3 cups Quick Cooking Oats
½ cup Coconut (optional)
½ cup Nuts (optional)
½ cup Peanut Butter
2 tsp. Vanilla

In microwave safe bowl, melt butter. Add sugar, cocoa, salt and milk. Blend well. Cook uncovered for 5 minutes, stirring once at 2½ minutes. Mix remaining ingredients in bowl. Pour into greased 13 x 9 inch pan. Cool several hours.

Variations can easily be made with this recipe, replace the coconut and/ or nuts with dried fruit, marshmallows, krispies, anything you like, be creative! Freezes well, too!

MONSTER COOKIES

Becca Ann - Age 9

3 eggs
1¼ cup brown sugar
1 cup white sugar
½ tsp. vanilla
1¼ tsp. syrup or water
2 tblsp soda powder

1 stick margarine or butter
1 cup peanut butter
4½ cups oatmeal
1 (6-oz.) pkg. chocolate chips
1 (8-oz.) pkg. M & Ms

Mix in given order. Drop large scoop on cookie sheet. Bake at 350 degrees for 12 minutes.

MONSTER COOKIES

Wyatt - Age 13
Kara - Age 10

6 eggs
2 cups sugar
2 cups brown sugar
2 sticks butter
2 T. vanilla extract
2½ cups flour

3 cups chunky peanut butter
6 cups oatmeal
4 tsp. baking soda
12 oz. semi-sweet chocolate
  chips
12 oz. bag M&M's

Mix ingredients in order given. You will need a very large bowl. Spoon onto a ungreased cookie sheet with a tablespoon. Bake at 350 degrees for 10 minutes. Makes a lot of cookies! Dough can be refrigerated or frozen and baked at a later time.

MONSTER COOKIES

Jack Patrick - Age 8
Nicholas Lawrence - Age 8
Noah Matthew - Age 5

3 eggs
½ cup brown sugar
1 cup white sugar
1 tsp. vanilla
1 tsp. corn syrup
2 tsp. baking soda

¼ lb. butter
1½ c. peanut butter
4½ c. oatmeal
1 c. chocolate chips
1 c. m & m's

Mix in order given. Drop on greased cookie sheet with ice cream scoop or large tablespoon and flatten. Place 6 at a time on a cookie sheet. Bake at 350 degrees for 12 minutes. Wrap individually. These are a real hit! Delicious!

MRS. FLOYD'S COOKIES

Mrs. Floyd's 2nd Grade Class
Countryside School

12 eggs
1 cup oil
2 cups sugar

1 tblsp. vanilla
9 cups flour
3 tsp. baking powder

Preheat oven to 375°. Mix oil and sugar together. Gently beat in the eggs. Mix the baking soda and flour together. Add the vanilla to the oil and sugar mixture. Slowly add in the flour. The mixture should end up like bread dough. Roll into a small ball and then roll it like a snake shape like a pretzel. Bake for 10-12 minutes on an ungreased pan. After cookies have cooled, drizzle with icing (powdered sugar, a bit of almond extract, and water. Can color with food coloring).

MUDDY MOO MIX

Meagan Reigh - Age 12

(12-oz.) bag chocolate chips
1 box Rice Chex
½ cup margarine or butter

1 box powered sugar
1 cup creamy peanut butter

In a microwave, melt chocolate chips, margarine and peanut butter. Microwave for an additional 30 seconds. Stir. Put Rice Chex into a large bowl. Pour chocolate mix over the top. Mix well. Put powdered sugar in bowl and toss. Place on cookie sheet to set up. Enjoy!!

98890-09

NATHAN'S SNOWBALL COOKIES

Nathan Wayne - Age 7

2 cups flour
2 cups finely chopped pecans
1/4 cup sugar
1 cup butter (softened)

1 tsp. vanilla
1 pkg. Hershey's Kisses,
 unwrapped
powdered sugar

Heat over to 350 F. Beat butter, sugar, and vanilla in large bowl until creamy. Gradually add flour and nuts to butter mixture, beating until blended. Mold a rounded tablespoon of dough around each chocolate Kiss, covering completely. Shape into balls. Place on an undressed cookie sheet. Bake 8 to 10 minutes or until very lightly browned. Cool 5 minutes; roll in powdered sugar while still warm and again when cool. Enjoy!

NEW JERSEY SHORE SALTWATER TAFFY

Ella Albright - Age 11

1 cup Sugar
1 tblsp Cornstarch
2/3 cup light Corn Syrup
1 tblsp Butter
1/2 cup Water

1/4 tsp. Salt
3 drops Food Coloring
1 tsp. Flavoring/Extract (try
 orange or vanilla)

Mix sugar and cornstarch in saucepan. Stir in corn syrup, butter, water and salt. Cook mixture over medium heat until it reaches 254° on a candy thermometer. Remove pan from heat and stir in a few drops of food coloring and flavoring of your choice. Pour taffy onto buttered baking sheet. Cool taffy for two or three minutes, until you can handle it comfortably. If it gets too cool, you can warm it in a 350° oven for three or four minutes. Divide taffy into two or three balls. Butter your hands, and pull lump of taffy until it is about 15 inches long. Double it up and pull again. Repeat until it is light in color and firm enough to hold a shape. Stretch it into a rope about 3/4 inch in diameter and snip off 1-inch bits with oiled kitchen scissors. Wrap each piece in wax paper.

NO BAKE BUTTERSCOTCH COOKIES

Alexis Elizabeth - Age 10
Ashley Dianna - Age 8
Nicole Frances - Age 5

1/3 cup Peanut Butter
1 pkg. Butterscotch Chips

6 cups Corn Flakes
1/2 cup Walnuts (optional)

Measure Corn Flakes (and nuts) and place in a large bowl. Melt peanut butter and chips over low heat until melted. Pour over Corn Flakes. Mix gently until all flakes are coated. Kids can have fun dropping the flake batter by spoonfuls onto wax paper or foil. Allow to harden in cool place.

NO BAKE CHOC-OAT SUNBUTTER COOKIES
(Peanut and tree nut free - safe for nut allergies)

Owen & Lyla Joy Ruff

2 cups sugar
¹/₂ cup milk
¹/₄ cup margarine
¹/₂ cup cocoa

¹/₂ cup SunButter
3 cups Quick Oats
1 tsp. vanilla

Over low heat in a large saucepan, combine sugar, milk, margarine, and cocoa. Stir frequently until boiling. Boil one minute. Remove from heat. Add SunButter, oats and vanilla. Stir well. Drop by teaspoonfuls onto wax paper and allow to cool.

NO BAKE COOKIES

Chase Elizabeth - Age 13

1 cup sugar
1 cup white karo syrup
1 cup chunky peanut butter

5 cups "Special K" cereal
(6-oz.) chocolate bits
(6-oz.) butter scotch bits

Makes 2¹/₂ dozen. In a saucepan, cook sugar and syrup until sugar is dissolved. Do not boil! Remove from heat. Add "Special K" and mix well. Spread on greased cookie sheet. Melt chocolate and butterscotch bits together. Once melted, spread over the mix evenly like frosting. Refrigerate ¹/₂ hour. Cut into small squares. Remove from pan, store in refrigerator.

NO CHILL ROLL-OUT COOKIES

Sophie Clark - Age 6
Ian Clark - Age 4

1 cup Butter
1 cup Sugar
1 Large Egg

2 tsp. Baking Powder
1 tsp. Vanilla
3 cups Flour

Heat oven to 400°. In large bowl, cream butter and sugar. Beat in egg and vanilla. Mix baking powder into flour. Add flour 1 C. at a time, mixing after each addition. For chocolate dough, stir in 3 oz. melted unsweetened chocolate after the flour is added. Divide dough into 2 balls. Roll out to ¹/₄" thick and cut with cookie cutters. Bake 6¹/₂ - 7 minutes.

98890-09

OATMEAL CHOCOLATE CHIP COOKIES

Reina Hershner - Age 6
Reed Hershner - Age 3

¾ cup shortening - softened
1 cup brown sugar
1 egg
¼ cup water
½ cup sugar
½ tsp. baking soda

1 tsp. vanilla
1 cup flour
1 tsp. salt
3 cups uncooked Quaker oats
1 12 oz. bag of semi-sweet
  chocolate chips

Place shortening, sugar, egg, water, and vanilla in a mixing bowl and beat thoroughly. Add flour, salt, and baking soda. Mix well. Blend in oats and chocolate chips. Drop by teaspoons onto greased cookie sheets. Bake at 350° for 12-15 minutes. Makes 5 dozen.

OATMEAL RAISIN COOKIES

Ryan Michael - Age 7

¾ cup butter, softened
¾ cup white sugar
¾ cup packed light brown
  sugar
2 eggs
1 tsp. vanilla extract

1¼ cups all-purpose flour
1 tsp. baking soda
¾ tsp. ground cinnamon
½ tsp. salt
2¾ cup rolled oats
1 cup raisins

Preheat oven to 375 degrees F (190 degrees C). In large bowl, cream together butter, white sugar, and brown sugar until smooth. Beat in the eggs and vanilla until fluffy. Stir together flour, baking soda, cinnamon, and salt. Gradually beat into butter mixture. Stir in oats and raisins. Drop by teaspoonfuls onto ungreased cookie sheets. Bake 8 to 10 minutes in the preheated oven, or until golden brown. Cool slightly, remove from sheet to wire rack. Cool completely.

OREO SPIDER COOKIES

John W. - Age 13

Oreo Cookies
Pull & Peel Licorice

M & Ms
Vanilla Frosting

First, pull Oreo cookies apart. Then, cut the pull and peel licorice in half. After that, pull eight strands of the pull and peel licorice and put it on the Oreo where the frosting has stayed to the cookie for the spider legs. Then put the other cookie on top of the cookie with the frosting and licorice. Next, make two little dots of vanilla frosting on the cookie where the eyes will be. Finally, put two M&Ms on top of the frosting for the spider eyes.

OREO TRUFFLE BALLS

Riley - Age 7
Ella - Age 6, Matthew - Age 5
Avery - Age 3

1 (16-oz.) pkg. Oreo cookies, divided
1 (8-oz.) pkg. Cream Cheese, softened

2 (8-oz.) pkg. Semi-Sweet Baking Chocolate, Melted

Crush 9 of the cookies to fine crumbs in food processor; reserve for later Crush 9 of the cookies to fine crumbs in food processor, set aside; Crush remaining 36 cookies to fine crumbs; place in medium bowl. Add cream cheese; mix until well blended. Roll cookie mixture into 42 balls, about 1-inch in diameter. Dip balls in chocolate; place on wax paper-covered baking sheet. Sprinkle with reserved cookie crumbs. Refrigerate until firm, about 1 hour.

PA'S FAVORITE SNICKERDOODLES

Julia Elizabeth - Age 5

2 cups all-purpose flour
2 tsp. cream of tartar
1 tsp. baking soda
1/4 tsp. salt
1/2 lb. unsalted butter, softened

1 1/2 cups sugar
2 large eggs
1/4 cup sugar (for mixture)
4 tsp. ground cinnamon (for mixture)

Preheat oven to 350°. Grease cookie sheets. Sift flour, cream of tartar, baking soda and salt together. In a separate bowl, beat butter and sugar together until very fluffy. Then, add eggs and beat until well combined. Stir the flour mixture into the butter mixture until well blended and smooth. Pull off pieces of the dough and roll between your palms to form 1 1/4-inch balls. Roll balls in a mixture of sugar and cinnamon. Space about 2 3/4 inches apart on the sheets. Bake for 8 to 11 minutes.

PARTY MIX

Travis James - Age 12
Jakob Daniel - Age 10
Trey Vincent - Age 7

1 c. Butter melted
2 c. Brown sugar
1/2 tsp. Corn syrup
1/2 tsp. baking soda
1/2 tsp. vanilla

18 oz. Crispix
16 oz. nuts (peanuts, cashews or combo. of both)
4 c. Pretzels

In a saucepan, melt butter and then add brown sugar and corn syrup. Boil 1 minute. Add baking soda and vanilla. Stir and pour over Crispix, nuts and pretzels in a bowl. Put into a large brown grocery bag. Micro-

(continued)

98890-09

wave 3 times for 1 minute. Shake after every time. Spread on wax paper to cool. After cooling, serve as a Party Mix in a bowl.

PEANUT BLOSSOM KISS COOKIES

Anna - Age 7
Luke - Age 5
Ashley - Age 3, Jake - Age 2

1³/₄ cup flour
1 tsp. baking soda
¹/₂ tsp. salt
¹/₂ cup brown sugar
¹/₂ cup white sugar
¹/₂ cup butter, softened

¹/₂ cup peanut butter
1 egg
2 T. milk
white sugar
48 chocolate candy kisses

Combine all above ingredients except Kisses in large bowl; beat on low until well mixed. Shape into rounded teaspoon size balls and roll in white sugar. Place on ungreased cookie sheet. Bake at 375 degrees for 10-12 minutes (cookies should still be light in color). Remove from oven; place one kiss on top of each cookie. Press down lightly.

PEANUT BLOSSOMS

Megan Suppes - Age 13

48 Hershey's Kisses
¹/₂ cup Shortening
³/₄ cup Creamy Peanut Butter
¹/₃ cup Granulated Sugar
¹/₃ cup Packed Light Brown
 Sugar
1 Egg

2 tblsp Milk
1 tsp. Vanilla Extract
1¹/₂ cup Flour
1 tsp. Baking Soda
¹/₂ tsp. Salt
¹/₄ cup Granulated Sugar (for
 decoration)

Heat oven to 375 degrees. Remove wrappers from chocolates. Beat shortening and peanut butter in large bowl until well blended. Add ¹/₃ cup granulated sugar and brown sugar. Beat until fluffy. Add egg, milk and vanilla; beat well. Stir together flour, baking soda and salt; gradually beat into peanut butter mixture. Shape dough into 1 inch balls. Roll in granulated sugar. Place onto ungreased cookie sheet. Bake 8-10 minutes or until lightly browned. *Immediately press chocolate kisses into center of each cookie. Cookie will crack at edges. Cool completely on wire rack.

PEANUT BUTTER & JELLY BARS
(The Ultimate Kids Food - for Dessert!)

William John - Age 4
Charles Thomas - Age 2

½ lb. unsalted butter at room temperature, plus more for greasing the pan
1½ cups sugar
1 tsp. pure vanilla extract
2 extra-large eggs, at room temperature
2 cups creamy peanut butter, such as Skippy (18 oz.)

3 cups all-purpose flour, plus more for dusting the pan
1 tsp. baking powder
1½ tsp. kosher salt
1½ cups raspberry jam or other jam (18 oz.)
⅔ cups salted peanuts, coarsely chopped

Preheat the oven to 350 degrees. Grease and flour a 9 x 13 x 2 inch baking pan. In the bowl of an electric mixer fitted with a paddle attachment, cream the butter and sugar on medium speed until light yellow, about 2 minutes. With the mixer on low speed, add the vanilla, eggs and peanut butter and mix until well-combined. In a small bowl, sift together the flour, baking powder and salt. With the mixer on low speed, slowly add the flour mixture to the peanut butter mixture. Mix until just combined. Spread two-thirds of the dough in the prepared pan, using a knife to spread it evenly. Spread the jam evenly over the dough. Drop small globs of the remaining dough evenly over the jam. Don't worry if the jam isn't completely covered; the dough will spread when it bakes. Sprinkle with the chopped peanuts and bake for 45 minutes, until golden brown. Cool and cut into squares. I sometimes omit the peanuts as some kids don't like them. This is a great recipe to take to a party or to just make and enjoy at home. Our family loves 'em!

PEANUT BUTTER BARS - THE BEST!

Andy Gates - Age 12

2 cups powdered sugar
4½ cups Rice Krispies
1 (18-oz.) jar peanut butter (heat to thin)

¼ lb. butter, melted
12 oz. chocolate chips

Mix everything except the chocolate chips and spread in a 9 x 13 pan. Next, melt the chocolate chips and spread across the top. Let the chocolate harden then cut it up into squares.

98890-09

PEANUT BUTTER COOKIES

Elise Marie - Age 13

2½ cup flour
½ tsp. salt
1 tsp. baking soda
1 cup margarine
1 cup sugar

1 cup brown sugar
2 eggs, beaten
1 tsp. vanilla
1 cup peanut butter
12 oz. chocolate chips (optional)

Cream the margarine and sugars. Add the beaten eggs, peanut butter, and vanilla. Beat well. Add dry ingredients and blend. Roll into balls and press a fork on top. Place on ungreased cookie sheet. Bake at 375° for 10 minutes. Let cool. Yummy!

PEANUT BUTTER CRISPIX BARS

Jack D. Pullen - Age 7

¾ cup peanut butter
1 cup semi-sweet chocolate
 chips

¼ cup butter
8 cups Crispix Cereal
2 cups powdered sugar

Melt peanut butter, chocolate chips, and butter in a large bowl. Slowly stir in Crispix cereal until well coated. In a plastic bag (gallon size), pour powdered sugar and crispix mix. Shake gently until cereal is well covered with powdered sugar. Let cool for 20 minutes and serve.

PEANUT SNOWMEN COOKIES

Michael John - Age 6

1 (16-oz.) pkg. vanilla flavored
 candy coating
1 lb. peanut shaped peanut
 butter sandwich cookies

96 miniature chocolate chips
assorted candies, pretzel sticks,
 and fruit roll snacks

Line cookie sheet with waxed paper. Place ¼ of candy coating in the microwave on high for 30 seconds. Stir and continue to microwave in 15 second increments until coating can be stirred smooth. Dip each side of 8 cookies into mixture to coat. Place on paper-lined cookie sheets. Add chocolate chips for eyes and mouth. Repeat with remaining candy coating cookies. Decorate as desired with assorted candies. Let cookies stand at room temperature for 30 minutes or until coating is set.

POKEMON CHOCOLATE BAR

Kamren Christopher - Age 5½
Keaten Lawrence - Age 7

8 (1-oz.) baking chocolate bars
2 tsp. sugar
2 tsp. butter

splash orange juice to desired
 taste

(continued)

Melt 8 (1 oz) bars of unsweetened baking chocolate in a sauce pan on low heat being careful not to boil. For best results, stir chocolate until completely melted. Stir in sugar and butter. Add a splash or two of Tropicana Healthy Kids orange juice to desired taste. Spoon chocolate into an ice cube tray and refrigerate until just hard. Once molded, gently cut around the cubes to loosen the candy. Bag the candy in individual candy bags and tie with ribbon. If you want to be creative: Try a new ingredient, re-name your candy, design your own label, and attach with ribbon. Voila, you have just created your very own chocolate brand. You are now ready to package and distribute!

POPCORN CANDY TREATS

Alex - Age 10
Miah - Age 4
Mandy - Age 2

vegetable cooking spray
3 tblsp. vegetable oil
1/3 cup popcorn kernels
3 tblsp. butter
1 tsp. pure vanilla extract
6 (12-oz.) cups mini
  marshmallows
6 fun size caramel peanut
  chocolate bars, cut into 1/4-inch
  pieces (Snickers)

3 chocolate chip cookies,
  crumbled
1/3 cup chopped salted almonds
1/2 cup chocolate candies (M&
  Ms)

Spray the inside of a large mixing bowl with vegetable cooking spray, and lightly spray a baking sheet. Set aside. In a 3 quart or larger, heavy-bottomed pan, heat the oil and popcorn over medium-high heat. Cover the pan and shake gently. Cook until all the kernels have popped, about 3 minutes. Place the popcorn in the prepared bowl. In a medium saucepan, heat the butter over low heat. Add the vanilla extract and marshmallows. Stir constantly until the marshmallows have melted and the mixture is smooth, about 5 minutes. Pour the melted marshmallow mixture over the popcorn. Using a spatula, sprayed with cooking spray, stir until the popcorn is coated. Spread the mixture over the prepared baking sheet. Sprinkle with the chocolate bar pieces, cookies, almonds and chocolate candies. Using a spatula, gently press the toppings into the popcorn. Allow the mixture to dry for 1 hour. Break into 2-inch pieces and serve.

POTATO CHIP COOKIES

Cassidy Barbara - Age 2 1/2

1 cup butter or margarine
1/2 cup sugar
1 3/4 cup flour, sifted
1 cup crushed potato chips

1 tsp. vanilla
1/2 cup chopped nuts (optional)
powdered sugar

(continued)

98890-09

Cream butter and sugar together, add vanilla. Add flour, nuts, chips in that order. Drop by teaspoon on ungreased baking sheet two inches apart. Bake at 350 degrees 12-15 minutes. Flatten with back of spoon while cooling. Sprinkle with powdered sugar.

PUMPKIN CHOCO CHUNK COOKIES

Daniel Mies

1 cup pumpkin purée
2 T. dark brown sugar
1/4 cup granulated sugar
1/4 cup unsalted butter, room temperature
1 egg, room temperature
1/2 tsp. baking soda
1/4 tsp. salt
1 tsp. ground cinnamom
1/4 tsp. ground cloves
1/4 tsp. ground nutmeg
1 tsp. vanilla
1/4 cup whole-wheat flour
1 cup all-purpose flour
1/2 cup semi-sweet chocolate chunks
1 tsp. baking powder

Have your grown-up helper preheat the oven to 350 degrees. Prepare your baking sheets with parchment paper. In a medium size bowl, mix together the pumpkin, sugars, and butter. Add the egg and stir well. Add the baking soda and powder, as well as the salt, cinnamon, cloves, and nutmeg. Stir in the vanilla. Carefully fold in the flours and stir just until mixed. Add the chocolate chips and stir gently. Drop onto the prepared cookie sheets by rounded teaspoons of dough. You can place them relatively close because they will not spread when baking. Place in the preheated oven and bake for 12-15 minutes, or until firm and golden on top. Allow the cookies to cool slightly before serving. Enjoy with a big glass of milk!

PUMPKIN COOKIES

Alan Kass - Age 12

2 cups all-purpose flour
1-1/3 cups quick or old fashioned oats
1 tsp. baking soda
1 tsp. ground cinnamon
1/2 tsp. salt
1 cup (2 sticks) butter or margarine
1 cup packed brown sugar
1 cup granulated sugar
1 cup 100% pure pumpkin
1 large egg
1 tsp. vanilla extract
3/4 tsp. chopped walnuts
3/4 cup raisins
decorating icings

Preheat oven to 350 degrees. Grease baking sheets. Combine flour, oats, baking soda, cinnamon, and salt in medium bowl. Beat butter, brown sugar, and granulated sugar until light and fluffy. Add pumpkin, egg, and vanilla extract. Mix well. Add flour mixture. Stir in nuts and raisins. Drop 1/4 cup dough onto prepared baking sheet. Spread into 3 inch circle. Repeat with remaining dough. Bake for 14-16 minutes or

(continued)

until cookies are firm and lightly browned. Cool on baking sheets for 2 minutes. Decorate!

QUICK CHOCOLATE CHIP COOKIES

Jessie Jacquelyn - Age 8

1 pkg. white cake mix
½ cup salad oil
2 T. water
2 eggs, slightly beaten

1 (6-oz.) pkg. semi-sweet
chocolate pieces
½ cup unsalted peanuts/walnuts

Preheat oven to 350°. Blend: cake mix with oil, water and eggs until thoroughly mixed and smooth. Stir: chocolate pieces and nuts into batter, evenly distributing them. Measure: onto greased cookie sheet, one teaspoon of batter at a time to make 3 dozen cookies. Bake: 12-15 minutes; remove from oven and cool one minute, place cookies on rack to finish cooling.

REESE'S CHOCOLATE CHIP COOKIES

Elena Pivek - Age 13

Chocolate chip cookie dough
Miniature Reese's cups

Mini muffin cups
Mini muffin pan

Preheat the oven to 375 degrees. Take a tablespoon of cookie dough and put it into the muffin cups. Put the cookie dough into the oven for four minutes. After the four minutes are up, take the cookie dough out. Place a Reese's cup into the cookie dough, it should fit and be placed very easily. After that, place it in the oven for five minutes. Allow thirty minutes to cool. Enjoy!

REINDEER COOKIES

Bennett John - Age 4
Annabelle Kady - Age 2

1 pkg. Nutter Butters
1 pkg. chocolate chips
2 cups small twisted pretzels

1 cup m&m's
1 pkg. white icing

A perfect holiday treat for the kids... Break off the "top" of the pretzels, forming two "reindeer ears". With the white icing, "glue" the reindeer ears to the top of a nutter butter. Proceed to "glue" two chocolate chips under the ears, forming two eyes. At the bottom of the nutter butter, "glue" on an m&m nose. Snack on any remaining ingredients and Enjoy!

254

98890-09

RICE KRISPIE TREATS

Lucciana Tru - Age 1

6 cups Rice Krispies cereal
3 tblsp butter melted
1 (10-oz.) bag Large
  marshmallows OR

4 cups of miniature
  marshmallows

In large saucepan melt butter over low heat. Add marshmallows and stir until completely melted. Remove from heat. Next, add KELLOGG'S RICE KRISPIES cereal. Stir until well coated. Using buttered spatula or wax paper, evenly press mixture into 13 x 9 x 2-inch pan coated with cooking spray. Cool. Cut into 2-inch squares. Best if served the same day. Yields 12 squares. This is an old standby but Kids really love these and adults too!

SAND TARTS

Ashley Lynn - Age 3

½ cup Butter
1 cup Sugar
1 Egg, beaten

1¾ cup Sifted Flour
2 tsp. Baking Powder

Cream the butter and sugar together and stir in the egg. Sift the flour and baking powder together and then blend it with butter, sugar and egg to make a soft dough. Refrigerate to chill. When cold, place on well-floured board and roll out ⅛ inch thick. Cut out cookies and bake them at 350° for 10-15 minutes. Decorate with butter cream icing.

SCOTCHAROOS

Allison Elizabeth - Age 13

1 cup sugar
1 cup light Karo syrup
1 cup peanut butter

6 cups Rice Krispies
1 (12-oz.) pkg. chocolate chips
1 (6-oz.) pkg. butterscotch chips

Combine sugar and Karo in 3 quart sauce pan. Cook until it bubbles. Then, add peanut butter. Stir until blended. Add Rice Krispies and press into a 9 x 13 inch pan. Melt butterscotch and chocolate chips together. Spread over Rice Krispies mix.

SNAPPING TURTLES

Kelsey Ann - Age 13

1 (14-oz.) bag soft caramels
1 (10-oz.) bag pretzel nuggets
12 oz. semi-sweet chocolate,
  finely chopped

2 cups nuts, finely chopped

(continued)

Unwrap the caramels. Using a rolling pin roll out each one into an ⅛ inch thick oval. Wrap a rolled out caramel around each pretzel and seal. In a double boiler over simmering water, melt half of the chocolate, stirring occasionally until smooth. Add the remaining chocolate. Remove the top of the double boiler from the saucepan and stir until smooth. Place the nuts in a shallow bowl. Line a baking sheet with wax paper. Using a fork dip a caramel covered pretzel in the chocolate to coat. Take off any excess chocolate. Transfer the pretzel to the nuts and toss to coat. Place on the prepared sheet. Repeat. Let stand till set- about 3 hours.

SNOWMAN S'MORE

Ally - Age 13

3 marshmallows
29 mini chocolate chips

graham crackers

Put 20 mini chocolate chips in a bowl and microwave for 30 seconds. Take one marshmallow and dip one side of the marshmallow into the bowl of melted chocolate and stick it on the graham cracker. Take the other two marshmallows and stick one side of the marshmallow into the bowl of melted chocolate and stick the marshmallows on top of each other. Put 3 chocolate chips on the bottom 2 marshmallows. Place the remaining 6 chocolate chips on the top marshmallow to make a face.

SOFT AND CHEWY CHOCOLATE PEANUT BUTTER COOKIES

Angelina Pascente - Age 12

1 pkg. (2 layer size) Devil's Food Cake mix
4 oz. Philadelphia Cream Cheese, softened

½ cup peanut butter
2 eggs

Preheat oven to 375°. Place ingredients in large bowl. Beat with electric mixer on low speed 1 minute, then beat on medium speed for 1 minute or until mixture pulls away from side of bowl and forms soft dough. Shape into 44 (1 inch) balls. Place, 2 inches apart, on baking sheets. Flatten each ball, in criss-cross pattern, with tines of fork dipped in sugar. Bake 7-8 minutes or just until edges of cookies are set. (Do not over bake). Cool on baking sheet 2 minutes. Remove to wire racks; cool completely. Jazz it up: Add ½ cup chopped Planter's Cocktail Peanuts to dough before shaping into balls and bake as directed. Frozen Nutty Buddies: For each frozen sandwich, spread 1 cookie with 1 tblsp. thawed Cool Whip; cover with second cookie. Roll edge in chopped Planters Cocktail Peanuts. Place in airtight container. Freeze up to 3 months. Serve frozen.

256

98890-09

SOME MORE S'MORE BARS

Mary Lillie - Age 13

3 tblsp butter
8 whole graham crackers
6 oz. sweetened condensed milk
1½ cup semi sweet chocolate
  chips

1½ tsp. vanilla extract
1 dash salt
1¼ cups mini marshmallows

Note: Must be chilled for at least 4 ½ hours before serving. Line a 8-inch square baking pan with aluminum foil, it should be hanging over the sides. Grease the foil with baking spray or butter. Put the butter into a saucepan and melt over medium heat, when melted, move the pan onto a heat-proof surface and let it cool for five minutes. Put six of the graham crackers into a Gallon sized zipper bag and press out the air. Crush the crackers with a rolling pin to make itsy-bitsy crumbs, you should have about 1 cup of crumbs. Pour the crumbs into the baking pan and press them down using plastic wrap, wax paper, or aluminum foil until you make one solid even layer of crumbs. Heat the condensed mild and chocolate chips over medium heat and stir them with a wooden spoon until melted and smooth. Move off of heat. Add the vanilla and salt and stir until blended. Pour the chocolate mix over the crumb crust and spread it evenly. Break the other two graham crackers into small pieces and scatter on top along with the marshmallows. Cover s'mores with plastic wrap and refrigerate for at least 4 ½ hours. Enjoy!

SPECIAL K TREATS

Nicholas Ryan - Age 7

1 c. sugar
1 c. light corn syrup
1 c. peanut butter

6 c. Special K cereal
6 oz. chocolate chips
6 oz. butterscotch chips

Mix sugar and light corn syrup. Cook over medium heat. Stir until mixture boils. Remove from heat. Add peanut butter and Special K cereal. Press evenly in a 9 x 13 pan. Melt chocolate chips and butterscotch chips. Spread over bars. Cool and cut.

SUPER QUICK OATMEAL COOKIES

Ethan Richard - Age 5 months

2 cups Sugar
½ stick Butter
½ cup Milk
½ cup Peanut Butter

3 cups Plain Oatmeal
1 T. Hershey's Cocoa
½ tsp. Vanilla Extract

Boil sugar, cocoa, and milk for one minute. Remove from heat. Add butter, peanut butter, vanilla, and oatmeal. Mix together. Drop generous spoonfuls onto wax paper. As it cools, it will firm up. Then eat!

TASTY TREATS

Daniella Dolores - Age 12

2 cups mini marshmallows   1½ T. butter or margarine
3 cups Cocoa Krispies cereal

Melt margarine or butter in medium saucepan over low heat. Add marshmallows and stir until completely melted. Remove from heat. Place medium saucepan on cooling rack. Add KELLOGG's COCOA KRISPIES cereal. Stir until well coated. Using wax paper, press mixture evenly into 9 x 9 inch pan sprayed with cooking spray. Cut into 2 inch squares when cool.

TOMMY TURTLES

Alexander John - Age 2

1 cup corn syrup   1 tsp. vanilla
1 cup butter   2-lb. milk chocolate
2¼ cups brown sugar   7 cups whole pecans
¼ tsp. salt
(14-oz.) can of sweetened
  condensed milk

Alexander loves to make Tommy turtles with help from his mommy. Combine all ingredients except for the vanilla, chocolate, and the pecans together in a saucepan. While stirring constantly, bring to 238 degrees on a candy thermometer (soft boil stage). Remove from heat, wait 5 minutes and then add the vanilla. Pour the Caramel mixture into a buttered 13 x 9 dish and let cool. Melt 2 pounds of chocolate slowly. On parchment paper, layout groups of 5 pecans to form the turtle shapes (approximately 7 cups of whole pecans). Carefully scoop out a tablespoon of the Caramel mixture over the pecan groups. Spoon some of the chocolate on top to create the turtles.

YUMMY CHOCOLATE CHIP COOKIES

Megan Suppes - Age 13

2 sticks unsalted butter,   2 eggs
  softened   2¼ cup flour
¾ cup sugar   1 tsp. salt
¾ cup packed brown sugar   1 tsp. baking soda
1 tsp. pure vanilla extract   1 bag milk chocolate chips

Pre-heat oven to 350 degrees. In a bowl, combine flour, salt and baking soda. In a different bowl, beat butter and two sugars until smooth. Add eggs and vanilla and beat again. Add flour mixture to butter mixture in small amounts. Add chocolate chips. Place spoonfuls of batter on cookie sheet and bake for 11-12 minutes.

98890-09

YUMMY FLOURLESS PEANUT BUTTER COOKIES

Nicole Grace - Age 7

1 cup peanut butter   **1 egg**
1 cup white sugar

Preheat oven to 350 degrees F. Combine ingredients and drop by teaspoonfuls on cookie sheet. Bake for 8 minutes. Let cool. Recipe doesn't make very many, so you could double recipe as you desire.

Recipe Favorites

Recipe Favorites

This&That

Helpful Hints

- Never overcook foods that are to be frozen. Foods will finish cooking when reheated. Don't refreeze cooked, thawed foods.

- When freezing foods, label each container with its contents and the date it was put into the freezer. Always use frozen, cooked foods within 1–2 months.

- To avoid teary eyes when cutting onions, cut them under cold running water or briefly place them in the freezer before cutting.

- Fresh lemon juice will remove onion scent from hands.

- To get the most juice out of fresh lemons, bring them to room temperature, and roll them under your palm against the kitchen counter before cutting and squeezing.

- Add raw rice to the salt shaker to keep the salt free flowing.

- Transfer jelly and salad dressings to a small plastic squeeze bottle – no more messy, sticky jars!

- Ice cubes will help sharpen garbage disposal blades.

- Separate stuck-together glasses by filling the inside glass with cold water and setting both in hot water.

- Clean Corning Ware® by filling it with water and dropping in two denture cleaning tablets. Let stand for 30–45 minutes.

- Always spray your grill with nonstick cooking spray before grilling to avoid sticking.

- To make a simple polish for copper bottom cookware, mix equal parts of flour and salt with vinegar to create a paste.

- Purchase a new coffee grinder and mark it "spices." It can be used to grind most spices. However, cinnamon bark, nutmeg, and others must be broken up a little first. Clean the grinder after each use.

- In a large shaker, combine 6 parts salt and 1 part pepper for quick and easy seasoning.

- Save your store-bought-bread bags and ties—they make perfect storage bags for homemade bread.

- Next time you need a quick ice pack, grab a bag of frozen peas or other vegetables out of the freezer.

THIS & THAT

100 DAYS SNACK MIX

Mrs. Schroeder's First Grade Class
Countryside School

100 Cheez-It Crackers	100 chocolate chips
100 colored Goldfish	100 pieces of popcorn
100 M&Ms	100 raisins
100 mini marshmallows	100 Cheerios
100 Cocoa Puffs	100 butterscotch chips
100 Skittles	100 pieces of Chex cereal
100 pretzels	100 plain Goldfish
100 Mint M&Ms	

Get a REALLY big bowl. Each child pours his/her contribution into the bowl. The teacher gently and carefully, but thoroughly mixes all ingredients. Spoon some into small cups for the children. Settle in and enjoy snack and a story!

ANTS ON A LOG

Alexis Patricia - Age 7

celery	peanut butter
raisins	

Take out a long piece of celery and spread peanut butter on the inside of the celery. Then place the raisins on the peanut butter.

BLUEBERRY STREUSEL COFFEECAKE

Timothy Sebastien - Age 5
Sophia Claire - Age 3

Coffeecake

¾ c. sugar	2 c. flour
¼ c. butter	2 tsp. baking powder
1 egg	¼ tsp. salt
½ c. milk	2 c. blueberries
½ tsp. almond extract	

Preheat oven to 370 degrees. Beat sugar, butter and egg until they are creamy, about three or four minutes. Add milk and almond extract and mix well. Add baking powder, salt and flour, and mix gently until not quite just combined. Fold in blueberries. (I always add just a little nutmeg to the batter and topping because nutmeg makes everything taste better!) Pour batter into a 10" springform pan.

(continued)

Streusel Topping

¼ c. sugar
¼ c. brown sugar
⅓ c. flour

½ tsp. cinnamon
¼ c. butter

Make the topping by mixing sugars, flour and cinnamon. Cut in the cold butter until crumbly. Crumble over the batter. Doubling the topping wouldn't be unheard of in our house. Bake at 370 degrees for 45 or so minutes (my oven always takes a little longer).

CARAMEL FRUIT DIP

Anna - Age 7
Luke - Age 5
Ashley - Age 3, Jake - Age 2

(8-oz.) softened cream cheese
½ cup brown sugar
⅓ cup powdered sugar

3 tsp. milk
1 tsp. vanilla

Beat all ingredients until smooth. Serve with apples, melon balls, strawberries, grapes or bananas.

CHALK

Timothy Sebastien - Age 5
Sophia Claire - Age 3

2⅔ c. plaster of paris
1 c. tempera paint

1 c. water

Mix all ingredients together and let stand for five minutes. Pour into molds or empty toilet paper tubes. Let dry for at least 24 hours.

CHEX MIX

Trevor Michael - Age 7
Morgan Kate - Age 4
Elise Nicole - Age 1

1 (12-oz.) Box of Rice Chex
   Cereal
1 (12-oz.) Box Corn Chex Cereal
1 (12-oz.) Box of Crispix Cereal

1 lb. Butter
2 lbs. Light Brown Sugar
1 cup Light Karo Syrup
1 tblsp Vanilla

Mix cereals in stock pot. In pan on stove, combine 1 lb. butter, 2 lbs. light brown sugar, 1 cup light Karo syrup. Bring to a boil. Simmer for 5 minutes stirring often. Remove from heat and add 1 TBSP. vanilla. Mix again. Pour over cereal and mix well. Put in stock pot, cover and shake. Pile on 2 cookie sheets. Bake in oven for 1 hour on 200°. After you take out of oven, pour onto counter top, and break apart while still hot. Cool on counter, then store covered!

262

98890-09

CHEX MUDDY BUDDIES

Kevin Russell - Age 6

9 cups Chex Cereal
6 oz. Chocolate Chips
1/2 cup Peanut Butter

1/4 cup Butter or Margarine
1/2 tsp. Vanilla
1 1/2 cups Powder Sugar

Pour cereal into large bowl. Set aside. Heat chocolate chips, peanut butter and butter in 1 qt. saucepan over low heat, stirring frequently, until melted. Remove from heat, stir in vanilla. Pour chocolate mixture over cereal in bowl, stirring until evenly coated. Pour into large plastic food-storage bag. Add powdered sugar. Seal bag. Shake until well coated. Spread on waxed paper to cool. Makes 9 cups.

CHOCOLATE DRIZZLED POPCORN

Timothy Sebastien - Age 5

2 T. Olive Oil
1/3 c. Popcorn kernels

1 tsp. Salt
1 c. chocolate melting discs

Find a large metal bowl. Pour just enough oil in the bottom of the bowl to cover it, then add kernels atop it. Cover the bowl with tin foil, and poke some holes in it. Turn the stove on to medium/medium high, and start shaking. Shake, shake, shake until it all stops popping. Immediately add just enough salt to taste. If you do it while the popcorn is hot, it sticks better without being overly salty. Lay the popcorn on the nonstick surface in a thin layer, like a silpat or waxed paper. While it is cooling (you want the popcorn to be cool when you put the chocolate on it), melt the chocolate over low heat in a heavy pan or double boiler. Use a spatula to scoop up just a little of the chocolate, and then drizzle the chocolate over the popcorn. You'll need to shake the spatula like you're trying to get dust off a rug to get the last of the chocolate off it, but that also makes for the best drizzles. Doing small bits of chocolate at a time works best. If you get clumps of chocolate, no worries. Just use your spatula to mix up the popcorn, distributing the chocolate. You can put on as much or as little chocolate as you like. You can also mix white and regular chocolates to make it extra fancy.

CHOCOLATE FLUFF SAUCE

Chase Elizabeth - Age 13

1 cup Whipping Cream
1/2 cup sugar

1/4 cup deoste cocoa
1 tsp. vanilla

Mix ingredients in bowl. Cover and chill overnight in the refrigerator. Whip using chilled beaters until firm. Best served with angel food cake.

CHOCOLATELY GRAHAMS MIX

Ethan Richard - Age 5 months

3 cups Cinnamon Teddy
Grahams
2 cups Banana Chips
3 cups Golden Grahams Cereal

1 large box Malted Milk Balls
1 medium can Honey Roasted
Peanuts

Mix all of the ingredients together and enjoy!

COLORED SAND FOR PICTURES

Timothy Sebastien - Age 5
Sophia Claire - Age 3

sidewalk chalk   salt

Scrape chalk dust with a table knife to get the desired amount of chalk dust. Combine equal parts chalk dust and salt. Store the colored sand in plastic bags or shaker bottles (clean baby food jars or yogurt containers with holes punched in the tops work fine). Make a design on paper with glue and sprinkle with colored sand to decorate.

COOKED PLAY DOUGH FOR KIDS
(Non-edible)

Ethan Richard - Age 5 months

1 cup Flour
2 tsp. Cream of Tartar
1 T. Vegetable Oil

1 cup Water
½ cup Salt
Food Coloring

Combine flour, cream of tartar, oil, water, and salt in a saucepan. Add food coloring by drops until desired color is reached. Heat, stirring constantly until a ball forms. Remove ball from pan and knead thoroughly until smooth. Play!

CRANBERRY RELISH
(Zach's Holiday Cranberry Relish)

Susan B. Johnson
Zachary Thad Johnson

2 cup cranberries
1 med. orange quartered

1 med. apple quartered
1 cup sugar

Grind cranberries, apple, and orange in food grinder - not food processor. Add sugar and chill overnight. Add more sugar as needed for taste. (This relish has been made by Zach every Christmas since he was 7 years old and he continues to make it in his own home not that he is grown with his own family)

264

CUPCAKE ICING

Puneet Grewal - Age 9

blue, red, yellow and green food
  coloring

confectioners' sugar
water

Mix until the desired consistency and color. Get creative!

DANCING RAISINS
(Kitchen Experiment)

Kyle Thomas - Age 8
Brandon Paul - Age 5

1 clear jar or container
1 can clear, fizzy drink (Sprite or
  7-up)

1 handful of raisins

Pour the drink into a clear container. Drop a handful of raisins into the liquid. Watch the raisins start to dance. This works because the raisins are more dense than the liquid so they sink. Then the carbon dioxide bubbles stick to the raisin's wrinkles. Raisins covered with bubbles are less dense than the liquid so they rise. At the surface of the liquid, the bubbles burst. The raisins become dense again, so they sink. The raisins will continue to rise and fall or "dance" for about half and hour.

EASY AND DELICIOUS ALFREDO SAUCE

Diana Kaitlyn Cox
Cameron Gabriel Cox

1 pint Heavy cream
½ stick Real butter
3-6 cloves Garlic - chopped
  finely or pressed

2 cups Fresh Parmesan cheese

Melt butter in large sauce pan. Stir in garlic (chopped finely or pressed) until tender. Add cream and Parmesan cheese. Stir and bring to a boil. Turn down the heat but continue cooking. If sauce is too thin, then add more cheese. Pour over your favorite pasta, enjoy!

FLOAT THE EGG
(Kitchen Experiment)

Kyle Thomas - Age 8
Brandon Paul - Age 5

1 large clear glass
1 egg

10 T. salt

Gently lower an egg into a large glass of water. It will sink because it is more dense than water. Rescue the egg. Then pour 10 T. salt into

(continued)

the water and stir until it all dissolves. This salt and water solution is called brine. Put the egg in the brine. Now it should float because the salt has made the water more dense than the egg. Amazing!

FLUBBER

Jessica Lynn - Age 6
Ryan Robert - Age 4

1 box cornstarch   **2 cups water**

What a fun experiment to do with kids! Pour entire box of cornstarch into a large bowl. Slowly add the water and mix. It will be difficult. Try to pick up the mixture with your hands and roll into a ball quickly. Once you stop manipulating the mixture, it will turn into liquid and run down your hands. Also try to quickly punch the mixture that is in the bowl. You will notice that your hand will bounce off of the mixture, as it seems to feel solid! Now SLOWLY stick your finger into the bowl and watch it sink. AMAZING! You might need a little less or a little more water. You will be able to determine once you start playing with the mixture.

FRUIT DIP

Alethia Ann

½ cup Brown Sugar   **1 cup Sour Cream**

Mix brown sugar with sour cream. Serve with fresh fruit. Alethia first made this dip when she was 10 years old. Now that she has a little boy of her own named Cooper, she substitutes ¼ cup Agave Nectar for the brown sugar.

GO FISH

Julia Elizabeth - Age 5

1 pretzel rod   **1 Swedish fish**
1 pc. licorice rope

Tie one end of the licorice to the pretzel. Tie the other end of the licorice to the Swedish fish. Enjoy!

GO FISH II

Julia Elizabeth - Age 5

1 box Jell-O Gelatin Dessert,   **6 Swedish fish**
Berry Blue   **6 glass custard cups**

Make Jell-O according to package directions. Divide among custard cups and place in refrigerator. Once Jell-O starts to gel -- but before it

(continued)

completely sets, place one Swedish fish in each custard cup. Place fish upright and toward the bottom of the cup, so it appears to swim. Continue to refrigerate until Jell-O sets. Enjoy!

GORP (GOOD OLD FASHIONED RAISINS AND PEANUTS)

Erin - Age 8

dry roasted peanuts
raw sunflower seeds
raisins
chopped dates or other dried
  fruits

unsweetened coconut chips
carob chips
roasted soy nuts
pumpkin seeds

Mix the nuts, seeds and fruit. Vary ingredients according to supply and tastes. A great trail snack -- a nutritious alternative to "empty calorie" snacks. Keeps well. (This is from "Whole Foods for the Whole Family" La Leche League International Cookbook, 1981.)

GRAHAM CRACKER HOUSE

Ally - Age 13

Graham Crackers
Frosting
raisins

sprinkles
chocolate chips
pretzel sticks

Spread frosting on edges of graham crackers. Put graham crackers together to build a house. You can customize your house with the rest of the listed ingredients or come up with your own!

GRANDMA'S PLAYDOUGH

Timothy Sebastien - Age 5
Sophia Claire - Age 3

1½ c. water
3 T. oil
1 c. salt

2 c. flour (fluff up flour and
  spoon into cup)
2 T. alum

In a saucepan, bring water and oil to a boil, then add food coloring. Remove from heat. Using a wooden spoon, stir in flour, salt and alum, mixing well. Complete mixing by hand, kneading until smooth and a good texture. Store in a plastic bag or covered plastic container to keep soft. Playdough keeps well at room temperature for a few weeks. Refrigeration seems to keep it longer.

HONEY BUNS

Eileen Mary - Age 12

1 pkg. split hot dog buns
peanut butter
2-3 bananas

honey
sunflower seeds

Slice bananas and set aside. Spread peanut butter on buns. Put 3 banana slices on top. Drip with honey and sprinkle with sunflower seeds. Yummy!! This is great for a teddy bear picnic! Invite your friends & their bears!

ICE CREAM KIDS CAN MAKE!

Timothy Sebastien - Age 5
Sophia Claire - Age 3

½ c. whole milk (don't use skim)
1 tsp. sugar
¼ tsp. vanilla

6 T. rock salt
1 pint size Ziploc bag
1 gallon size Ziploc bag
ice cubes

Fill the large bag half full of ice, and add the rock salt. Seal the bag. Put the milk, vanilla, and sugar into the small bag, and seal it. Place the small bag inside the large bag, and seal again carefully. Shake up the mixture until it is ice cream, about five minutes. Wipe off the top of the small bag, then open carefully and enjoy!

JAM FILLED CRUMB BARS

Jenna C. - Age 13

1¾ cups flour
½ cup chopped nuts
¾ cup butter
½ cup powdered sugar

¼ tsp. lemon zest
½ - 1 cup jam (any flavor)
1 tblsp. flour

Preheat oven to 375°. Stir 1¾ cups of flour and chopped nuts together. In separate bowl, beat butter until soft and add powdered sugar and zest. Beat until fluffy. Add flour and nut mixture. Using a mixer, beat on slow until crumbly. Press about ⅔ of the crumbs in pan as crust. Spread Jam. Mix remaining dough with tablespoon of flour and crumble over top. Bake for 25-30 minutes.

JELL-O JIGGLERS

Francesca Michele - Age 4

2 pkgs. Knox unflavored gelatin
1½ cups cold water, divided

1 (6-oz.) pkg. Jell-o (any Flavor)
1 cup boiling water

(continued)

98890-09

Mix together unflavored gelatin packages and 1 cup of cold water, set aside. Add Jell-O to 1 cup of boiling water and stir until dissolved. Add to cold mixture. Add additional ½ cup cold water. Pour into pan (13X11 inch). Chill in refrigerator until set: use cookie cutters to shape into fun molds and shapes.

MARINARA DIPPING SAUCE

Lane - Age 8
Mackenzie - Age 5

1 (14-oz.) can tomato sauce
1 (6-oz.) can tomato paste
3 tsp. crushed garlic

2 tblsp. sugar
3 tsp. Italian seasoning

Combine all ingredients in a bowl and allow to stand for 10 minutes before using. Serve warm with fresh refrigerator breadsticks. Can also be used to top pasta or as a pizza sauce.

MOM'S CHILDHOOD PLAYDOUGH

Timothy Sebastien - Age 5
Sophia Claire - Age 3

1 c. flour
½ c. salt
1 c. cool water

2 tsp. cream of tartar
1 T. oil
few drops of food coloring

Combine all ingredients and mix well. Cook over medium heat until dough forms a ball. Knead 10 to 15 times. Store in a plastic bag or container with lid. Have fun!

NIBBIL'N FISH

Erin - Age 8

2½ cups Cheerios
1½ cups pretzel sticks
1 cup Goldfish crackers

1 cup peanuts
⅓ cup cooking oil
2 T. Worcestershire sauce

First combine Cheerios, pretzel sticks, Goldfish crackers and nuts into a 13 x 9 inch baking pan. Stir together oil and Worcestershire sauce. Combine with Cheerios mix. Mix well. Bake in 300 degree oven for 30 minutes. Stir every 15 minutes. Cool and store mix in tightly covered container.

NUTS & BOLTS
(a.k.a. Little Things)

Joseph Patrick - Age 4

1¼ lb. Margarine
¼ cup Worcestershire sauce
3 tsp. Garlic salt
3 tsp. Onion salt
3 tsp. Celery salt
1 lb. Mixed salted nuts
1 (12-oz.) pkg. Shredded wheat
  squares

1 (16-oz.) pkg. Rice cereal
1 (7-oz.) pkg. Cheerios
1 box Corn Chex
1 (6-oz.) pkg. Small pretzels
1 pkg. Cheese tidbits or Cheez
  Its

My great Aunt Rose makes this for parties and my Mother helps me with the margarine and Worcestershire sauce and salt measurements...but I do all the pouring and mixing of the other ingredients! It is very easy! All you do is...melt the margarine, add the sauce and assorted salts. Let stand to marry the flavors. Pour over all cereals, nuts, and pretzels and bake uncovered for 2 hours at 250 degrees. It's yummy!

NUTTY PROFESSOR

Taylor L- Age 13

Peanut Butter
Honey
Olive Oil

Cinnamon
Frosted Flakes

Number of Servings: 8 Calories Per Serving: 300 Nutrition Info: GOOD!!! Take some peanut butter and put it on a piece of foil. Pour a tip of honey, cinnamon and olive oil onto the peanut butter. Next, roll into balls and sprinkle with frosted flakes. Set it in the freezer for 2 minutes.

OVEN BAKED ZUCCHINI STICKS

Laura Rizzo

canola oil or cooking spray
½ c. whole-wheat flour
½ c. all-purpose flour
2 tblsp. cornmeal
1 tsp. kosher salt
½ tsp. fresh ground black
  pepper

½ tsp. chili powder
½ tsp. garlic powder
1½ lb. zucchini, cut into ½" x
  3" sticks
2 egg whites, lightly beaten

1. Preheat oven to 475 degrees F. 2. Coat a large baking sheet with cooking spray. Combine flours, cornmeal, and seasonings in a large sealable plastic bag. Dip zucchini in egg white, shake in the bag to coat, and arrange, not touching, on the baking sheet. Coat all exposed sides with cooking spray. 3. Bake on the center rack for 7 minutes. Turn the zucchini and coat any floury spots with cooking spray. Continue

(continued)

98890-09

to bake until golden and just tender, about 5 minutes more. Serve hot.
4. Serve with lowfat ranch dressing for dipping, if desired

OYSTER CRACKER GOODIES

Nikolas Southard

2 pkgs. oyster crackers
²⁄₃ cup salad oil
1 pkg. Hidden Valley Ranch
  dressing

1 tsp. dill weed
Garlic to taste

Pour oyster crackers into a large bowl. In a separate, mix oil, Ranch dressing mix, dill weed, and garlic. Pour mixture over oyster crackers and mix thoroughly with hands. Store in airtight container.

PEANUT BUTTER IS SO LAME
(TIP FOR PEANUT ALLERGIES)

Auntie Gina

In with the Sunflower Seed
  Butter

Out with the peanut butter

So many wonderful recipes call for peanut butter, making these favorite treats unavailable to those of us with peanut allergies (as well as our siblings, children, and family and friends we cook for!) How tragic! FINALLY there's a solution -- Sunflower Seed Butter! Since it has the same look, color and consistency as PB, you can substitute it in recipes (as long as they don't call for chunky). It's so yummy, I hear it tastes almost identical-- without those icky peanuts. Sunflower Seed Butter is available at more and more stores (I currently get mine at Trader Joes) right NEXT to that grody, un-cool, totally weak peanut butter. Hooray!

PEANUT BUTTER NUTS AND BOLTS

Eileen Mary - Age 12

1 can cocktail peanuts
1 pkg. Rice Chex cereal
1 pkg. pretzel sticks

½ cup peanut butter
½ pkg. Cheerios cereal
½ cup oil

Mix peanut butter and oil. Heat in microwave or stove top until smooth. Pour all ingredients into a roasting pan. Mix well. Bake for 15-20 minutes at 300 degrees. Store in airtight container.

PUPPY CHOW

Jennifer Sue - Age 12

1 box Rice Chex cereal
1 bag chocolate chips
5 heaping tblsp peanut butter

1 stick butter
powdered sugar

First get a bowl that is microwave safe and place the bag of chocolate chips, peanut butter, and one stick of butter in the bowl. Place the bowl in the microwave for 3 minutes and 30 seconds. When the mixture is melted, mix and place on top the Rice Chex. Mix. After mixed well, put the powdered sugar on top. Lastly, put the mix in the fridge until it cools down.

PUPPY CHOW

Reina Hershner - Age 6
Reed Hershner - Age 3

9 cups Toasted Rice Cereal
  (Rice Chex)
1 cup semi-sweet chocolate
  chips

$\frac{1}{2}$ cup peanut butter
$\frac{1}{4}$ cup butter
1 tsp. vanilla
$1\frac{1}{2}$ cups powdered sugar

In a large bowl, measure out cereal. In a small saucepan, combine chocolate chip, peanut butter, and butter and melt over low heat until creamy. Once creamy, add vanilla. Pour mixture over cereal and stir until cereal is evenly covered. Pour cereal mix into a brown bag or 2 gallon resealable bag and add powdered sugar, seal bag and shake until cereal mixture is covered. Place on wax paper to dry. Store in an airtight container.

RAISIN AND RICE FRIED PUDDING

Anthony Raven - Age 6
Jaydon Mateo - Age 5
Brandon Michael - Age 2

$\frac{1}{3}$ cup white rice
$\frac{3}{4}$ cup raisins
1 tblsp cooking oil or cooking
  spray

1 tblsp butter
2 tblsp milk
2 cups water

In a medium saucepan, bring the water to a boil. Add the rice and cook until done (about 25 minutes). Turn off the heat, drain any access water if necessary. While the rice is still hot, add the butter, milk and raisins. Mix thoroughly and wait a few minutes for the raisins to soften. Meanwhile, heat the oil in a medium frying pan. Place the raisin and rice mixture into the pan and press down gently with a spoon or spatula to spread the rice evenly. Do not mix. On medium heat allow to fry on one side until a golden brown crust forms on the bottom (about 10 minutes).

(continued)

98890-09

Carefully lift the pudding with a spatula and flip it to the other side. Cook for an additional 10 minutes or until the other side is golden brown. You can cut the finished pudding into serving size portions and sprinkle the top with a little bit of sugar. Wait a few minutes for the pudding to cool before you eat as the inside will be very hot.

SHISH KABOB MARINADE

William Michael - Age 3

1 cup soy sauce
½ cup brown sugar
½ cup apple cider vinegar

½ cup pineapple juice
½ tsp. garlic powder
1 - 2 tsp. salt

Mix and bring to a boil. Marinate beef chunks for at least 4 hours.

SIMPLE SNACK MIX

Emily M - Age 13

1 cup whole grain cereal
¼ cup nuts

¼ cup dried fruit
¼ cup pretzels or any crackers

This recipe is fun and easy to make, just for your fast little critters. All you need to do is get a mixing bowl and mix all of the ingredients; your snack mix is completed.

SNACK ATTACK

Ryan Michael - Age 7
Haleigh Faith - Age 5

2 cups o-shaped cereal
1 cup stick pretzels

1 cup soft raisins

Pour the ingredients together into a bowl. Stir with a large spoon. Store in a resealable bag or a plastic container. Enjoy!

SNACK MIX

Ms. Anastacio's Class

plastic bags
pretzels
marshmallows

raisins
chocolate chips

Put 10 pretzels in a bag. Add 15 marshmallows, 22 raisins, 17 chocolate chips in the bag. Shake the bag. EAT!

SNACK MUNCHIES

Laney Marie Staszcuk - Age 5

18 level oz. granola without raisins
17 level oz. mixed nuts
1 (15-oz.) pkg. raisins
1 (14-oz.) bag milk chocolate M&M's

1 (14-oz.) bag peanut M&M's
12-1/4 level oz. Honey-Nut Cheerios
89 level oz. Cheerios

In a large bowl, combine all ingredients. Store snack mix in a covered container or large resealable plastic bags. Yield: 4-1/2 quarts.

SPICED ALMONDS

Issac Noah - Age 7

1/2 cup Packed brown sugar
1 tsp. Pumpkin pie spice
1/2 tsp. Curry powder

1/4 tsp. Salt
1 Egg white
1 lb. Blanched Almonds

In a small bowl, combine brown sugar and seasonings; set aside. In another bowl whisk egg white until foamy. Add almonds to egg whites and toss to coat. Add sugar/spice mixture and toss to coat. Spread on a greased foil-lined baking sheet. Bake at 325 degrees for 20-25 minutes or until lightly browned. Stir once during baking. Cool completely and store in an airtight container. Enjoy!

SPRAY SIDEWALK CHALK

Timothy Sebastien - Age 5
Sophia Claire - Age 3

cornstarch
water

food coloring

Mix equal parts cornstarch and water. Add food coloring to the mixture. Store in an empty spray bottle, and enjoy outside on a summer day. Discard unused spray chalk the same day, and rinse the bottle!

STRAWBERRY YOGURT PARFAIT

Maura Grogan

4 medium Strawberries
10 small Grapes
1 container Strawberry Yogurt

1/2 cup Strawberry Yogurt
Cheerios

Cut Strawberries and Grapes into bite pieces. Mix all ingredients and serve. Great for breakfast or snacktime. Must love strawberries!

98890-09

SWEETY DIP

Benjamin Wilson - Age 9

2 cups sour cream
1½ tsp. cinnamon
½ tsp. nutmeg

1 T. sugar
2 tsp. honey

Stir all ingredients until it is smooth, not bumpy. Sprinkle a dash of cinnamon on top before serving. Serve chilled. Makes a great dip for fruit, graham crackers, and pretzels. Good anytime you need to satisfy your sweet tooth! Be careful - it's addicting! Your family and friends will love it.

TODDLER TRAIL MIX

Sydney Ella - Age 1½

Teddy Grahams (your favorite
  kind)
Raisins

Cinnamon Chex
M&Ms (just a few)

Combine equal parts of one or all in your child's favorite cup or bowl as a fun snack. Sydney LOVEs the M&Ms and eats her trail mix out of a red plastic cup. Yum!

TRADITIONAL PLAY DOUGH

Michael Jacob - Age 6

1 cup flour
1 cup warm water
2 tspn cream of tartar

1 tspn oil
¼ cup salt
Food coloring - optional

Mix all ingredients, adding food coloring last. Stir over medium heat until it forms a dough ball. Remove from pan and knead until blended smooth. Place in plastic bag or airtight container when cooled. Will last for a long time.

TRAIL MIX HOMEMADE

Sierra Birdsell

bag of pretzels
bag of M&M's

2 boxes of raisins

Fill a bowl ¾ full with pretzels. Add M&M's and raisins and mix well.

UNCOOKED FRUITY PLAYDOUGH

Timothy Sebastien - Age 5
Sophia Claire - Age 3

1 c. flour
½ c. salt
3 T. oil
1 small pkg. unsweetened drink
  mix (e.g., Kool-Aid)

½ c. hot water
2 tsp. cream of tartar

Dissolve drink mix in hot water, then add oil. Combine dry ingredients in a separate large bowl. Pour liquid ingredients into dry, then mix. Knead until well blended. Store in an airtight container.

WHITE CHOCOLATE PARTY MIX

Timothy Sebastien - Age 5
Sophia Claire - Age 3

4 c. Cheerios
6 c. Rice Chex
3 c. waffle cut pretzels
3 c. M&Ms

2 c. Craisins
1½ lb. premium white chocolate
  (not almond bark)

Place the white chocolate in a very heavy saucepan or in a double boiler and melt over medium low heat. Cover the pot to ensure the heat is being evenly distributed and not just cooking the bottom part. After about a few minutes, turn off the heat and begin stirring. Stir until it is all fully melted, which will take a few minutes. While the chocolate is melting, place the remaining ingredients in a large bowl. Gently mix the dry stuff together without breaking anything (read: Rice Chex). Use the spatula to drizzle the white chocolate onto the dry stuff. Only do about a quarter or so of the chocolate at a time and mix well in between or you'll end up with massive gobs of chocolate and lots of dry other stuff. You'll want to put waxed paper on a counter. If you have a damp counter, the waxed paper sheets will stay in place while spreading the mix rather than sliding all over the counter. Once the ingredients are mixed, pour it out onto the waxed paper and use the spatula to spread it out so that it hardens into manageable chunks. Once it hardens (less than an hour in the middle of summer for me), you'll want to break it up a little more, but not too much.

WHITE CREAMY ICING

Chase Elizabeth - Age 13

1 stick margarine
½ cup shortening
1 cup sugar

½ cup milk
3 T. flour
½ tsp. vanilla

Cream margarine and shortening together. Add sugar and mix well. Add milk and flour alternately. Add vanilla and beat well.

98890-09

YOGURT POPSICLE

Crystal Marie - Age 13

Dixie Cups   **Popsicle Sticks**
Your Favorite Yogurt

Pour the yogurt into the Dixie cups. Then put the popsicle sticks inside of the Dixie cups so its straight up. Take all of the Dixie cups filled with yogurt into the freezer for about a half hour. Congratulations! You have made a tasteful and healthy snack in a short period time! Enjoy!

YOGURT SNACK

Shivani S - Age 9
Sanjiv N - Age 6

1 cup Vanilla Yogurt   **1 tblsp honey**
1 tblsp Toasted Wheat Germ **1 banana**

Add the wheat germ, honey and banana to the yogurt for a healthy, sweet snack! Wheat germ is full of folic acid and vitamin E and provides a great crunch to the yogurt.

Recipe Favorites

Recipe Favorites

INDEX OF RECIPES

APPETIZERS & BEVERAGES

SOUPS & SALADS

VEGETABLES & SIDE DISHES

MAIN DISHES

BREADS & ROLLS

DESSERTS

COOKIES & CANDY

THIS & THAT

How to Order

Get additional copies of this cookbook by returning
an order form and your check or money order to:

Kids Feeding Kids Club
P.O. Box 313
Barrington, IL 60011-0313
www.kidsfeedingkids.info

Please send me _____ copies of:
Kids Feeding Kids Cookbook
at **$20.00** plus **$4.00** for s/h per book.
Enclosed is my check or money order for $_____.

Mail Books To:

_____
Name

_____
Address

_____   _____   _____
City   State   Zip

Please send me _____ copies of:
Kids Feeding Kids Cookbook
at **$20.00** plus **$4.00** for s/h per book.
Enclosed is my check or money order for $_____.

Mail Books To:

_____
Name

_____
Address

_____   _____   _____
City   State   Zip